Hands-On Business Intelligence with DAX

Discover the intricacies of this powerful query language to gain valuable insights from your data

Ian Horne

BIRMINGHAM - MUMBAI

Hands-On Business Intelligence with DAX

Copyright © 2020 Packt Publishing

Commissioning Editor: Sunith Shetty
Acquisition Editor: Reshma Raman
Content Development Editor: Nazia Shaikh
Senior Editor: Ayaan Hoda
Technical Editor: Dinesh Chaudhary
Copy Editor: Safis Editing
Project Coordinator: Aishwarya Mohan
Proofreader: Safis Editing
Indexer: Priyanka Dhadke
Production Designer: Nilesh Mohite

First published: January 2020

Production reference: 1300120

Published by Packt Publishing Ltd.
Livery Place
35 Livery Street
Birmingham
B3 2PB, UK.

ISBN 978-1-83882-430-3

www.packt.com

To my mum and dad for all their love, and for always being there. To my lovely wife Catherine and my wonderful sons Ollie and Josh, for their continuous love, support and inspiration. To all my family and friends who took an interest, and encouraged me to write this book.

– Ian Horne

Packt.com

Subscribe to our online digital library for full access to over 7,000 books and videos, as well as industry leading tools to help you plan your personal development and advance your career. For more information, please visit our website.

Why subscribe?

- Spend less time learning and more time coding with practical eBooks and Videos from over 4,000 industry professionals

- Improve your learning with Skill Plans built especially for you

- Get a free eBook or video every month

- Fully searchable for easy access to vital information

- Copy and paste, print, and bookmark content

Did you know that Packt offers eBook versions of every book published, with PDF and ePub files available? You can upgrade to the eBook version at www.packt.com and as a print book customer, you are entitled to a discount on the eBook copy. Get in touch with us at customercare@packtpub.com for more details.

At www.packt.com, you can also read a collection of free technical articles, sign up for a range of free newsletters, and receive exclusive discounts and offers on Packt books and eBooks.

Contributors

About the author

Ian Horne is head of data services with a global organization. He is a **business intelligence (BI)** professional with over 30 years of experience and specializes in the design, development, and maintenance of corporate databases, data warehouses, associated ETL processes, and end user reporting. He has extensive knowledge of the Microsoft BI stack, including SQL Server, SSRS, SSAS, Power BI, and, of course, DAX. Ian holds a diploma in computing and a Bachelor of Science degree from the Open University. In his spare time, he creates training videos on Power BI, DAX, and other data-related matters, which he shares through his YouTube channel, Data World TV.

About the reviewers

Felipe Vilela has a master's degree in BI and data warehousing from IESB University and has several certifications from MicroStrategy and others, such as Tableau and Alteryx. He has worked for more than 10 years on BI projects with big US companies and has also been a technical reviewer for two of Packt's MicroStrategy books.

Juan Tomás Oliva Ramos is an environmental engineer from the University of Guanajuato, Mexico, with a master's degree in administrative engineering and quality. He now works in the Tecnologico Nacional de México campus Purísima del Rincón, Guanajuato. He has more than 5 years experience in the management and development of patents, technological innovation projects, and technological solutions through the statistical control of processes. He has been a teacher of statistics, entrepreneurship, and technological development since 2011. He has developed prototypes via programming and automation technologies for the improvement of operations, all of which have been registered for patents.

Packt is searching for authors like you

If you're interested in becoming an author for Packt, please visit authors.packtpub.com and apply today. We have worked with thousands of developers and tech professionals, just like you, to help them share their insight with the global tech community. You can make a general application, apply for a specific hot topic that we are recruiting an author for, or submit your own idea.

Table of Contents

Preface

DAX provides an extra edge by extracting key information from the data that is already present in your model. With this book, you will leverage DAX's functionality and flexibility in the **business intelligence (BI)** and data analytics domain.

You'll start with the basics of DAX, along with the importance of good data models, and how to write efficient DAX formulas by using variables and good formatting. You will learn how DAX queries work using an example-based approach. You will learn how to optimize your BI workflow by writing efficient and powerful DAX queries with easy-to-follow explanations and examples. You will learn how to manipulate and load datasets of different complexities within various Microsoft products, such as Power BI, SQL Server, and Excel Power Pivot. You will learn how to build and extend your data models to gain additional insights. Later, you will delve into progressive DAX syntax and functions to understand complex relationships in DAX. You will cover important DAX functions, specifically those related to tables, date and time, filtering, and statistics. You will then move on to more advanced topics, such as how the formula and storage engines work to be able to optimize your queries.

By the end of this book, you will be able to employ DAX to enhance your data model by extracting new information and gaining deeper insights.

Who this book is for

This book is for data analysts, business analysts, BI developers, or any SQL users who want to get the best out of DAX in the BI and data analytics domain using an example-rich guide. You will learn how to use DAX queries in Power BI, Excel, and SQL Server to carry out efficient analysis. Some understanding of BI concepts is mandatory.

What this book covers

Chapter 1, *What is DAX?*, gives you an overview of the DAX language, what it is, and how, as a BI pro, you can use it to create new information from existing data. It will introduce the different calculation types, calculated columns and measures, and the CALCULATE function, probably the most important DAX function.

Chapter 2, *Using DAX Variables and Formatting*, teaches you about using variables in DAX formulas and how these can make your DAX code easier to read and potentially more efficient. You will also look at recommended formatting styles for DAX code. Finally, you'll look at error handling and how using variables can make this easier.

Chapter 3, *Building Data Models*, talks about the importance of building a well-defined data model, both from the point of view of a BI professional and in terms of making DAX easier to use.

Chapter 4, *Working with DAX in Excel, Power BI, and SSAS*, looks at the three different platforms that support DAX – Excel, Power BI, and SSAS Tabular. You will look at loading data in more depth and the different ways DAX is used in each.

Chapter 5, *Getting it into Context*, moves beyond the basics and builds upon what you learned about evaluation contexts in the first chapter. You will learn about the difference between the row context and the filter context and how these affect DAX functions. You will also take a more in-depth look at the CALCULATE function.

Chapter 6, *Progressive DAX Syntax and Functions*, explores the structure of DAX syntax, and you'll look at the groups of functions currently available in DAX. You'll take a more in-depth look at relationships, aggregation functions, and parent-child functions, all with hands-on examples.

Chapter 7, *Table Functions*, concerns the DAX table functions and includes details of the syntax of each function, as well as an explanation of how each works. Finally, you'll get hands-on with some practical examples of the functions being used.

Chapter 8, *Date, Time, and Time Intelligence Functions*, is where you will learn about the DAX date, time, and time intelligence functions, with details of the syntax of each function, including an explanation of how each works. Finally, you'll get hands-on with some practical examples of the functions being used.

Chapter 9, *Filter Functions*, moves on to the DAX filter functions, with details of the syntax of each function, including an explanation of how each works. Finally, you'll get hands-on with some practical examples of the functions being used.

Chapter 10, *Statistical Functions*, covers the DAX statistical functions, with details of the syntax of each function, including an explanation of how each works. Finally, you'll get hands-on with some practical examples of the functions being used.

Chapter 11, *Working with DAX Patterns*, is the final chapter of part 2, and you will look at some examples of DAX being used in the form of DAX patterns. Each pattern will have a walkthrough involving a practical example that breaks down the code and gives a detailed explanation of how it works.

Chapter 12, *Optimizing Your Data Model*, delves into the VertiPaq engine and how it can be used to help you optimize your data model. You'll also look at some ways in which you can optimize your data model along with how and why this may improve performance.

Chapter 13, *Optimizing Your DAX Queries*, shows you some techniques that will help to make your DAX calculations more efficient, including a look at some tools to help you analyze query performance. You'll also look at the two DAX calculation engines: the storage engine and the formula engine.

To get the most out of this book

You should be familiar with general BI concepts. A basic understanding of using Power BI, Excel, and SQL Server to carry out efficient analysis is mandatory.

Download the example code files

You can download the example code files for this book from your account at www.packt.com. If you purchased this book elsewhere, you can visit www.packtpub.com/support and register to have the files emailed directly to you.

You can download the code files by following these steps:

1. Log in or register at www.packt.com.
2. Select the **Support** tab.
3. Click on **Code Downloads**.
4. Enter the name of the book in the **Search** box and follow the onscreen instructions.

Once the file is downloaded, please make sure that you unzip or extract the folder using the latest version of:

- WinRAR/7-Zip for Windows
- Zipeg/iZip/UnRarX for Mac
- 7-Zip/PeaZip for Linux

The code bundle for the book is also hosted on GitHub at `https://github.com/PacktPublishing/Hands-On-Business-Intelligence-with-DAX`. In case there's an update to the code, it will be updated on the existing GitHub repository.

We also have other code bundles from our rich catalog of books and videos available at `https://github.com/PacktPublishing/`. Check them out!

Download the color images

We also provide a PDF file that has color images of the screenshots/diagrams used in this book. You can download it here: `http://www.packtpub.com/sites/default/files/downloads/9781838824303_ColorImages.pdf`.

Conventions used

There are a number of text conventions used throughout this book.

`CodeInText`: Indicates code words in text, database table names, folder names, filenames, file extensions, pathnames, dummy URLs, user input, and Twitter handles. Here is an example: "Mount the downloaded `WebStorm-10*.dmg` disk image file as another disk in your system."

A block of code is set as follows:

```
Return % =
DIVIDE (
    SUM ( Sales[ReturnQuantity] ),
    SUM ( Sales[SalesQuantity] )
)
```

Bold: Indicates a new term, an important word, or words that you see on screen. For example, words in menus or dialog boxes appear in the text like this. Here is an example: "Select **System info** from the **Administration** panel."

 Warnings or important notes appear like this.

 Tips and tricks appear like this.

Get in touch

Feedback from our readers is always welcome.

General feedback: If you have questions about any aspect of this book, mention the book title in the subject of your message and email us at customercare@packtpub.com.

Errata: Although we have taken every care to ensure the accuracy of our content, mistakes do happen. If you have found a mistake in this book, we would be grateful if you would report this to us. Please visit www.packtpub.com/support/errata, selecting your book, clicking on the Errata Submission Form link, and entering the details.

Piracy: If you come across any illegal copies of our works in any form on the Internet, we would be grateful if you would provide us with the location address or website name. Please contact us at copyright@packt.com with a link to the material.

If you are interested in becoming an author: If there is a topic that you have expertise in and you are interested in either writing or contributing to a book, please visit authors.packtpub.com.

Reviews

Please leave a review. Once you have read and used this book, why not leave a review on the site that you purchased it from? Potential readers can then see and use your unbiased opinion to make purchase decisions, we at Packt can understand what you think about our products, and our authors can see your feedback on their book. Thank you!

For more information about Packt, please visit packt.com.

Section 1: Introduction to DAX for the BI Pro

This section covers the basics of DAX, along with the importance of good data models and how to write efficient DAX formulas by using variables and good formatting. You will understand how DAX queries work using an example-based approach. You will also learn how to optimize the BI workflow by writing efficient and powerful DAX queries with easy-to-follow explanations and examples:

- Chapter 1, What Is DAX?
- Chapter 2, Using DAX Variables and Formatting
- Chapter 3, Building Data Models
- Chapter 4, Working with DAX in Power BI, Excel, and SSAS
- Chapter 5, Getting It into Context

What is DAX? 1

In this chapter, you will begin your journey to mastering the use of DAX with a brief introduction to the DAX language itself. We'll look at what it is and why, as a **Business Intelligence (BI)** professional, you need to learn it if you want to unleash the full power of Excel Power Pivot, Analysis Services, or Power BI.

By the end of this chapter, you will be introduced to the different groups of functions and operators available and the differences between calculated columns and measures, and you will have started your understanding of evaluation contexts. This chapter will round off with a look at how you can alter how filters affect measures by using one of the most important DAX functions, the CALCULATE function.

This chapter is broken down into the following sections:

- Introducing DAX
- Working with data types and operators
- Working with calculated columns and measures
- Evaluation contexts – part 1
- Using the CALCULATE function

Introducing DAX

DAX, or **Data Analysis Expressions** to give it its full name, is a collection of constants, operators, and functions that are used to build expressions that return one or more values. It was originally developed by the SQL Server Analysis Services team as part of their *Project Gemini*, the development of a new in-memory database technology that would let Excel users work with massive amounts of data. It was introduced initially in 2009 as an add-in to Microsoft Excel 2010 and eventually went on to become the Power Pivot add-in for Excel that we have today.

Today, DAX consists of more than 250 functions, and regularly receives updates to existing functions as well as receiving new functions. It is a language used by the following products in Microsoft's business intelligence stack:

- Excel Power Pivot
- Power BI
- **SQL Server Analysis Services (SSAS)** Tabular
- Azure Analysis Services

DAX is not a programming language in the traditional sense but is instead a functional language, which means that it makes calls to a function as part of an expression. The result of an expression will, depending on the function, return either a single value or a table as output. The output from an expression can be used to nest functions, by using it as the input parameter to another function.

DAX can only be used to filter or query a physical table; it cannot add, delete, or update data in a table. However, if you are using Power BI or SSAS Tabular, it can use the result of a DAX expression to add a new table to a data model. Unfortunately, this method cannot be used to add tables to an Excel Power Pivot data model without using a workaround, which itself has limitations.

As Power Pivot was originally built as an add-in to Excel, many of the DAX functions are very similar to functions in Excel, which creates a level of familiarity for BI professionals who are already using Excel.

In *Table 1-1*, you will see that while some functions are almost identical in syntax, others are not. In Excel, the AND function can compare up to 255 logical conditions, while the equivalent function in DAX is limited to just two. Even where functions are identical, the ones in Excel will work with a range of cells, whereas the DAX equivalent will work with columns in a table:

Excel Function	DAX Function	Comments
SUM (cell range)	SUM (table[column])	Excel works with a range of cells; DAX works with the column of a table.
MIN (cell range)	MIN (table[column])	Excel works with a range of cells; DAX works with the column of a table.
MAX (cell range)	MAX (table[column])	Excel works with a range of cells; DAX works with the column of a table.

MEDIAN (number1, [number2], ...)	MEDIAN (table[column])	Excel works with a list of numbers of cells; DAX works with the column of a table.
AND (logical1, [logical2], ...)	AND (logical1, logical2)	Excel supports up to 255 logical conditions; DAX only supports 2 logical conditions.

Table 1-1: Comparison of Excel and DAX functions

If you are already working with formulas in Excel, then you will be accustomed to working with cells and ranges of cells. However, if you are to successfully transition to working with DAX, you will need to learn to work with the rows and columns of data in tables.

DAX consists of the following function groups:

- Aggregate
- Count
- Date and Time
- Time intelligence
- Information
- Logical
- Mathematical
- Statistical
- Text
- Parent/Child

While DAX functions appear similar to functions found in Excel, they have their own unique characteristics, such as being able to perform calculations that vary by context. They can also return tables as well as values and they can work across the relationships of a data model.

As a BI professional, you may be asking whether it's necessary to learn DAX to be able to use tools such as Power BI or Excel Power Pivot; and the simple answer is no. If you have a well-designed data model filled with good quality data and your reporting requirements are simple, you can get started by dragging and dropping a numeric field onto the report canvas in Power BI, or by adding it to a pivot table in Excel. Behind the scenes, a DAX measure is automatically created, and this is known as an implicit measure.

However, when you want to add columns to existing tables, based on data already in those tables, or you want to create some summary tables, you will probably have to go back to your IT department to get them to add these to an existing database or data warehouse.

The power of DAX is that it enables you, as a BI professional, to add these elements to your data model yourself. Using DAX functions, you can add new columns to an existing table, such as an age range field, based on a person's age.

You can also create explicit measures, which allow you to create aggregated summaries of data, such as record counts. Furthermore, these measures will be dynamically calculated based on any filters or slicers that you add to your Power BI dashboard or Power Pivot worksheet. As you make changes to these filters and slicers, the measures are recalculated dynamically.

With Power BI and Analysis Services, DAX can even be used to create new tables in your data model. Unfortunately, this feature is not available with Excel Power Pivot models.

Quite simply, DAX gives you, as a BI professional, the power to gain deeper insights into your data that you wouldn't otherwise be able to get. When you start to look at the more powerful DAX functions, such as the time-intelligence functions, you can start to carry out some truly amazing analysis of your data. It becomes easy to look at a year-on-year comparison of sales or to look at percentage growth across product ranges for different dates.

While the syntax of DAX is simple, mastering its use can be a challenge. If you are coming from an Excel background, you should be prepared to adopt a different mindset. You will need to study the theory that will be delivered in the following chapters and gain a solid understanding of the following fundamental concepts:

- Calculated columns and measures
- Context
- Syntax
- Functions

Each of these will be looked at in detail throughout this book, with plenty of hands-on examples to help you to understand each concept. When you have done this, you will be ready to put what you have learned into practice. Ultimately, the key to truly mastering the art of using DAX is down to lots of practice and experience.

Working with data types and operators

In DAX, you define the data type for columns of data in a table. In this section, we will look at the different data types that are available and delve into the implicit data type conversions that take place when data is used in a DAX expression. We will also look at the different groups of available operators.

Data types

Choosing the correct data type when building your data model helps to ensure that the size of your model is kept to a minimum. It can also help with performance when it comes to refreshing the data in your model.

When you load new data into your model, the modeling engine will attempt to pick the most efficient data type for a column, based on the values that it is importing for that column. However, it is worth checking the data types that it selects, as it may not always choose the most appropriate data type for your data needs. For example, if a column currently contains only integer numbers, the modeling engine will pick the Whole Number data type. If this column subsequently contains fractional values, then the fractional part of these numbers will be lost when the data is imported. Worse still, if the column subsequently contains non-numeric data in the column, then you will get errors when the data is refreshed.

You should always use the correct data type, as some DAX functions have special data type requirements. Although DAX may implicitly convert a data type for you, there are some cases where it will not.

Implicit conversions are described later in this article. *Table 1-2* gives details of the different data types available in DAX:

Data Type	Stored As	Comments
Whole Number	64-bit (8 byte) integer value	Integers between -9,223,372,036,854,775,808 and 9,223,372,036,854,775,807.
Decimal Number	64-bit (8 byte) real number	Negative numbers between -1.79E +308 and -2.23E -308, zero, and positive number between 2.23E -308 and 1.79E + 308; the number of significant digits is limited to 15 decimal digits, with the separator occurring anywhere within the number.

Currency (Fixed Decimal Number in Power BI)	64-bit (8 byte) real number	Numbers that have four decimal digits of fixed precision between -922,337,203,685,477.5808 and 922,337,203,685,477.5807.
Date/Time	64 bit (8 byte) real number	Underneath the covers, the Date/Time value is stored as a Decimal Number type. Supports dates from March 1, 1900 through to December 31, 9999.
Text	A Unicode character string	Represents strings, numbers, or dates in a text format; maximum length is 268,435,456 Unicode characters or 536,870,912 bytes.
True/False	Boolean	A Boolean value that is either True or False.
Blank	N/A	Creates a blank with the BLANK function, and verify blanks with ISBLANK.
Table	N/A	Represents a table in the data model.

Table 1-2: Data types in DAX

DAX functions have specific requirements for the type of data used for inputs and outputs. If the data in a column passed as an argument is not compatible with the data type required by the function, DAX will try to implicitly convert it into the required data type. If this is not possible, it will return an error.

The type of implicit conversion that DAX performs is determined by the operator, it will convert the data into the type required before it performs the requested operation. *Tables 1-3* through to *1-6* list the operators and show the implicit conversion that takes place when the data type in the row is combined with the data type in the column.

Table 1-3 shows the implicit conversion that takes place when a value with the data type in the row is added to a value with the data type in the column:

Addition (+)	Whole	Currency	Decimal	Date/Time
Whole	Whole	Currency	Decimal	Date/Time
Currency	Currency	Currency	Decimal	Date/Time
Decimal	Decimal	Decimal	Decimal	Date/Time
Date/Time	Date/Time	Date/Time	Date/Time	Date/Time

Table 1-3: Addition

Table 1-4 shows the implicit conversion that takes place when a value with the data type in the row is subtracted from a value with the data type in the column:

Subtraction (-) Row – Column	Whole	Currency	Decimal	Date/Time
Whole	Whole	Currency	Decimal	Decimal
Currency	Currency	Currency	Decimal	Decimal
Decimal	Decimal	Decimal	Decimal	Decimal
Date/Time	Date/Time	Date/Time	Date/Time	Date/Time

Table 1-4: Subtraction

Table 1-5 shows the implicit conversion that takes place when a value with the data type in the row is multiplied by a value with the data type in the column:

Multiplication (*)	Whole	Currency	Decimal	Date/Time
Whole	Whole	Currency	Decimal	Whole
Currency	Currency	Decimal	Currency	Currency
Decimal	Decimal	Currency	Decimal	Decimal

Table 1-5: Multiplication

Table 1-6 shows the implicit conversion that takes place when a value with the data type in the row is divided by a value with the data type in the column:

Division (/) Row / Column	Whole	Currency	Decimal	Date/Time
Whole	Decimal	Currency	Decimal	Decimal
Currency	Currency	Decimal	Currency	Decimal
Decimal	Decimal	Decimal	Decimal	Decimal
Date/Time	Decimal	Decimal	Decimal	Decimal

Table 1-6: Division

In addition to the implicit conversions of numeric types shown in the preceding tables, DAX will automatically convert numbers into strings and strings into numbers depending on the requirements of the operator.

For the concatenation operator (&), DAX will convert numeric values into string values:

```
Measure 1-1 = 2 & 3
```

In this example, the DAX measure will evaluate to the string value, "23".

For an arithmetic operator such as addition (+), string values will be converted into a numeric value where possible:

```
Measure 1-2 = "2" + "3"
```

In this example, the DAX measure will evaluate to the numeric value 5.

However, there is the potential for errors to occur when allowing for automatic conversion as described. For example, where you are passing string values to an arithmetic operator that cannot be converted into a number, your expression will generate an error. Therefore, you must ensure that correct data types are used for the columns that are used with operators. Exception handling should be done if there is any possibility of errors occurring.

Operators

There are four groups of operators in DAX:

- Arithmetic
- Comparison
- Concatenation
- Logical

Table 1-7 shows the different types of operator available within the arithmetic group, along with an example illustrating typical use:

Operator	Meaning	Example
+	Addition	3 + 7 = 10
-	Subtraction or sign	10 - 7 = 3
*	Multiplication	10 * 7 = 70
/	Division	10 / 5 = 2
^	Exponentiation	3 ^ 4 = 81

Table 1-7: DAX arithmetic operators

When using arithmetic operators it is important to consider the order in which they need to be applied. If necessary, use parentheses to override the precedence of an operator. *Table 1-8* shows the order of precedence for each of the different DAX arithmetic operators:

Operator	Description
^	Exponentiation
-	Sign
* and /	Multiplication and division
+ and -	Addition and subtraction

Table 1-8: DAX arithmetic operator precedence

The following gives an example of where parenthesis can be used to override the precedence of an operator:

*5*2+6 = 16*

Here, the *5* is multiplied by the *2* to give *10*, before the *6* is added to give *16*. The multiplication operator (*) has higher precedence than the addition operator (+), so that part of the calculation is calculated first.

However, take a look at this example:

5(2+6) = 40*

Here, the use of the parentheses around *2+6* gives it higher precedence and causes it to be calculated before the result is multiplied by *5*.

Table 1-9 shows the different types of comparison operators available, with an example illustrating the operator being used:

Operator	Meaning	Example
=	Equal to	[Firstname] = "Ian"
==	Strictly equal to	[Number] == 0 true only when number equals 0 and false if blank
>	Greater than	[Number] > 100
<	Less than	[Number] < 100
>=	Greater than or equal to	[Number] >= 100
<=	Less than or equal to	[Number] <= 100
<>	Not equal to	[Firstname] <> "Ian"

Table 1-9: DAX comparison operators

When using comparison expressions, you should consider the following points:

- Boolean values are treated as greater than string values.
- String values are treated as greater than numeric or date/time values.
- Numeric and date/time values are treated the same.

Table 1-10 shows the concatenation operator, with some examples illustrating how it is used:

Operator	Meaning	Example
&	Joins two values together to form one text value	"abcd" & "efg" = "abcdefg" 2 & 3 = "23"

Table 1-10: DAX concatenation operator

It is important to note that, as we have seen in the previous section on data types, when using the concatenation operator, DAX will implicitly convert numeric values to string values.

Table 1-11 shows the different types of logical operators available, with examples of each operator being used:

Operator	Meaning	Example
&&	Logical AND: If both expressions are TRUE, return TRUE; otherwise return FALSE.	(true) && (true) = true (true) && (false) = false
||	Logical OR: If either expression is TRUE, return TRUE; when both expressions are FALSE, return FALSE.	(true) || (true) = true (true) || (false) = true (false) || (true) = true (false) || (false) = false
IN	Logical OR: Creates a logical OR condition between each value included in a list of values.	Channel(ChannelName) IN ('Store', 'Online', 'Catalog')

Table 1-11: DAX logical operators

In addition to the preceding logical operators, DAX also has the logical AND and OR functions that replicate the functionality of the AND operator (&&) and OR operator (||) respectively.

The advantage of using these functions over the equivalent operators in a complex expression is that it is easier to format and read the code. However, one drawback is that the functions only accept two arguments, restricting you to comparing two conditions only. To be able to compare multiple conditions, you will need to nest the functions. In this case, it might be better to use the AND operator (&&) instead.

The following gives an example of the syntax for the AND function:

```
Measure 1-3 =
IF (
    AND (
        20 > 10,
        -20 < -10
    ),
    "All true",
    "One or more false"
)
```

The following gives an example showing the syntax of the AND function nested to compare three conditions:

```
Measure 1-4 =
IF (
    AND (
        AND (
            10 > 9,
            5 < 10
        ),
        20 > 10
    ),
    "All true",
    "One or more false"
)
```

The following gives an alternative example of the one given, using the equivalent AND operator (&&):

```
Measure 1-5 =
IF (
    10 > 9
        && 5 < 10
        && 20 > 10,
    "All true",
    "One or more false"
)
```

Any column in a table can have blank values, which are the result of the data source containing NULL in values. How a blank value affects the result of a DAX expression depends on the data type expected and the operator being used. In some instances, a blank value will be converted into a zero or an empty string, while in others, it will propagate through as a blank. *Table 1-12* shows how different DAX operators handle blank values:

Expression	DAX
BLANK + BLANK	BLANK
BLANK & "Hello"	Hello
BLANK + 2	2
BLANK * 2	BLANK
2 / BLANK	Infinity
0 / BLANK	NaN
BLANK / BLANK	BLANK
FALSE OR BLANK	FALSE

FALSE AND BLANK	FALSE
TRUE OR BLANK	TRUE
TRUE AND BLANK	FALSE
BLANK OR BLANK	BLANK
BLANK AND BLANK	BLANK

Table 1-12: Handling blank values in DAX

The BLANK data type represents nulls, blank values, empty cells, and missing values. The BLANK function is used to generate blanks, while the ISBLANK function is used to verify a blank value.

Working with calculated columns and measures

Understanding the difference between a calculated column and a measure (also known as a calculated field) is an important concept that you will need to learn to begin mastering DAX. At first, they may seem very similar, and indeed there are some instances where both can be used to obtain the same result. However, they are different and serve different purposes. Likewise, they also impact resources in different ways. Calculated columns allow you to extend a table in your data model by creating additional columns. Measures allow you to aggregate the values of rows in a table and take into account any current filters or slicers that are applied.

Calculated columns

You can create new columns by using DAX expressions if you want to extend a table in your Power BI, Excel Power Pivot, or Analysis Services Tabular data model. These are referred to as calculated columns. In Excel, each row of a column in a worksheet can be defined by using a different expression. However, calculated columns evaluate the same expression throughout the column of a table, calculating the appropriate value on a row-by-row basis.

To create a new calculated column in Power BI Desktop, follow these steps:

1. Start on the report page and highlight the table that you want to add a new column to from the list of tables shown in the **Fields** pane on the right-hand side.
2. Right-click on the table name and select **New column** from the menu, as shown in *Figure 1-1*:

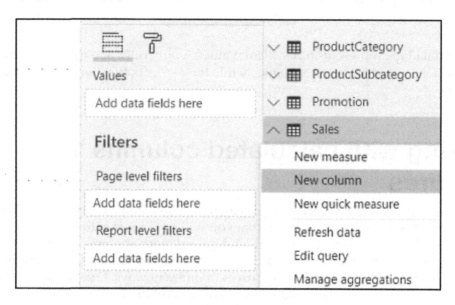

Figure 1-1: Adding a new column from the Fields pane

Alternatively, you can highlight the table and click on the **New Column** button on the **Calculations** section of the **Home** ribbon or the **Calculations** section of the **Modeling** ribbon, as shown in *Figure 1-2*:

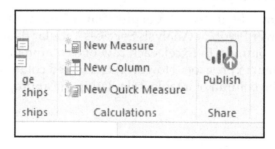

Figure 1-2: Adding a new column from the Home ribbon

Or you can highlight the table and click on the **New Column** button on the **Calculations** section of the **Modeling** ribbon, as shown in *Figure 1-3*:

Figure 1-3: Adding a new column from the Modeling ribbon

3. Open the formula editor, and enter the DAX expression that will define your **New Column**. *Figure 1-4* shows the formula editor in Power BI Desktop:

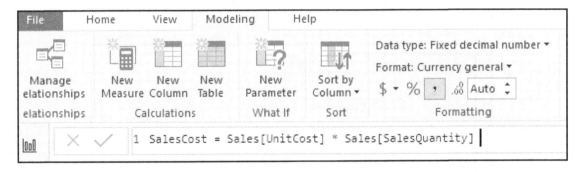

Figure 1-4: The formula editor in Power BI Desktop

To create a new column in Excel Power Pivot and Analysis Services, we do the following:

1. Go into your data model and select the table you want to add the new column to.
2. Select a cell in the last column labeled **Add Column**.

3. In the formula editor, write the expression that defines your new column. *Figure 1-5* shows the formula editor in Excel. Unlike Power BI, in Excel Power Pivot and Analysis Services, the DAX expression begins with the assignment symbol (=) and not the column name:

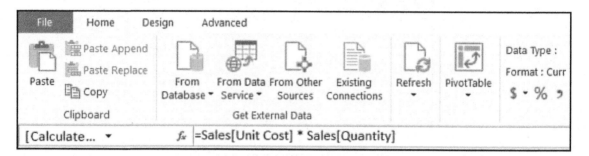

Figure 1-5: The formula editor in Excel Power Pivot

4. To rename a new column, once you have entered the expression, right-click on the column name and select **Rename Column** from the menu, as shown in *Figure 1-6*:

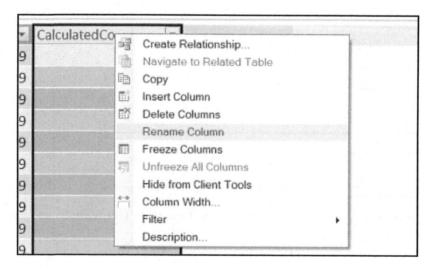

Figure 1-6: Renaming a column

It is important to know that, once created, calculated columns are treated just like another column in a table. And once generated, a calculated value cannot be changed. Calculated columns can be used in any part of a report and they can be used to define relationships.

Calculated columns are computed during a data refresh and stored in memory with the rest of your data model. This is an important point to note when you are planning and building your data model. On the one hand, with complex expressions, the time taken to compute them is at the point you refresh the data and not when you are querying the data. This can improve the user experience, especially with complex expressions, but you need to remember that each calculated column will take up space in memory. Although this might not be an issue with a smaller table, it could have a significant impact on memory use when you are dealing with large tables. If you have complex expressions behind your calculated columns, then this could also slow down the time it takes to refresh the data in your data model.

You would be well advised not to have too many calculated columns in your data model and to consider whether it would be possible to use a measure instead, especially if it does not impact the user experience too adversely.

Measures

The other way you can extend your data model is by using measures (also referred to as calculated fields in Excel 2013). Unlike calculated columns, which are evaluated row by row using the context of the current row, measures are used to summarize data by aggregating the values of rows in a table. They work within the current filter context, which means they are affected by the current filters, slicers applied, and the highlighted sections of charts or visuals.

There are two types of measures: implicit and explicit. Implicit measures are created behind the scenes when you drag a field to the **Values** area of the **PivotTable Fields** list, as shown in *Figure 1-7*:

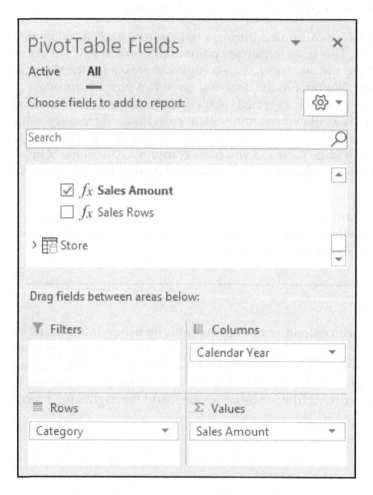

Figure 1-7: Creating an implicit measure in the PivotTable Fields dialog

They are also created when you drag a visual on to the desktop of Power BI, as shown in *Figure 1-8*:

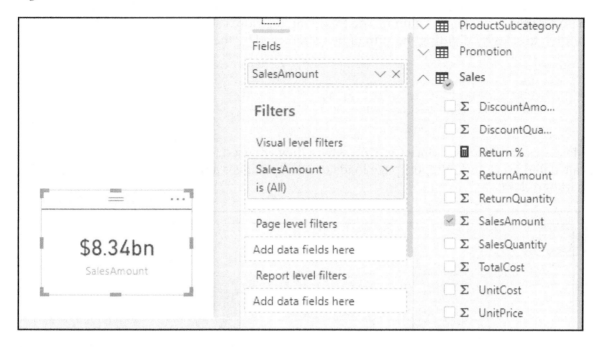

Figure 1-8: Creating an implicit measure with a visual in Power BI Desktop

An explicit measure, on the other hand, is a measure that is specifically created by you.

A measure must be created if you want to conduct an operation on aggregate values instead of values on a row-by-row basis. For example, if you need to calculate the percentage ratio of two columns, you will need to create a measure that calculates the ratio based on the sum of each column. The following measure calculates the percentage of returns to sales by dividing the sum of items returned by the sum of items sold:

```
Return % =
DIVIDE (
    SUM ( Sales[ReturnQuantity] ),
    SUM ( Sales[SalesQuantity] )
)
```

Measures are calculated once for everywhere they are used in a report. They are re-calculated every time a report page loads or a user changes a filter or slicer or highlights part of a chart:

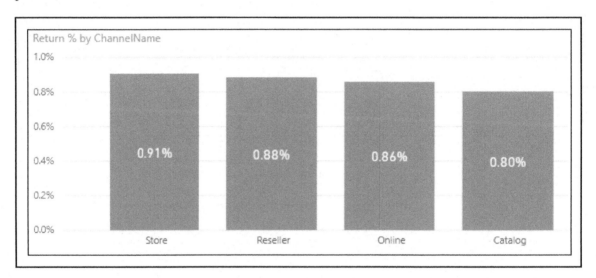

Figure 1-9: A measure being used in a column chart

In *Figure 1-9*, a measure is used to calculate the number of returns over the number of sales. This is used for the value in the column chart, with the sales channel used for the axis. In this example, the measure is calculated four times, once for each time the filter context changes to reflect each of the four different stores.

To create a new measure in Power BI Desktop, follow these steps:

1. Start on the report page and highlight the table that you want to add the new measure to, from the list of tables shown in the **Fields** pane on the right-hand side.

2. Next, right-click on the table name and select **New measure** from the menu, as shown in *Figure 1-10*:

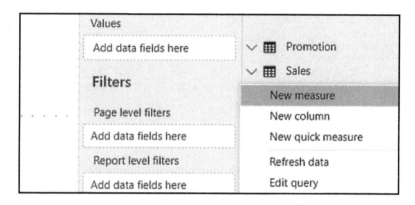

Figure 1-10: Creating a new measure from the Fields pane

To create a new measure in Excel Power Pivot and Analysis Services, we do the following:

1. Go into your data model and select the table you want to add the measure to.
2. Select a blank cell in the calculation area.
3. In the formula editor, write the expression that defines your new measure. *Figure 1-11* shows a couple of measures in the calculation area of an Excel table:

$9.99	$0.00	$5.09	$9.99	£5.09
$9.99	$0.00	$5.09	$9.99	£5.09
$9.99	$0.00	$5.09	$9.99	£5.09
$9.99	$0.00	$5.09	$9.99	£5.09
$9.99	$0.00	$5.09	$9.99	£5.09
				Sales Amount: $4,21...
				Sales Rows: 12,535

Figure 1-11: Measures in the calculation area of a Excel Power Pivot table

The syntax used to create a measure differs slightly depending on the tool you are using. With Power BI, you use the = assignment operator, whereas with Excel and Analysis Services, you use the := assignment operator. If you use the := assignment operator in Power BI, it will automatically be converted into the = operator.

So, for example, *Figure 1-12* shows an example of the syntax used to create a measure in Power BI Desktop:

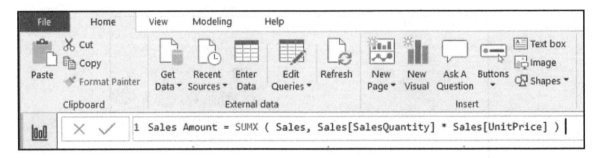

Figure 1-12: A measure being created using the formula editor in Power BI Desktop

On the other hand, *Figure 1-13* shows an example of the syntax used to create a similar measure in Excel:

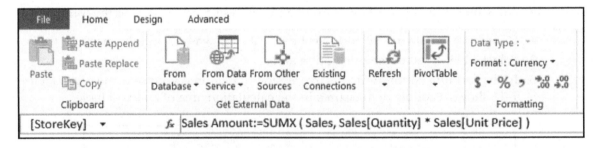

Figure 1-13: A measure being created using the formula editor in Excel Power Pivot

Although DAX requires measures to be defined within a table, they can be moved between tables without affecting their functionality. In fact, it is good practice to keep general measures under one table with a name such as **Key Measures**.

Calculated columns versus measures

Although they may look similar, calculated columns and measures operate very differently. They both use DAX expressions, but they differ in the point at which they are calculated and in the context of their evaluation:

- The values of calculated columns are calculated during a data refresh and they are evaluated using the current row context. They also take up memory and disk space and can slow down data loading times during data refreshes. However, once loaded, they do not impact performance.
- A measure is executed every time a value uses it in a report or chart. Measures are re-calculated every time a page loads. They are also re-calculated when filters or slicers are changed or a user highlights different parts of a chart or visual. A measure does not add to the space used by a data model, but it may impact the speed of user interactions. Measures operate on aggregates that are defined by the current filter context.

You will need to **use a calculated column** whenever you want to do the following:

- Use the value in a slicer.
- Use the value in rows or columns of a pivot table.
- Use the value on the axes of a chart.
- Use the value as a filter condition in a DAX query.
- Define an expression that is bound to the current row.

You will need to **define a measure** whenever you want to do the following:

- Use a value that reflects a user's selection of filters, slicers, or highlighted visuals.
- Calculate a ratio.
- Calculate a percentage.

It is sometimes possible to calculate the same value using either a calculated column or a measure, using different DAX expressions. In most cases, where this is possible, you should use a measure, as this will not increase the size of your data model and use extra memory or disk space. This is especially important if you are working with a table that contains a large number of records.

When naming measures, you should not include the table name in the measure name. Although a measure is created under a table, it does not strictly belong to that table. If you do not include the table name, it can easily be moved between tables if necessary. It also makes it easier to identify as a measure. On the other hand, calculated columns should include the table name.

Evaluation contexts – part 1

Understanding the concept of the evaluation context in DAX is probably the most important concept you will need to learn, if you are to master the use of DAX. In this section, we will have a brief introduction to the concept and will take a more in-depth look in later chapters.

Evaluation contexts are the basis of advanced DAX functionality. They are used to determine the evaluation of a DAX formula and the corresponding result that's given, which will vary depending on the current context. It is this ability that enables you to perform dynamic analysis, in which the results of a DAX formula can change to reflect the current row or a cell selection, or any filters or slicers that may be applied. Understanding context and using context effectively is essential for building powerful DAX formulas and being able to effectively troubleshoot problems with DAX expressions.

There are two types of evaluation contexts in DAX:

- Row context
- Filter context

You may also see references to a query context in Microsoft documentation, but this is essentially another form of filter context.

Row context

The easiest way to think of row context is as the current row in a table. It applies when you add a calculated column to a table. When you use an expression to define your calculated column, it is executed for every row in the table. For example, if you have a table with a thousand rows in it, the expression will be evaluated one thousand times, once for every row in the table, each with a different row context.

The row context can use values from the same row of the table or rows from related tables:

	DeliveryDat...		Order Date	Due Date	Delivery Date	Quantity	Unit Price	Unit Discount	Unit Cost	Net Price	Sale Amount	
3967	20070318		12/03/2007	25/03/2007	18/03/2007	2	$36.83	$2.58	$18.78	$34.25	£73.66	
3968	20070321		12/03/2007	19/03/2007	21/03/2007	3	$36.83	$2.58	$18.78	$34.25	£110.49	
3969	20070314		03/03/2007	14/03/2007	14/03/2007	2	$70.13	$4.91	$32.25	$65.22	£140.26	
3970	20070310		03/03/2007	14/03/2007	10/03/2007	4	$70.13	$4.91	$32.25	$65.22	£280.52	
3971	20070312		06/03/2007	16/03/2007	12/03/2007	2	$369.00	$25.83	$188.13	$343.17	£738.00	
3972	20070314		06/03/2007	13/03/2007	14/03/2007	4	$44.00	$3.08	$22.43	$40.92	£176.00	
3973	20070306		22/02/2007	01/03/2007	06/03/2007	2	$188.50	$13.20	$86.68	$175.31	£377.00	
3974	20070329		19/03/2007	29/03/2007	29/03/2007	3	$168.00	$11.76	$85.65	$156.24	£504.00	
3975	20070411		31/03/2007	13/04/2007	11/04/2007	3	$25.00	$1.75	$11.50	$23.25	£75.00	
3976	20070211		03/02/2007	12/02/2007	11/02/2007	4	$68.00	$4.76	$31.27	$63.24	£272.00	
3977	20070215		06/02/2007	12/02/2007	15/02/2007	2	$1,818.90	$127.32	$836.45	$1,691.58	£3,637.80	
3978	20070215		06/02/2007	14/02/2007	15/02/2007	3	$149.00	$10.43	$75.96	$138.57	£447.00	
3979	20070219		07/02/2007	19/02/2007	19/02/2007	2	$99.99	$7.00	$50.98	$92.99	£199.98	
3980	20070315		09/03/2007	21/03/2007	15/03/2007	2	$89.00	$6.23	$40.93	$82.77	£178.00	
3981	20070318		10/03/2007	23/03/2007	18/03/2007	2	$599.00	$41.93	$275.46	$557.07	£1,198.00	
3982	20070316		10/03/2007	20/03/2007	16/03/2007	4	$599.00	$41.93	$275.46	$557.07	£2,396.00	

[Sale Amount] ▾ f_x = Sales[Quantity] * Sales[Unit Price]

Sales Amount: $4,219,917.90
Sales Rows: 12,535

Figure 1-14: A calculated column being created in Excel Power Pivot

Figure 1-14 shows a calculated column called **Sale amount** that multiplies the value in the **Quantity** column by the value in the **Unit Price** column. Once the data is loaded into the data model from the data source, the calculated column is populated by iterating through each row of the table and calculating the value based on the values contained in the **Quantity** column and the **Unit Price** column, for that row. In other words, the value of the calculated column is generated based on the row context as defined by that individual row.

If you have a relationship between tables, the expression used to define a calculated column can also access the columns of a related table by using the RELATED function:

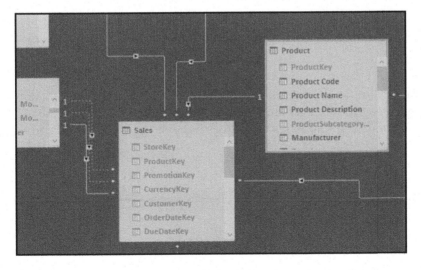

Figure 1-15: The one-to-many relationship between Product and Sales

In *Figure 1-15*, we can see that there is a one-to-many relationship between the **Product** table and the **Sales** table. By creating a calculated column with the following expression, it's possible to add the total weight to the **Sales** table by multiplying the value of the **Quantity** column by the value of the **Weight** column in the related **Product** table:

```
=
IF (
    ISBLANK ( RELATED ( 'Product'[Weight] ) ),
    0,
    [Quantity] * RELATED ( 'Product'[Weight] )
)
```

The following screenshot, *Figure 1-16*, shows the new total weight column added to the **Sales** table, with values generated for each row:

		Order Date	Due Date	Delivery Date	Quantity	Unit Price	Unit Discount	Unit Cost	Net Price	Sale Amount	Total Weight
1	510	02/05/2007	15/05/2007	10/05/2007	1	$9.99	$0.00	$5.09	$9.99	£9.99	5.5
2	511	02/05/2007	08/05/2007	11/05/2007	1	$9.99	$0.00	$5.09	$9.99	£9.99	5.5
3	512	02/05/2007	09/05/2007	12/05/2007	1	$9.99	$0.00	$5.09	$9.99	£9.99	5.5
4	514	02/05/2007	11/05/2007	14/05/2007	1	$9.99	$0.00	$5.09	$9.99	£9.99	5.5
5	710	01/07/2007	09/07/2007	10/07/2007	1	$9.99	$0.00	$5.09	$9.99	£9.99	0.3
6	711	01/07/2007	10/07/2007	11/07/2007	1	$9.99	$0.00	$5.09	$9.99	£9.99	0.3
7	712	01/07/2007	11/07/2007	12/07/2007	1	$9.99	$0.00	$5.09	$9.99	£9.99	0.3
8	713	01/07/2007	12/07/2007	13/07/2007	1	$9.99	$0.00	$5.09	$9.99	£9.99	0.3
9	708	01/07/2007	14/07/2007	08/07/2007	1	$9.99	$0.00	$5.09	$9.99	£9.99	0.3
10	709	01/07/2007	07/07/2007	09/07/2007	1	$9.99	$0.00	$5.09	$9.99	£9.99	0.3
11	710	01/07/2007	08/07/2007	10/07/2007	1	$9.99	$0.00	$5.09	$9.99	£9.99	0.3
12	711	01/07/2007	09/07/2007	11/07/2007	1	$9.99	$0.00	$5.09	$9.99	£9.99	0.3
13	712	05/07/2007	14/07/2007	12/07/2007	1	$9.99	$0.00	$5.09	$9.99	£9.99	0.3
14	713	05/07/2007	15/07/2007	13/07/2007	1	$9.99	$0.00	$5.09	$9.99	£9.99	0.3
15	714	05/07/2007	16/07/2007	14/07/2007	1	$9.99	$0.00	$5.09	$9.99	£9.99	0.3
16	716	05/07/2007	18/07/2007	16/07/2007	1	$9.99	$0.00	$5.09	$9.99	£9.99	0.3

Sales Amount: $4,219,917.90
Sales Rows: 12,535

Figure 1-16: The total weight column added to the Sales table

In the preceding example, the ISBLANK function has been used in conjunction with the IF function to return a zero when a value is not returned from the related table. This would happen when a product in the **Sales** table does not exist in the related **Product** table.

Filter context

The filter context is more complex to understand than the row context, but it can be defined simply as the set of filters that are applied to a data model before the evaluation of a DAX expression begins, which will alter the value returned.

The easiest way to illustrate the filter context is by using a PivotTable:

Sales Amount	Column Labels ▾			
Row Labels ▾	CY 2007	CY 2008	CY 2009	Grand Total
Audio	$12,856.27	$12,240.48	$22,019.91	$47,116.66
Cameras and camcorders	$399,051.85	$268,123.49	$194,420.20	$861,595.54
Cell phones	$53,762.84	$81,481.47	$105,493.78	$240,738.09
Computers	$338,170.40	$310,194.59	$255,491.12	$903,856.11
Games and Toys	$11,735.03	$10,516.64	$20,580.90	$42,832.57
Home Appliances	$463,074.67	$415,946.41	$547,267.18	$1,426,288.26
Music, Movies and Audio Books	$14,179.41	$19,454.06	$13,455.01	$47,088.48
TV and Video	$324,892.14	$125,036.20	$200,473.85	$650,402.19
Grand Total	$1,617,722.61	$1,242,993.34	$1,359,201.95	$4,219,917.90

Figure 1-17: Pivot table showing total sales amount by calendar year for product categories

In *Figure 1-17*, the PivotTable shows the total sales amount of products by calendar year for each product category. The highlighted cell, showing $310,194.59, has a filter context for the calendar year **2008** and the product category of **computers**.

The filter context has the following sources of filter:

- Row selection
- Column selection
- Slicer selection
- Filter selection
- A PivotTable filter

Figure 1-18 shows a Power BI report that has slicers for product category and channel. The total sales amount shown in the card visual is the total sales amount with a filter context for the product category of **Cell phones** and where the sales channel is equal to **Catalog**:

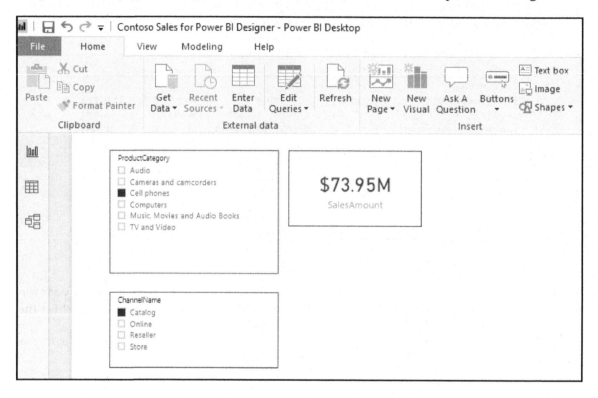

Figure 1-18: Power BI report with slicers for product category and channel

The filter context will automatically propagate through relationships defined in the data model. In Excel Power Pivot and SQL Analysis Services, only the one-to-many direction is supported, but Power BI has the facility for relationships to be bi-directional.

With a one-to-many relationship, a filter applied to the one side of the relationship automatically filters the rows of the table on the many side of the relationship. If the table on the many side has another table that has a one-to-many relationship with it, the filters do not affect that table, unless you set the relationship to be bi-directional (in Power BI only). We will look at relationships between tables in more detail when we come to looking at data modeling.

Using the CALCULATE function

So far, we have only looked at implicit filter context, a context created when you use filters or slicers on a Power BI report or add rows and columns to a PivotTable in Excel. However, it is also possible to create an explicit filter context using the DAX CALCULATE function.

The CALCULATE function in DAX evaluates an expression, as an argument, with a context that is modified by the filters that are passed in one or more additional arguments to the function. It is possibly the most important and complex function in the whole of the DAX language. Although it appears very simple when you first look at it, how it can be used and how it can alter an existing filter context can quickly become confusing.

While other functions can remove either part or all of an existing filter context, the CALCULATE function, along with the associated CALCULATETABLE function, are unique in DAX in that they are the only functions that can alter the context. It is this ability that makes them so powerful and so useful to you as a BI professional.

The following is the syntax of the CALCULATE function:

```
CALCULATE ( <expression>, <filter1>, <filter2>, ... )
```

The function has only one mandatory argument: the expression that is to be evaluated. It will then take one to many optional filter arguments. These optional filter arguments are combined to form the overall filter, which is applied to the expression given as the first argument.

Some restrictions apply to Boolean expressions used as arguments:

- Expressions cannot reference a measure.
- Expressions cannot use a nested CALCULATE function.
- Expressions cannot use any function that scans a table or returns a table, including aggregation functions.

However, expressions can use functions that look up single values or calculate a scalar value.

The power of the CALCULATE function comes from its ability to alter the existing filter context of the expression passed in the first argument, by the *n* number of filter conditions specified by the following arguments. This is done according to the following:

- If the filter context specified by a filter condition already exists, it will override the existing filter context with the new one specified in the expression.
- If the filter context does not exist at all, it will add a new one according to the filter conditions specified.

As you can see, the syntax for the CALCULATE function is straightforward but following what it is doing is more complex. The best way to show this is through a hands-on example.

In the following example, we have what is possibly the most common scenario for using the CALCULATE function, which is to take a value and calculate what percentage it is of an overall total.

Let's start by creating a new measure to calculate the sum of a column called **SaleQuantity** in a table called **Sales**, by using the following DAX expression:

```
SumOfSalesQuantity =
SUM ( Sales[SalesQuantity] )
```

In the screenshot shown in *Figure 1-19*, the measure has been added to a table in Power BI, along with the manufacturer. The manufacturer becomes the filter context for the measure, giving a breakdown of sales quantity by manufacturer:

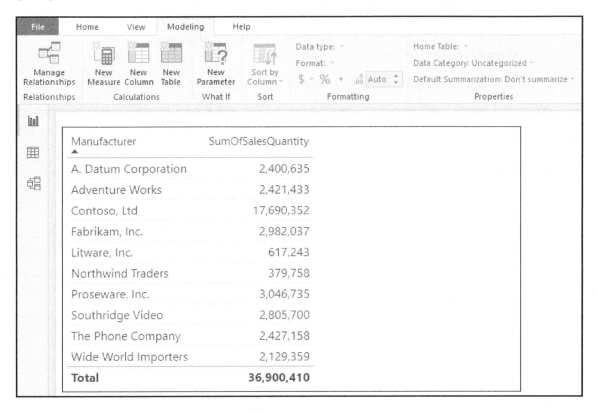

Figure 1-19: The SumOfSalesQuantity measure added to a table in Power BI Desktop

Now, to be able to calculate the sales quantity of each manufacturer as a percentage of the overall sales quantity, each row will need to know what the overall sales quantity is. To do this, you need an expression that will amend the filter context by removing the manufacturer from the filter. This is where the CALCULATE function comes in.

The next step is to create another measure, which again will calculate the sum of the **SalesQuantity** column, but uses the ALL function to amend the current filter context:

```
TotalSalesQuantity =
CALCULATE (
    SUM ( Sales[SalesQuantity] ),
    ALL ( 'Product'[Manufacturer] )
)
```

In this code, we see the following:

- The first argument calculates the total sum of values in the **SalesQuantity** column of the **Sales** table.
- The next argument, the first filter argument, will effectively amend the current filter context by using the ALL function to remove any existing filters on the **Manufacturer** column of the **Product** table.

Figure 1-20 shows this measure added to the Power BI table:

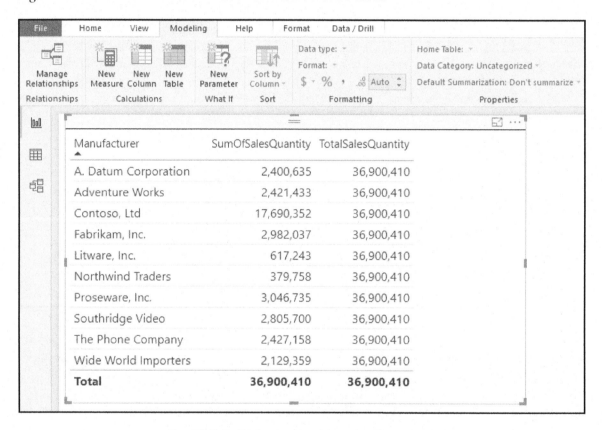

Figure 1-20: The TotalSalesQuantity measure added to a table in Power BI Desktop

As you can see, for each row, the filter context has been altered by the **TotalSalesQuantity** measure and returns the overall sales quantity, regardless of the manufacturer.

With these two new measures, it is possible to create a measure to calculate the sales quantity of each manufacturer as a percentage of the overall sales quantity:

```
%SalesQuantity =
DIVIDE (
    // The sum of sales quantity measure - current filter context
    [SumOfSalesQuantity],
    // The sum of sales quantity measure - current filter context altered
    // to include ALL manufacturers
    [TotalSalesQuantity]
)
```

In this example, we use the DIVIDE function. This function divides the value returned by the measure passed as the first argument (the numerator), by the value returned by the measure passed as the second argument (the denominator). The DIVIDE function also allows for an optional third argument that specifies the alternative value to be returned when division by zero results in an error. When this third argument is not provided, as in this example, the default alternative of BLANK is returned.

Figure 1-21 shows this percentage measure added to the Power BI table:

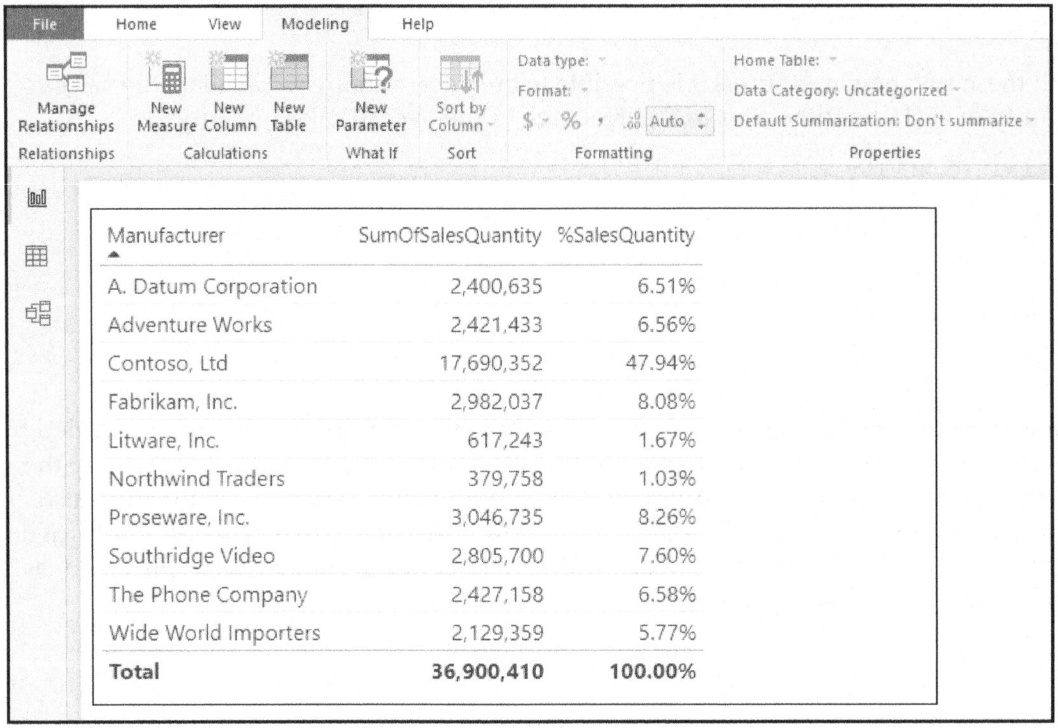

Figure 1-21: The %SalesQuantity measure added to a table in Power BI Desktop

Finally, it's possible to rewrite this measure as a self-contained measure that doesn't require the intermediate measures of **SumOfSalesQuantity** and **TotalSalesQuantity.**

Let's have a look at the following example, which demonstrates this:

```
%SalesQuantity2 =
DIVIDE (
    // The sum of sales quantity - current filter context
    SUM ( Sales[SalesQuantity] ),
    // The sum of sales quantity - current filter context altered
    // to include ALL manufacturers
    CALCULATE (
        SUM ( Sales[SalesQuantity] ),
        ALL ( 'Product'[Manufacturer] )
    )
)
```

This is a relatively simple example of the CALCULATE function being used. In Chapter 5, *Getting it into Context*, there will be some more complex examples when we look at evaluation contexts in more detail.

Summary

In this chapter, we covered a brief introduction to the DAX language, looking at what it is and why learning it is important if you want to get the most out of Excel Power Pivot, SSAS Tabular, or Power BI. You should now have an understanding of the different data types and operators available in DAX and how these operators implicitly convert data to the required type. You have learned about calculated columns and measures, including the differences between them and how and when you can make use of them.

You have also learned how to make use of these features in DAX to expand your data model, creating new information from existing data and giving you even greater insights into your data. Finally, you have learned about the evaluation context, with the row context and the filter context, and how you can modify an existing filter context using the CALCULATE function.

In the next chapter, we will move on to look at using variables in DAX formulas and how these can make your DAX code easier to read, as well as potentially more efficient.

Using DAX Variables and Formatting

2

In this chapter, we will focus on how to use DAX variables and the overall impact of using them in your code. The usage of DAX variables will not only improve the re-usability of your code but potentially make it more efficient as well. Apart from this, we will talk about the recommended formatting rules for DAX code and how using these features will help us identify and debug errors in our code.

Then, you will be introduced to the VAR and RETURN keywords and will learn how to effectively use them within your DAX code. We will also go through a practical example of using variables and formatting rules to debug a DAX measure that is not working correctly.

This chapter has been broken down into the following sections:

- Getting started with DAX variables
- Formatting your DAX code
- Debugging errors in your DAX code

Getting started with DAX variables

Variables were first introduced into the DAX language with Power BI in 2015 and with the 2016 versions of Excel and SSAS Tabular.

Variables allow you to store hard coded values or the results that are returned by a DAX expression. They can store both scalar values and tables and can be used within the definitions of calculated columns, measures, and tables.

A variable is declared using the VAR keyword, and the overall process of declaring and using a variable uses the following syntax:

```
VAR <variableName> = <DAX expression>
RETURN <DAX expression including variableName>
```

When defining an expression, you can use as many variables as you need; each variable is declared using its own VAR keyword. Variables can be used for declaration purposes when defining other variables, as well as to return values in the expression given after the RETURN keyword.

The RETURN keyword is used to define the return expression, which is then used to define the calculated column, measure, or table.

Once a variable has been declared and initialized, it cannot be assigned another value. So, for example, the following would produce an error:

```
VAR varOne = 1
VAR varOne = varOne + 1
RETURN varOne
```

Instead, you should declare a second variable and then use the first variable as part of the second variable's declaration. Then, you can use the second variable in the expression being used with the RETURN keyword, as shown in the following example:

```
VAR varOne = 1
VAR varTwo = varOne + 1
RETURN varTwo
```

Variables in DAX are not declared with data types; they are automatically allocated to the type of the value being assigned to them.

In the following example, the varTextExample variable is being assigned with the data type of text:

```
VAR varTextExample = "Hello World"
RETURN varTextExample
```

In the next example, the varTableExample variable is being assigned as a table, which, in this case, is a copy of the **Products** table that has been filtered so that it only includes products where the **ClassName** is equal to **Deluxe**:

```
VAR varTableExample = FILTER ('Product', 'Product'[ClassName] = "Deluxe")
RETURN varTableExample
```

When using variables of different types with an operator, they will follow the same rules of implicit data type assignment, which we described in `Chapter 1`, *What Is DAX?*. In the following example, the first variable, `varOne`, is assigned the numeric data type, while the second variable, `varTwo`, is assigned the text data type. The third variable, `varThree`, is declared by combining the first two variables using the concatenate operator, and is automatically assigned with a data type of **text**:

```
NumberAndText1 =
VAR varOne = 1
VAR varTwo = "2"
VAR varThree = varOne & varTwo
RETURN varThree
```

Figure 2-1 shows the output of the **NumberAndText1** measure, which was defined using the concatenate operator in the preceding code:

Figure 2-1: The result of the NumberAndText1 measure

In the following example, both the first and second variables are assigned, just like in the previous example. However, on this occasion, the third variable combines the first two variables using the addition operator. This time, it is automatically assigned as a **numeric** data type:

```
NumberAndText2 =
VAR varOne = 1
VAR varTwo = "2"
VAR varThree = varOne + varTwo
RETURN varThree
```

Figure 2-2 shows the output of the **NumberAndText2** measure, which was defined using the addition operator in the preceding code:

Figure 2-2: The result of the NumberAndText2 measure

When it comes to naming variables, you cannot use names that are already in use by tables, or names that are used as DAX keywords. In addition, the following are the limitations when it comes to naming a variable:

- Variable names cannot contain blank spaces
- Delimiters such as square brackets and apostrophes are not allowed
- The supported characters are a-z, A-Z, 0-9
- 0-9 cannot be used as a first character
- A double underscore (__) is allowed as a prefix of a name

Variable nesting

It is possible to nest variables within the declaration of another variable, which offers multiple levels of scope. Each level of variable nesting starts with the VAR keyword and ends with the RETURN keyword. An expression may only refer to variables that have been declared within the same level of scope or higher.

The following measure definition is an example of variable nesting:

```
NestedVariableExample1 =
// The first level of scope is defined by the first VAR keyword
VAR varLevelOneA = "Level 1"
VAR varLevelOneB =
    // The second level of scope is defined using the VAR
    // keyword in the definition of this variable.
    // Variables within this scope can access variables from
    // this level or from the first level of scope.
    VAR varLevelTwoA = varLevelOneA & " and Level 2"
    VAR varLevelTwoB = varLevelTwoA
```

```
    // The second level of scope is closed with the RETURN keyword
    RETURN varLevelTwoB
// Control is passed back to the first level of scope.
// Variables defined in the second level of scope cannot be
// directly referenced by this first level.
RETURN varLevelOneB
```

Figure 2-3 shows the output of the **NestedVariableExample1** measure that was defined using the preceding code:

Figure 2-3: The result of the NestedVariableExample1 measure

This example can be broken down as follows:

1. The first level of scope is defined with the first use of the VAR keyword.
2. The varLevelOneA variable is declared with the text *Level 1*.
3. The second level of scope is defined using the VAR keyword within the declaration of the second variable, varLevelOneB.
4. The varLevelTwoA variable is declared using the varLevelOneA variable (which it can access since it is from a higher level of scope) concatenated with the text *and Level 2*. The varLevelTwoA variable now holds the value *Level 1 and Level 2*.
5. The varLevelTwoA variable is declared using the value stored in varLevelTwoB, which it can access since it is defined at the same level. The varLevelTwoB variable now also holds the value *Level 1 and Level 2*.
6. The second level of scope is closed with the RETURN keyword, which returns the value stored in the varLevelTwoB variable to the varLevelOneB variable. The varLevelOneB variable now also holds the value *Level 1 and Level 2*.
7. The first level of scope is closed with the second RETURN keyword, which returns the value stored in the varLevelOneB variable to the **NestedVariableExample1** measure.

The following code takes variable nesting to the next level. See if you can follow what it is doing while using the previous example as a guide:

```
NestedVariableExample2 =
VAR varLevelOneA = "Level 1"
VAR varLevelOneB =
    VAR varLevelTwoA = " & Level 2"
    VAR varLevelTwoB =
        VAR varLevelThree = varLevelOneA & varLevelTwoA
        RETURN varLevelThree
    RETURN varLevelTwoB
VAR varLevelOneC =
    VAR varLevelFour = varLevelOneB & " & Level 3"
    RETURN varLevelFour
RETURN varLevelOneC
```

Figure 2-4 shows the output of the **NestedVariableExample2** measure that was defined using the preceding code:

Figure 2-4: The result of the NestedVariableExample2 measure

This example introduces a third level of scope within the declaration of the varLevelTwoB variable. This level has access to the variables declared in level 1 and level 2, as well as those declared at its own level. There is another level of scope that's created in the declaration of the varLevelOneC variable. This level of scope only has access to the variables that have been declared in its own level and those defined in level 1. It cannot access variables that have been declared in the scope of levels two and three.

Using variables with measures, calculated columns, and tables

Using variables when you define your measures will make your DAX code much easier to read. In some cases, it can also make your code perform more efficiently. We will look at the potential of improving code performance using variables in more detail when we look at optimizing DAX queries in Chapter 13, *Optimizing Your DAX Queries*.

The following code defines a measure that counts the number of products in a table, where the value of the **ClassName** column is equal to **Deluxe**:

```
Deluxe Products =
VAR varDeluxeProducts =
    FILTER ( 'Product', 'Product'[ClassName] = "Deluxe" )
RETURN COUNTROWS( varDeluxeProducts )
```

This example can be broken down as follows:

1. The measure is defined using the name **Deluxe Products**.
2. The VAR keyword is used to declare a variable called varDeluxeProducts.
3. The variable is defined using the FILTER function, which references the **Product** table and the filters for rows where the value in the **ClassName** column is equal to **Deluxe**.
4. The varDeluxeProducts variable inherits the table type and is used as the argument to the COUNTROWS function, which is used by the RETURN keyword to return the number of rows in the filtered table.

When using variables in an expression that is used to define a calculated column, you automatically have access to the values of the other columns in the same row.

The following example creates a new column called **UnitProfit** that calculates the profit for each product, based on the unit price minus the unit cost of each product:

```
UnitProfit =
VAR varUnitCost = 'Product'[UnitCost]
VAR varUnitPrice = 'Product'[UnitPrice]
RETURN varUnitPrice - varUnitCost
```

This example can be broken down as follows:

1. The column is defined with the name **UnitProfit**.
2. The first VAR keyword is used to declare a variable called varUnitCost, which stores the value held by the **UnitCost** column of the **Product** table for the current row.
3. The second VAR keyword is used to declare a variable called varUnitPrice, which stores the value held by the **UnitPrice** column of the **Product** table for the current row.
4. These two variables are then used with the RETURN keyword and the minus operator to take the value of the varUnitCost variable away from the value of the varUnitPrice variable, giving the value of unit profit.

The screenshot in *Figure 2-5* shows the **Product** table with the new **UnitProfit** column added:

UnitCost ▾	UnitPrice ▾	ProductKey ▾	ProductSu ▾	UnitProfit ▾
$10.69	$20.96	873	22	£10.27
$6.63	$13	879	22	£6.37
$6.63	$13	880	22	£6.37
$6.63	$13	881	22	£6.37
$6.63	$13	882	22	£6.37
$25.49	$50	887	22	£24.51
$25.49	$50	888	22	£24.51
$25.49	$50	889	22	£24.51
$25.49	$50	890	22	£24.51
$9.13	$17.9	833	22	£8.77
$11.68	$22.9	834	22	£11.22
$26.97	$52.9	835	22	£25.93
$8.11	$15.9	836	22	£7.79
$6.07	$11.9	837	22	£5.83
$7.9	$15.5	838	22	£7.6
$7.09	$13.9	841	22	£6.81

Figure 2-5: The Product table with the new UnitProfit column added

When using variables in the definition of a calculated column, it is important to remember that the RETURN keyword should only return a single value, and not a table.

Finally, variables can be used in the definition of an expression to create a new table.

The following example creates a new table called **Deluxe Products Top 20 Sellers** that shows the top 20 best-selling deluxe products by sales quantity. This new table contains columns for the product name, the total sales quantity, and the total sales amount:

```
Deluxe Products Top 20 Sellers =
VAR varDeluxeProducts =
    FILTER (
        'Product',
        'Product'[ClassName] = "Deluxe"
    )
```

```
VAR varDeluxeProductsSummarized =
    SUMMARIZE (
        varDeluxeProducts,
        'Product'[ProductName],
        "TotalSalesQuantity", SUM ( Sales[SalesQuantity] ),
        "TotalSalesAmount", SUM ( Sales[SalesAmount] )
    )
VAR varDeluxeProductsTop20Sales =
    TOPN (
        20,
        varDeluxeProductsSummarized,
        [TotalSalesQuantity]
    )
RETURN
    varDeluxeProductsTop20Sales
```

This example can be broken down as follows:

1. The table is defined with the name **Deluxe Products Top 20 Sellers**.
2. The first VAR keyword is used to declare a variable called varDeluxeProducts, which stores the values returned by the FILTER function. This function filters for rows in the **Product** table that have a **ClassName** equal to **Deluxe**.
3. The second VAR keyword is used to declare a variable called varDeluxeProductsSummarized, which stores the value returned by the SUMMARIZE function. This function takes the table stored in the varDeluxeProducts variable and groups it by the **ProductName** column. Then, it adds new columns, which calculate the sum of sales quantity and sum of the sales amount for each product.
4. Finally, the third VAR keyword is used to declare a variable called varDeluxeProductsTop20Sales. This variable uses the TOPN function to filter the varDeluxeProductsSummarized variable for the top 20 deluxe products, based on the value of **TotalSalesQuantity**.

The screenshot in *Figure 2-6* shows the contents of the new **Deluxe Products Top 20 Sellers** table:

ProductName	TotalSalesQuantity	TotalSalesAmount
Contoso Bluetooth Active Headphones L15 Red	62820	£8,157,691.437
Contoso Bluetooth Active Headphones L15 White	61420	£7,974,490.0305
Contoso Bluetooth Active Headphones L15 Black	58740	£7,628,441.0517
Proseware High-Performance Business-Class Laser Fax X200 Black	22052	£5,382,373.76
Contoso SLR Camera X143 Grey	21917	£13,933,838.86
The Phone Company PDA Phone 3.7 inches M340 Black	21758	£7,063,894.2
Contoso SLR Camera X142 Black	21653	£13,578,190.08
Contoso DVD 14-Inch Player Portable L100 Silver	21525	£5,508,665.5201
Contoso Integrated Business Phone With card L10 White	21477	£887,276.04
Contoso DVD 15-Inch Player Portable L200 Black	21465	£6,126,552.0323
Contoso 8GB Clock & Radio MP3 Player X850 Black	21456	£6,317,358.7215
SV DVD 15-Inch Player Portable L200 Black	21430	£6,117,263.6526
A. Datum Consumer Digital Camera E100 Pink	21384	£5,909,947.04
SV DVD 60 DVD Storage Binder L20 Red	21360	£481,252.1784
Contoso Integrated Business Phone With card L10 Black	21316	£880,913.46
The Phone Company PDA Wifi 4.7-inch L290 Black	21288	£7,960,806.2
Contoso DVD 15-Inch Player Portable L200 Silver	21267	£6,073,794.1516
Proseware Color Ink Jet Fax with 5.8 GHz Cordless Handset X250 Grey	21256	£4,771,595.4
A. Datum Super-zoom Digital Camera X300 Pink	21251	£6,065,263
Adventure Works LCD24W X300 Black	21227	£18,149,482.12
Total	**548062**	**£138,969,088.9357**

Figure 2-6: Table showing output from the new Deluxe Products Top 20 Sellers table

 When using variables in the definition of a calculated table, it is important to remember that you must return a table with the RETURN keyword and not a single value.

Formatting your DAX code

In addition to using variables to make your DAX code easier to read, it is also important to format your code in some way. While there is no official set of rules for formatting your DAX code, following some good formatting guidelines is essential if you want to make DAX easier to work with. Not only is poorly formatted DAX code difficult to read, but it is almost impossible to interpret. In addition, well-formatted DAX code is much easier to debug when things don't work as expected.

Since it is a functional language, a DAX expression will consist of a call to a DAX function, along with some parameters. These parameters can be static arguments, or they can be calls to other DAX functions. All but the simplest DAX expressions will consist of nested functions calls, often many layers deep.

The following example shows a relatively simple DAX expression that creates a measure to calculate the month-over-month percentage change in sales amount:

```
SalesAmount MoM% = DIVIDE(SUM('Sales'[SalesAmount]) -
CALCULATE(SUM('Sales'[SalesAmount]),DATEADD('Calendar'[DateKey].[Date], -1,
MONTH)),
CALCULATE(SUM('Sales'[SalesAmount]),DATEADD('Calendar'[DateKey].[Date], -1,
MONTH)))
```

Even with a simple measure like this, with no formatting, the DAX code is difficult to read and understand.

The following example is the same measure, but this time it is formatted and also makes uses of a variable to store the value of the previous month's sales amount:

```
SalesAmount MoM% 2 =
VAR varPrevMonth =
    CALCULATE (
        SUM ( 'Sales'[SalesAmount] ),
        DATEADD (
            'Calendar'[DateKey].[Date],
            -1,
            MONTH
        )
    )
RETURN
    DIVIDE (
        SUM ( 'Sales'[SalesAmount] ) - varPrevMonth,
        varPrevMonth
    )
```

Now, it is easier to understand what the measure is doing. This can be broken down as follows:

1. First, it calculates the total sales amount for a previous month's date.
2. It stores this value in the varPrevMonth variable.
3. Then, it takes a value of varPrevMonth away from the total sales amount for the current date.
4. Finally, it divides the value from the previous step by the value of varPrevMonth.

The following are a basic set of formatting rules that you should follow to make your DAX code easier to read:

- Always place a new function call on a new line.
- Place the first bracket for a function call on the same line as the function.
- If a function only has one argument, then place that on the same line as the function call.
- If a function has more than one argument, then place each argument on a new line.
- If an argument is on a new line, indent four spaces from the function call.
- The closing bracket for a function call should be lined up with the function call, and not indented.
- Keep commas separating arguments on the same line as the previous argument.
- If you have to spread a function call over more than one line, ensure that operators are the first characters.
- Use a space after brackets.
- Use a space after operators.
- Use a space after a comma, but not before it.

When referencing table names, calculated columns, and measures, follow these guidelines:

- Do not use a space between the table name and the column name.
- Only use single quotes for table names when required (that is, when table names have spaces).
- Ensure you always include the table name with column references. It should be written as `TableName[ColumnName]`.
- Do not include a table name with a measure reference. It should be written as `[MeasureName]`.

Although these simple rules may be difficult to follow at first, they will soon become second nature, and they will make a tremendous difference to you when working with your DAX code. As you will see in the next section, you will more than save on the extra time it takes to format your code with the time you save in debugging problems.

If you want some help formatting your DAX code, head on over to `www.daxformatter.com`, where you will find a very useful tool called **DAX Formatter.** This is a free tool that will transform your raw DAX into clean, readable code.

Go to the website and paste in your unformatted DAX code, as shown in *Figure 2-7*:

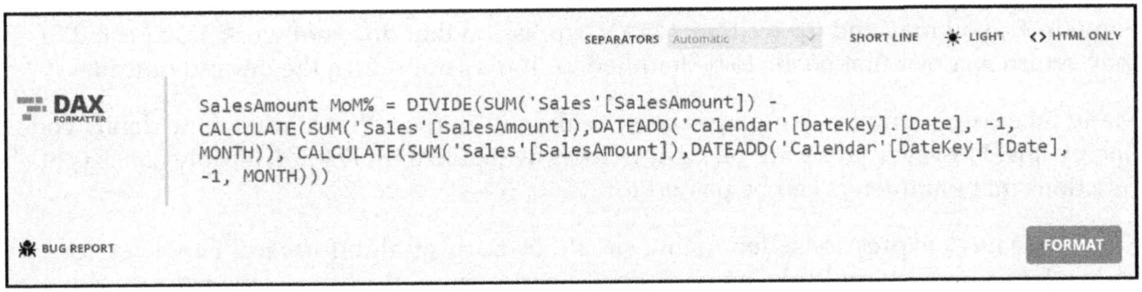

SEPARATORS Automatic   SHORT LINE   ☀ LIGHT   <> HTML ONLY

DAX FORMATTER

```
SalesAmount MoM% = DIVIDE(SUM('Sales'[SalesAmount]) -
CALCULATE(SUM('Sales'[SalesAmount]),DATEADD('Calendar'[DateKey].[Date], -1,
MONTH)), CALCULATE(SUM('Sales'[SalesAmount]),DATEADD('Calendar'[DateKey].[Date],
-1, MONTH)))
```

🐛 BUG REPORT   FORMAT

Figure 2-7: Pasting unformatted DAX into DAX Formatter

Here, I am using the month-over-month example we looked at earlier. Click on the **FORMAT** button; the formatting tool will format your code using a similar set of rules to the ones we looked at previously:

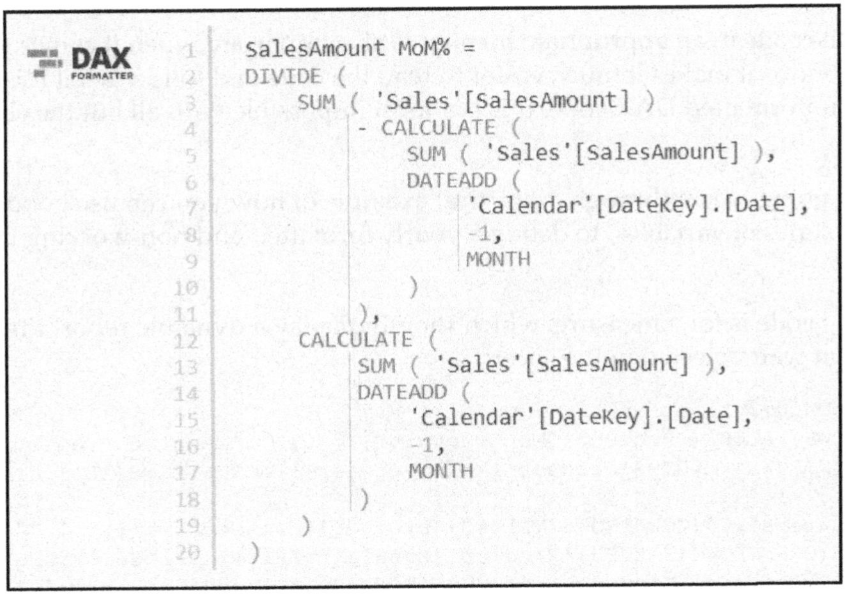

DAX FORMATTER

```
1   SalesAmount MoM% =
2   DIVIDE (
3       SUM ( 'Sales'[SalesAmount] )
4           - CALCULATE (
5               SUM ( 'Sales'[SalesAmount] ),
6               DATEADD (
7                   'Calendar'[DateKey].[Date],
8                   -1,
9                   MONTH
10              )
11          ),
12      CALCULATE (
13          SUM ( 'Sales'[SalesAmount] ),
14          DATEADD (
15              'Calendar'[DateKey].[Date],
16              -1,
17              MONTH
18          )
19      )
20  )
```

Figure 2-8: DAX code formatted using DAX Formatter

The screenshot in *Figure 2-8* shows the same code after it has been reformatted by the **DAX Formatter** tool. As you can see, it is very similar to the code we used in our earlier example. However, this time, the reformatted code does not use a variable; however, it does apply many of the formatting rules that were listed, and it is much easier to read and understand.

Debugging errors in your DAX code

Sometimes, you may end up writing a DAX expression that does not work as expected. It may return an error that needs to be handled, or it may not return the desired output.

Many other programming languages come with built-in tools that allow you to debug code line by line. However, there are no built-in tools available with DAX. It simply consists of functions that parameters can be passed to.

For simple DAX expressions, debugging should be fairly straightforward. However, for code where you have multiple layers of nested expressions, it may become necessary to break the expression down into smaller, more manageable parts. By reducing the code into smaller segments, you will be able to inspect different values and confirm which ones are returning the expected results and which ones are not. This is where using variables becomes invaluable when debugging code as it allows you to break your code down and assign each segment to its own variable. Then, you can change the expression for the RETURN keyword in order to return the values of different variables.

Formatting the code in an appropriate manner is also important when it comes to debugging code as it makes it much easier to read the code and follow what it is should be doing. With unformatted DAX code, this is almost impossible with all but the simplest of expressions.

Now, we are going to run through a practical example of how you can use good formatting, along with a series of variables, to debug a poorly formatted and non-working DAX measure.

The following code is for a measure, which should display a dynamic report title based on the values that were selected in the slicer:

```
SelectedManufacturers = IF
(COUNTROWS(VALUES('Product'[Manufacturer]))=0,"","Manufactured by
"&IF(COUNTROWS(VALUES('Product'[Manufacturer]))=COUNTROWS(ALL('Product'[Man
ufacturer])),"all
manufacturers",IF(COUNTROWS(VALUES('Product'[Manufacturer]))=1,"",CONCATENA
TEX(TOPN(COUNTROWS(VALUES('Product'[Manufacturer])),VALUES('Product'[Manufa
cturer]),'Product'[Manufacturer],ASC),'Product'[Manufacturer],",",'Product'
[Manufacturer],ASC)&" and
")&EXCEPT(VALUES('Product'[Manufacturer]),TOPN(COUNTROWS(VALUES('Product'[M
anufacturer])),VALUES('Product'[Manufacturer]),'Product'[Manufacturer],ASC)
)))
```

However, the visual that's been set up to display the measure does not appear to match what has been selected in the slicer, as shown in *Figure 2-9*:

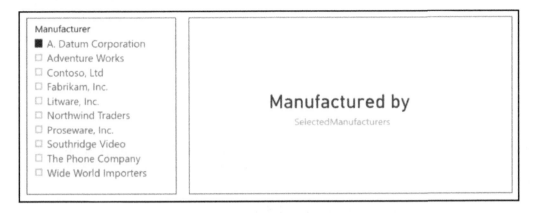

Figure 2-9: Visual not matching value selected in slicer

As it is, the measure has no formatting, and it is almost impossible to work out what it is doing. So, the first step is to apply some formatting, following the rules we mentioned in the previous section.

The following is the same measure, but with formatting applied:

```
SelectedManufacturers =
IF (
    COUNTROWS ( VALUES ( 'Product'[Manufacturer] ) ) = 0,
    "",
    "Manufactured by "
        & IF (
            COUNTROWS ( VALUES ( 'Product'[Manufacturer] ) )
                = COUNTROWS ( ALL ( 'Product'[Manufacturer] ) ),
            "all manufacturers",
            IF (
                COUNTROWS ( VALUES ( 'Product'[Manufacturer] ) ) = 1,
                "",
                CONCATENATEX (
                    TOPN (
                        COUNTROWS ( VALUES ( 'Product'[Manufacturer] ) ),
                        VALUES ( 'Product'[Manufacturer] ),
                        'Product'[Manufacturer], ASC
                    ),
                    'Product'[Manufacturer],
                    ", ",
                    'Product'[Manufacturer], ASC
                ) & " and "
            )
                & EXCEPT (
                    VALUES ( 'Product'[Manufacturer] ),
```

```
TOPN (
    COUNTROWS ( VALUES ( 'Product'[Manufacturer] ) ),
    VALUES ( 'Product'[Manufacturer] ),
    'Product'[Manufacturer], ASC
)
            )
        )
    )
```

While this is a start and makes the code easier to read, it still doesn't help isolate the cause of the problem. So, the next step is to convert the DAX code so that it can use variables. Follow these steps to do so:

1. Looking at the code, the first candidate that will be converted into a variable is the function call to get the list of selected manufacturers:

   ```
   VAR SelectedManufacturers =
       VALUES ( 'Product'[Manufacturer] )
   ```

2. Next, we need to create another variable that will hold the value for the number of selected manufacturers:

   ```
   VAR NumberOfSelectedManufacturers =
       COUNTROWS ( SelectedManufacturers )
   ```

3. Then, we need to create a variable that will hold the value for the total number of manufacturers that it is possible to select:

   ```
   VAR NumberOfPossibleManufacturers =
       COUNTROWS ( ALL ( 'Product'[Manufacturer] ) )
   ```

4. Finally, we need to create two additional variables that use code from the original DAX measure. The first, AllButLastSelectedManufacturer, should get a list of all the values that were selected in the slicer, except the last one. The last variable, LastSelectedManufacturer, should get the value of the last select item that was selected in the slicer:

   ```
   VAR AllButLastSelectedManufacturer =
       TOPN (
           NumberOfSelectedManufacturers,
           SelectedManufacturers,
           'Product'[Manufacturer], ASC
       )
   VAR LastSelectedManufacturer =
       EXCEPT ( SelectedManufacturers, AllButLastSelectedManufacturer )
   )
   ```

5. The final step is to create the return expression, where we will replace all of the existing expressions with the variables we created in *steps 1* to *4*. Once completed, the revised DAX code for the measure will be as follows:

```
SelectedManufacturers =
 VAR SelectedManufacturers =
     VALUES ( 'Product'[Manufacturer] )
 VAR NumberOfSelectedManufacturers =
     COUNTROWS ( SelectedManufacturers )
 VAR NumberOfPossibleManufacturers =
     COUNTROWS ( ALL ( 'Product'[Manufacturer] ) )
 VAR AllButLastSelectedManufacturer =
     TOPN (
         NumberOfSelectedManufacturers,
         SelectedManufacturers,
         'Product'[Manufacturer], ASC
     )
 VAR LastSelectedManufacturer =
     EXCEPT ( SelectedManufacturers, AllButLastSelectedManufacturer
)
 RETURN
     IF (
         NumberOfSelectedManufacturers = 0,
         "",
         "Manufactured by "
             & IF (
                 NumberOfSelectedManufacturers =
NumberOfPossibleManufacturers,
                 "all manufacturers",
                 IF (
                     NumberOfSelectedManufacturers = 1,
                     "",
                     CONCATENATEX (
                         AllButLastSelectedManufacturer,
                         'Product'[Manufacturer],
                         ", ",
                         'Product'[Manufacturer], ASC
                     ) & " and "
                 ) & LastSelectedManufacturer
             )
     )
```

While this doesn't fix the error, we are now in a much better place to start debugging the code. We'll start by creating a copy of the measure, but with the code after the RETURN keyword removed. Then, we can start inspecting the results of each variable by placing each variable after the RETURN keyword and testing them one by one. Since this is a measure and the first variable returns a table, it will need to be used with the COUNTROWS function so that it returns a single number instead. In this case, it should return the number of manufacturers we selected in the slicer.

So, the code for testing the first variable should look like this:

```
SelectedManufacturersTest =
 VAR SelectedManufacturers =
     VALUES ( 'Product'[Manufacturer] )
 VAR NumberOfSelectedManufacurers =
     COUNTROWS ( SelectedManufacturers )
 VAR NumberOfPossibleManufacturers =
     COUNTROWS ( ALL ( 'Product'[Manufacturer] ) )
 VAR AllButLastSelectedManufacturer =
     TOPN (
         NumberOfSelectedManufacurers,
         SelectedManufacturers,
         'Product'[Manufacturer], ASC
     )
 VAR LastSelectedManufacturer =
     EXCEPT ( SelectedManufacturers, AllButLastSelectedManufacturer )
 RETURN
     COUNTROWS ( SelectedManufacturers )
```

With Power BI Desktop, I can use a card visual to see the value of the variable that's being returned. For this variable, the result is as expected, as shown in *Figure 2-10*:

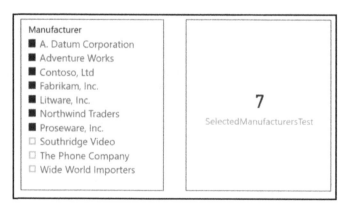

Figure 2-10: Debugging code using the COUNTROWS function

Using this method, it is possible to go through all of the variables to see if they return the values that we expected. In this case, when the AllButLastSelectedManufacturer variable is tested, it returns one more row than expected. In fact, the variable declaration should be one less than the value being returned by the NumberOfSelectedManufacturers variable.

So, the correct code should be as follows:

```
VAR AllButLastSelectedManufacturer =
    TOPN (
        NumberOfSelectedManufacturers - 1,
        SelectedManufacturers,
        'Product'[Manufacturer], ASC
    )
```

With the code for the measure corrected, it now returns the correct dynamic title based on the manufacturers selected in the slicer, as shown in *Figure 2-11*:

Figure 2-11: DAX code corrected to display dynamic title based on selected values of a slicer

Although this method of debugging is more complex compared to the other programming languages, it still provides us with a practical way to inspect and fix errors in our DAX code.

In this example, rather than looking at how the code for the measure works, you should focus more on the method that's being used to inspect the code and identify the cause of the problem.

Using variables allows you to break down your code into smaller parts and understand how it is working, especially in relation to interactions with filters, slicers, and other visuals.

Summary

In this chapter, you learned how to add variables to your DAX code using the VAR and RETURN keywords, as well as how using variables will make your code easier to read. You learned about nesting variables and about the different levels of scope in which variables can exist and interact with each other.

Then, you went through some practical examples of variables being used to create measures, calculated fields, and calculated tables. You also looked at the advantages of following set formatting rules when writing DAX code. Finally, you went through a practical example of how to use both of these features to help you debug your code.

In the next chapter, we will learn about the importance of data models and the different types of schema. We'll look at DAX data modeling concepts, how to load data into a data model, and how DAX can be used to extend a data model.

Building Data Models 3

In this chapter, you will learn about the importance of building a well-defined data model, both from the point of view of a BI professional and in terms of making DAX code easier to write.

By the end of this chapter, you will have learned about the basics of good data modeling and why it is important to have a well-structured data model. You'll learn about importing data from different data sources and transforming it into a structure that is easy for both you and your end users to understand. Then, we'll look at a couple of different schema designs as well as some data modeling concepts. There will also be some hands-on examples of loading data, creating relationships, and using DAX functions to extend your model through the addition of calculated columns, calculated tables, and measures. Finally, you'll learn how to extend your data model further by using DAX functions to create a custom data table.

This chapter has been broken down into the following sections:

- Introduction to data modeling
- Data modeling concepts in DAX
- Getting data into your data model
- Extending your data model
- It's a date

Introduction to data modeling

Before you start using a report or writing DAX expressions, you need to build the underlying data model. You can think of a data model like the chassis of a sports car. No matter how good the car looks, if it has a poorly designed chassis, it will give a poor driving experience. In the same way, no matter how good a report might look, if it's built using a poorly designed data model, then it won't be very easy to work with. Worse still, the report may contain inaccurate information.

In addition to making it easier to work with DAX expressions, a well-structured data model can also help to reduce the overall size of your Excel spreadsheet or Power BI Desktop file. Through careful planning, a well-designed data model can also improve performance.

The process of building a data model begins with importing data into tables and creating the relationships between them. Then, you refine the data model by removing or hiding columns that will not be used and by checking the remaining columns to ensure they use the correct data types and formats. You can refine the data model further by appending and merging tables to simplify the structure. Finally, you can add hierarchies and extend the data model by using DAX functions to create calculated columns and tables and measures.

A data model consists of the following elements:

- Data
- Tables
- Relationships
- Hierarchies
- Calculated columns
- Measures

To start with, a data model defines how you connect to your source data. You can import data from a large number of different data sources using many different file formats. The following are some examples of the file types you can connect to using Excel Power Pivot:

- Excel
- Text/CSV
- XML
- JSON

In addition, you can also connect to the following databases:

- SQL Server
- Microsoft Access
- SQL Server Analysis Services Database
- ODBC
- OLE DB

If you are using Power BI Desktop, you can choose from even more data sources. The screenshot in *Figure 3-1* shows the data connection screen in Power BI Desktop and shows the vast array of connection options available. Monthly updates to Power BI Desktop regularly increase this list with the addition of new data source connectors:

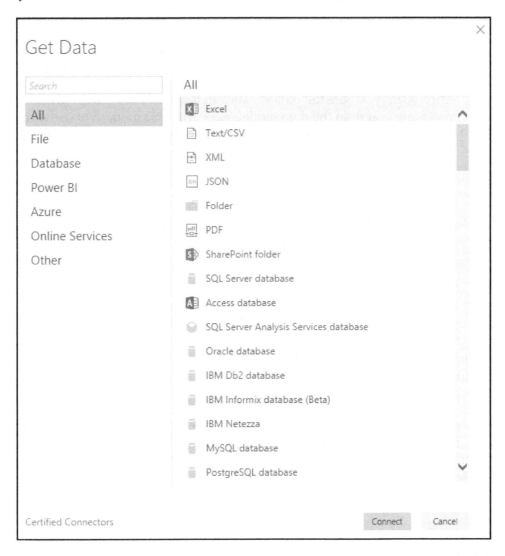

Figure 3-1: The data connection screen in Power BI Desktop

In addition, it is also possible to create custom connectors, meaning that you can connect to almost any data source.

In a typical data model, you might load data from several different sources. For example, you might load some of your data from a SQL Server database, some of it from an Access database, and some of it from Excel spreadsheets or flat files. You might even import data directly from a source system using an API service.

 When you import data into your model, you are loading a copy of it into memory. There is also the option to use a method of connecting called **DirectQuery**, where the data remains in the data source and only the metadata is kept in the data model. However, this method of connection comes with some limitations. These will not be covered in this book as they are out of scope.

Once imported, the data is stored in tables, much like in a database. However, before it is ready to use, you should do the following:

- Merge and append tables to simplify the data model.
- Create or amend relationships between the tables.
- Rename tables and columns to something more in line with business requirements.
- Remove columns that will not be used.
- Hide columns that are required but should not be seen by end users.
- Ensure the columns have been defined with the correct data types.
- Decide on the appropriate formats for columns.
- Add hierarchies.
- Create calculated columns, calculated tables, and measures.

Building a well-designed data model is important as it underpins your entire report. Getting it right from the start will make the process of building your report much easier. Not only will it potentially make your report more efficient, but it will also make your DAX code easier to write and understand.

Although your data model may look like other transactional databases, it serves a very different purpose. With a transactional database, the goal is to efficiently add, amend, and delete data. When designing a data model for business analysis purposes, the goal is to allow for efficient querying and aggregation of data.

The first step in building any data model for reporting purposes is to understand the business requirements. You need to know requirements such as where the data will be coming from, how the data will be filtered and sliced, and how the data will be aggregated.

 Before you start building a data model or report, consider what sort of analysis the business is trying to achieve. To be successful, you need to understand what questions the business is trying to answer.

Users who are new to building a data model for reporting and analysis usually make one or more of the following mistakes:

- **Importing data into a single flattened table**: This may be sourced from a SQL query that joins several tables together. It's also not uncommon for systems to export data as a single, de-normalized text file. The temptation here is to import this file as it is and build your report on top of the resulting single table data model.
- **Importing a complete copy of a source database**: This often results in a large number of tables when using the default relationships that were identified by the import process. Not only can these relationships be incorrect, but the data in the related tables may be of different granularity, resulting in inaccurate results in your reports. The data model can also be difficult to work with due to its size.
- **Not refining the data model**: Once you have imported some data, you should go through the process of refining your data model, as outlined earlier.

Ideally, you should aim to keep your data model as simple as possible, with just the right amount of data to be able to answer questions that are being asked by the business for a specific purpose. Do not be tempted to try and build a data model that supports all of the reporting needs of the business. You will end up with a very large and unwieldy data model that will be difficult to understand. It will use more memory than necessary and will perform less efficiently. It will also make the job of writing DAX expressions more difficult as you will struggle to understand how data flows around the relationships between tables.

Data modeling concepts in DAX

Before you can design and build a well-structured data model, there are some key concepts that you need to understand. In this section, we will look at these concepts in detail. Then, in the next section, we'll put them into practice when we build a simple data model as a hands-on example.

Fact tables and dimension tables

In its simplest form, a good data model's design will consist of a primary table (or fact table) containing the numerical figures that you want to aggregate and analyze. This is then joined to several lookup tables (dimension tables) that contain the descriptive data relating to the business entities that you want to use to slice and dice your data.

A **fact table**, as the name suggests, contains values relating to events or processes such as sales. It contains numerical data, which can be aggregated and analyzed to provide measurements, metrics, or other facts about the business. It is the primary table in a schema and has foreign keys that relate it to the dimension tables.

A **dimension table** is a lookup table that contains descriptive data relating to business entities such as customer, product, or date. It may contain groups and subgroups and allows you to slice and dice the information you have in the fact table. The primary key of a dimension table relates to a foreign key in the fact table.

Star schema and snowflake schema

With a simple data model, the fact table sits at the center and is surrounded by the dimension tables. This sort of data model is known as a star schema due to the fact that, when arranged, the tables form a star shape, as shown in *Figure 3-2*:

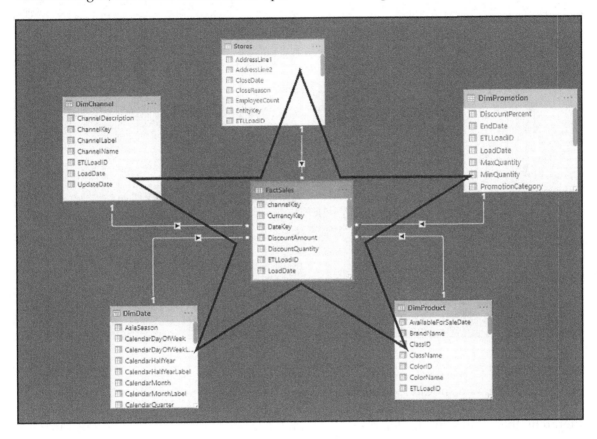

Figure 3-2: Example of a star schema data model

You may also have dimension tables that are related to other dimension tables in the form of a hierarchy chain. In this case, you end up with a snowflake schema, as shown in *Figure 3-3*:

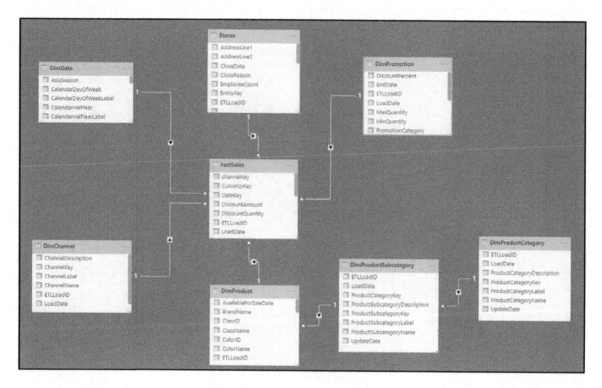

Figure 3-3: Example of a snowflake schema data model

Where possible, you should look to flatten these chains of dimension tables by merging them together to form a single dimension table. Once you've done this, you can create a hierarchy that allows you to step down through the levels of groups and subgroups in your reports.

You may also have tables in your data model that have a one-to-one relationship. In these cases, you should also consider flattening the data model by merging the tables into one. Not only will this reduce the overall size of your model in memory, but it may also improve performance.

Relationships

Once you have imported some data, the next step is creating the relationships between the tables. If you have imported data from a database where primary and foreign keys have already been defined, then these should be imported along with the tables. However, you may find that these relationships are not suitable for your data model. You may also have more than one relationship between tables, where only one will be active. In addition, you may also want to create new relationships.

A relationship is defined by a single column from each table. You cannot use multiple columns to define a relationship, but you can create new columns in each table that consist of multiple columns concatenated together. You can then use these to create the relationships:

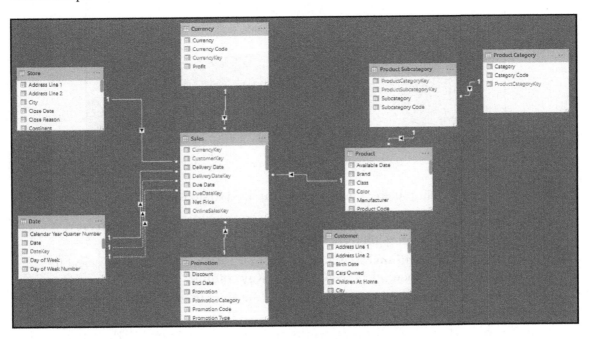

Figure 3-4: Creating relationships between tables in a data model

The screenshot in *Figure 3-4* is from a data model in Power BI Desktop. Both Excel Power Pivot and SSAS Tabular provide similar views of their data models. In this case, most of the relationships have already been defined. However, the relationship between the **Sales** table and the **Customer** table still needs to be created. To do this, you can drag the cursor from the **CustomerKey** field in the **Sale** table to the **CustomerKey** field in the **Customer** table.

Alternatively, you can create or maintain relationships through the **Manage Relationships** dialog, which can be found under the **Modeling** tab, as shown in *Figure 3-5*:

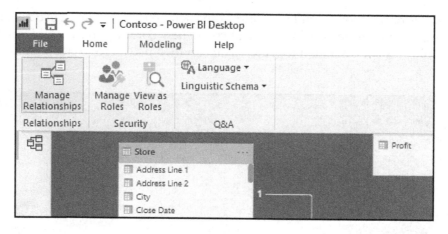

Figure 3-5: The Manage Relationships button in Power BI Desktop

To create a new relationship using this method, you need to do the following:

1. On the **Modeling** tab, click **Manage Relationships** to open the **Manage Relationships** dialog, then click on **New**.
2. In the **Create Relationship** dialog, in the first table drop-down list, select the **Sales** table and then select the **CustomerKey** column.
3. In the second table drop-down list, select the **Customer** table and select the **CustomerKey** column.
4. From the drop-down list for **Cardinality**, select **Many to one (*:1)**.
5. From the drop-down list for **Cross filter direction**, select **Single**.
6. Ensure the checkbox for **Make this relationship active** is ticked.
7. Your dialog box should look like the one shown in *Figure 3-6*. If it does, click on **OK**.

8. Click **Close** on the **Manage Relationships** dialog:

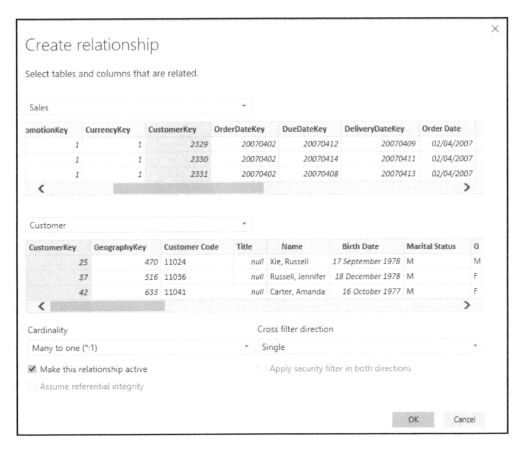

Figure 3-6: The Create Relationship dialog in Power BI Desktop

This should create an active relationship between the **Sales** and **Customer** tables. The cardinality of the relationship will be one-to-many between the **Customer** and **Sales** tables. This means that a single record in the **Customer** table may have many related records in the **Sales** table.

 On the one side of a one-to-many relationship, the table must have a distinct set of primary key values; otherwise, you will get an error. However, on the one side of a one-to-many relationship, the table does not need to have matching primary key values for all of the foreign key values in the table on the many side of the relationship. A data model does not enforce referential integrity in the way you might expect if you have experience of working with database models.

If you create a slicer that's connected to a dimension or lookup table and it contains a **(Blank)** record at the top, there must be records in the related fact or data table that have no corresponding record in the lookup table:

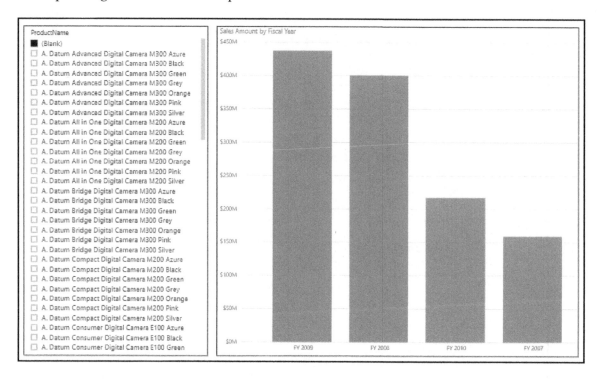

Figure 3-7: Slicer with a blank value showing

The screenshot in *Figure 3-7* shows an example of this. Here, we have a product slicer that is referencing the **Product** table and has **(Blank)** at the top. This means that there are records in the related **Sales** table that are for products that do not exist in the **Product** table.

One solution to this is to simply filter out blank records from the slicer. However, as shown in the preceding example, this would also remove a significant amount of data from the **Sales** table, meaning that data would also be removed from your reports. Where you encounter this situation, you should review your data model and, if necessary, the source data behind it.

Cardinality

Relationships in your data model can have the following cardinality:

- **One-to-many (*:1)**: The column of the table on the one side of the relationship, which is usually the lookup or dimension table, only has one instance of a value. This is usually the primary key for that table. The other related table, which is often a fact table, can have many instances of the value. This is known as the foreign key.
- **One-to-One (1:1)**: The column of the table on one side of the relationship has only one instance of a value, while the column of the table on the other side of the relationship also only has one instance of the value.
- **Many-to-many (*:*)**: You can have many-to-many relationships between tables, removing the need for unique values in tables. It also removes the need to create bridging tables for the purposes of establishing relationships. However, there may still be circumstances where creating bridging tables is the preferred solution.

Cross filter direction

When you create a relationship between two tables in SSAS Tabular and Power BI Desktop, you have the choice of bidirectional cross filters or single direction cross filters. With Excel Power Pivot, to maintain backward compatibility with earlier versions of Excel, you can only have relationships with single direction cross filters. The arrow on a relationship line, which is shown in the data model view, shows the direction in which the filter flows. Let's take a look at the directions that are stated:

- **Single direction**: If you filter records in the table on the one side of a relationship, the filtering choices are carried through to the table on the many side of the relationship. However, if you filter records in the table on the many side of the relationship, these are not carried through to the table on the one side of the relationship. In Excel Power Pivot, all relationships will have a single direction.
- **Both**: Unlike single direction cross filters, these filters flow in both directions. So, if you filter records in the table on either side of the relationship, they will be carried across to the table on the other side of the relationship. For filtering purposes, both tables in the relationship are treated like they are a single table. However, with bidirectional cross filters, it is possible to create an ambiguous set of relationships, especially when you have a complex pattern of tables. Because of this, you should avoid using bidirectional filters where possible.

Hierarchies

A hierarchy is a set of nested columns that are grouped together in a way that allows you to drill up and down a report visual using a single object from the field list. A typical example of a hierarchy is usually found in a date table, where a date hierarchy might consist of the year, month, week, and day fields. This could then be used with a report visual, where it would allow you to aggregate data by these values, giving you the ability to drill up and down by them.

In the following example, we're taking a data model where there are separate tables for products, product subcategories, and product categories. As it is, these can be used as they are to create a visual that allows you to drill up and down on a matrix to show data that's been aggregated by different levels. However, you need to use three objects from the field list to accomplish this. The screenshot in *Figure 3-8* shows an example of this:

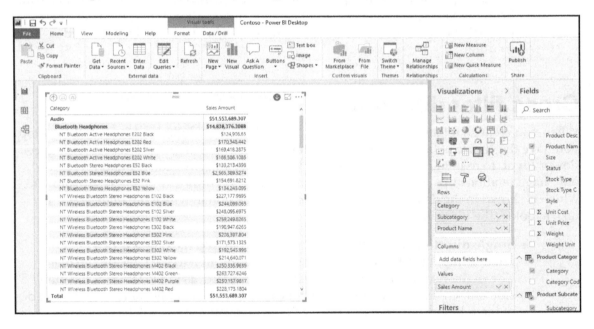

Figure 3-8: A visual using multiple fields to create a drill-down

In the **Date** table, a hierarchy has been created that includes the **Year**, **Quarter**, **Month**, and **Day** fields. Now, we only need to use one object from the field list to be able to drill up and down the matrix. This can be seen in the screenshot in Figure 3-9:

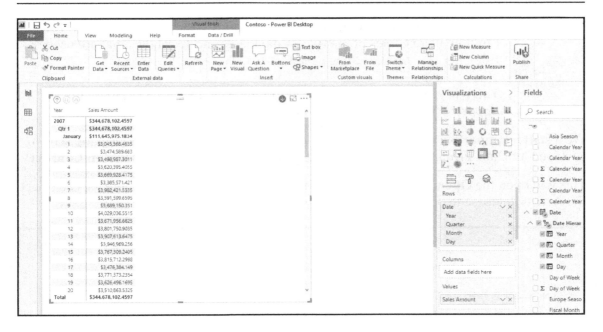

Figure 3-9: A visual using a date hierarchy to create a drill-down

In the next section, we'll go through a hands-on example where we'll merge the **Product Category**, **Product Subcategory**, and **Product** tables into one table and create a new hierarchy.

Getting data into your data model

Now, let's walk through a hands-on example of building a simple data model. We'll start by importing data from an Access database. Once the data has been imported, we'll refine the model by renaming the tables and columns, hiding unused data, and ensuring that we have created the appropriate relationships.

Building your first data model

In this example, we'll use Power BI Desktop to walk through the process of importing data and building a simple data model. In the next chapter, we'll look at how to import data using Excel Power Pivot and SSAS Tabular.

If you want to follow along with the examples in the rest of this book, you can download copies of the Access databases and Excel files that are used from: `https://github.com/dataworldtv/Hands-On-Business-Intelligence-with-DAX`.

You will also find a Power BI Desktop file there that has the tables already imported, to help get you started.

We'll start by importing data from an Access database. From the Power BI Desktop screen, click on **Get Data**. From the **Get Data** dialog, select **Access database** and click on **Connect**.

This will open the **Open file** dialog, as shown in *Figure 3-10*, and this is where we can select the Access database to open:

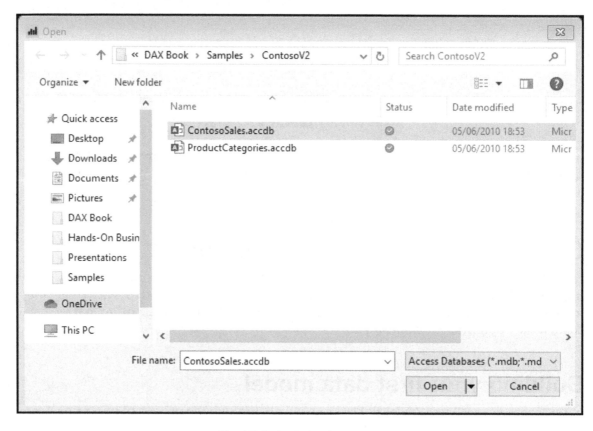

Figure 3-10: The Open file dialog for getting data

We'll start with the **ContosoSales** database. Click on **Open**, which will open the **Navigator** dialog. This is where we can select which tables we want to import. For now, we'll select the **DimDate**, **DimProduct**, **DimSubcategory**, and **FactSales** tables, as shown in *Figure 3-11*:

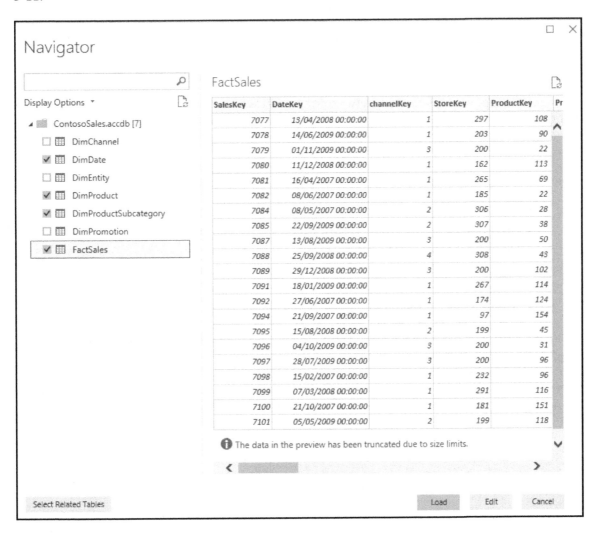

Figure 3-11: Selecting tables to import from the Navigator dialog

At this point, instead of clicking **Load**, click **Edit**, which will take us into the **Power Query Editor**. From here, we can choose which fields we want to load from each table. We can also rename the tables and fields to something more business-friendly.

On the left-hand side of the screen, we have a list of tables we're going to import. In the middle section of the screen, we can see the data from the highlighted table. Finally, on the right-hand side, we have some field properties. You will also see a list of steps that have been taken to transform the table, such as renaming columns. We'll follow this as we make changes, but for now, it should only have two steps for **Source** and **Navigation**.

For the next step, we will create a new group so that we can store our Access tables, and we will rename the table to something more appropriate for business end users. Remember, when you produce reports, your field names will be used for labeling, so it's important to have names that make sense to the business.

When renaming tables and fields, you should follow these simple rules:

- Avoid using all capital letters, for example, SALESAMOUNT.
- Do not use Pascal casing, for example, SalesAmount.
- Do not use Camel casing, for example, salesAmount.
- Separate words with a space, for example, Sales Amount.
- Remove any prefixes or suffixes, for example, FactSalesAmount.
- Avoid using abbreviated names or acronyms, for example, Sales Amt.

To create a group for our tables, we'll right-click in the blank area under the tables and select **New Group** from the context menu. We'll name this new group **Access Tables** and, once created, move the tables into this group by right-clicking on each table and selecting **Move To Group** from the context menu. Once the tables have been renamed and moved to the new group, the list of tables should look like the screenshot in *Figure 3-12*:

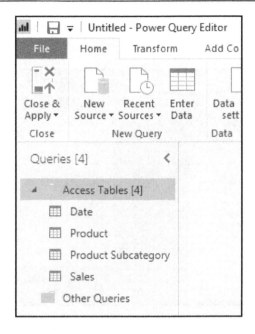

Figure 3-12: Tables imported and sorted into group

The next step is to go through each of the tables, remove any fields that are not needed, and rename those that are required. As you do this, you will notice that the new steps are added to the list of steps shown in the panel on the right-hand side, as shown in *Figure 3-13*:

Figure 3-13: Steps added to data import

If we were to go ahead and import the data at this stage, we would end up with the data model shown in *Figure 3-14*:

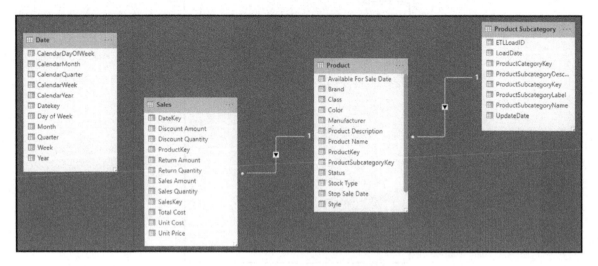

Figure 3-14: Data model after loading imported data from Access

At this stage, we have a snowflake schema since the product and product categories have been split over two tables. From both a storage and a performance point of view, it would be better if we could merge these two tables into one. To do this, we need to go back to the Power Query editor:

1. In the Power Query editor, select the **Product** table and click on **Merge Queries**, which can be found in the **Combine** section of the **Home** ribbon.
2. In the **Merge** dialog, highlight the **ProductSubcategoryKey** column for the **Product** table. Then, in the lower half of the dialog, select the **Product Subcategory** table from the drop-down box.
3. Next, select the **ProductSubcategory** column for the **Product Subcategory** table.

The screenshot in *Figure 3-15* shows what the **Merge** dialog should look like at this stage:

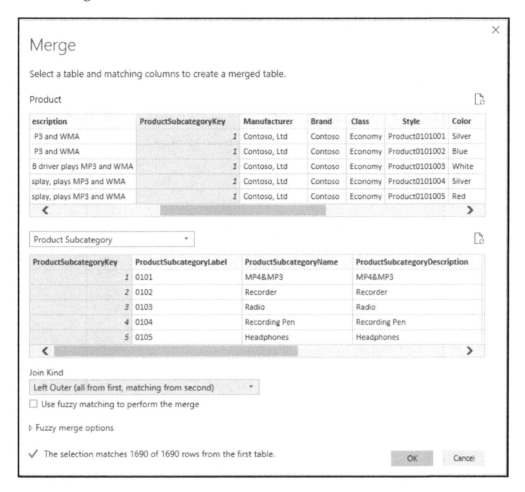

Figure 3-15: Merging data using the Merge dialog

4. Finally, check that the **Join Kind** is set to **Left Outer** and click **OK**.

Now, you will have a new column in the **Product** table called **Product Subcategory**. At this point, it will be a table type, which is indicated by the fact that each field contains a table for a value.

5. Click on the double arrow icon next to the field name.

6. A list of fields from the **Product Subcategory** table will be displayed. Click the **Select All Columns** checkbox to deselect the columns and select the **ProductSubcategoryName** field. Make sure the **Use original column name as prefix** checkbox is not ticked.

The screenshot in *Figure 3-16* shows what the merge should look like:

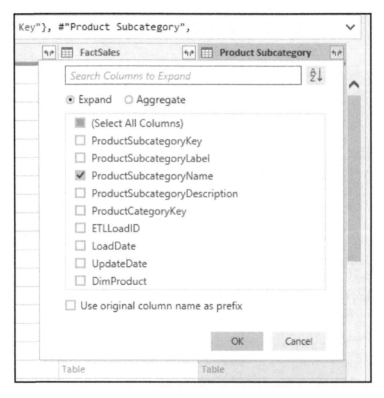

Figure 3-16: Selecting fields to include in the merge

7. Click on **OK**. This will complete the table merge, adding the **Product Subcategory** field to the **Product** table.

8. We no longer need to load the data from the **Product Subcategory** table, so right-click on the **Product Subcategory** table and uncheck **Enable load** from the context menu. You will get a warning about data loss, but you can click continue to ignore it.

9. Now, click **Close and apply** to load the data into the data model.

Now, if we look at the data model, we will see that the **Product Subcategory** table is no longer included in the model. **Product Subcategory** has been added to the **Product** table as a new column instead.

Now that we have **Product Subcategory** and **Product** in the same table, we can create a hierarchy by performing the following steps:

1. Right-click on the **Product** table and select **Create hierarchy** from the **Context** menu.
2. In the **Properties** pane, give the hierarchy a name, and in the advanced section, add **Product Subcategory Name** and **Product Name**, as shown in *Figure 3-17*:

Figure 3-17: Creating a hierarchy

3. Click on **Apply Level Changes** to create the new hierarchy.

The next step in building our data model is to hide the columns that are needed by the model but should not be shown to the end user. These will include the various key fields that are required for creating and maintaining relationships but are not needed for reporting purposes.

You should also hide the **Product Name** and **Product Subcategory Name** fields in the **Product** table to ensure that end users use the new **Products** hierarchy and not these fields when creating reports.

To hide a field, right-click on a field name and select **Hide from report view** from the context menu. Hidden fields are grayed out on the data model view.

Finally, we need to link the **Date** table by creating a new relationship. First, drag the **DateKey** field from the **Date** table to the **DateKey** field of the **Sales** table. This should automatically create a one-to-many relationship between the two tables.

We could also use this method to connect the **Date** table to the **Product** table, but, as shown in *Figure 3-18*, these relationships are inactive when they're created:

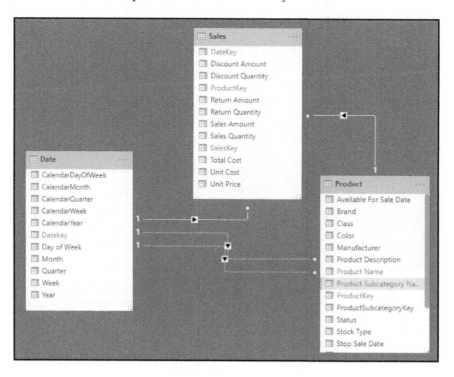

Figure 3-18: Inactive relationships between tables

While this is fine, and later in the book we will look how we can use DAX to work around this, for now we'll make a couple of copies of the **Date** table and use these to join the two dates we have in the **Product** table.

To do this, switch to the report view. From the **Modeling** ribbon, select **New Table** from the **Calculations** section. Type the following into the DAX editor:

```
Available Date = 'Date'
```

Repeat this process to create a second copy of the **Date** table, but this time, type in the following DAX expression:

```
Stop Date = 'Date'
```

Return to the model view. Here, you will see you have two new date tables. Create the relationship between the **Available Date** table and the **Product** table by dragging the **DateKey** field from the **Available Date** table to the **Available For Sale Date** on the **Product** table.

Repeat this process for the **Stop Date** table by dragging the **DateKey** field from the **Stop Date** table to the **Stop Sale Date** on the **Product** table.

You should now have a simple but well-structured data model like the one shown in *Figure 3-19*:

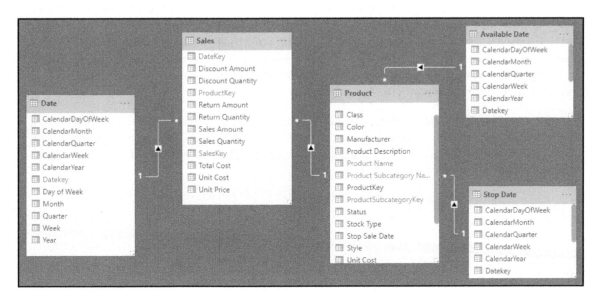

Figure 3-19: Example of a simple data model using multiple date tables

One final step that we can take to make the data model even better is to go through the tables and ensure that the fields have the correct data type and formatting. To do this, go to the model view. In the **Properties** pane, you will be able to see the various properties for each field. These include the following:

- Data type
- Format
- Percentage format
- Thousands separator
- Decimal places
- Currency format
- Sort by column
- Data category
- Summarize by
- Is nullable

In this hands-on example, we only built a small data model, but in doing so, we have covered several important data modeling concepts and looked at some best practices. When building a data model, it is important to consider the end user. Name tables and columns appropriately using language that the business understands.

Removing unnecessary columns from your data load and reducing the number of tables by merging and appending tables not only makes the data model more usable by the end user, but it also helps to reduce its size. Finally, making sure that you have defined your relationships correctly is important when it comes to building reports and ensuring that you get correct results. These are essential if your DAX expressions and the evaluation contexts are to work the way you expect.

Having a good data model makes using DAX easier since it makes it easier to understand how data and filters flow between tables when they are applied. This, in turn, helps you to understand the effect that the evaluation context has on data in your model and how this affects the execution of your DAX expressions.

Extending your data model

The true power of DAX for the BI professional is that it allows you to gain deeper insights into your data by giving you the ability to expand your data model. It allows you to create new data and extract new information from the data that already exists within your data model.

In this section, we're going to look at three different ways in which you can use DAX to extend your data model. By the end, we'll have added some examples of each of the following objects to our data model:

- Calculated columns
- Calculated tables
- Measures

Calculated columns are a very quick and easy way to add data to your model, but they have the disadvantage that they will increase its size and use more memory. Calculated tables will also add to the size of your data model, but they are a great way of adding lookup tables that may be missing from the model's source data. As we will see in the next section, they also offer an effective way to add custom date tables to your data model.

Measures are a particularly powerful way to gain insights. These range from a simple sum of a column, through to very complex measures that use values from across different tables. They are also a great way to expand your data model without increasing its size, and in many cases, they can be used instead of calculated columns.

Adding a calculated column

In Chapter 1, *What is DAX?*, we covered the process of creating a simple calculated column. So, for this example, we'll create something a little more complex.

From the Power BI desktop, do the following:

1. Switch to the **Data** view.
2. In the **Fields** pane, select the **Product** table. This will display the contents of the **Product** table in the view pane.

3. From the **Calculations** section of the **Home** ribbon, select **Create New Column**. This will bring up the DAX editor, as shown in *Figure 3-20*. Here, you can name the column and add the DAX expression that defines it:

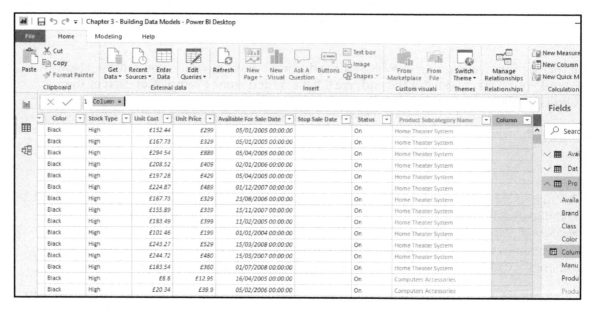

Figure 3-20: Creating a new calculated column

4. For this example, we're going to use the RELATED function to get the value of a field from a related table. We'll add a new column that contains the month and year when a product will be available.

5. Call the new column **Available From**. Remember that it's okay to use spaces in column names. In fact, this is the preferred style as it makes the name more business-friendly for report end users. Type the following DAX expression into the DAX editor:

```
Available From =
CONCATENATE (
    RELATED ( 'Available Date'[Quarter] ) & " ",
    RELATED ( 'Available Date'[CalendarYear] )
)
```

6. This will create a new column called **Available From** that will contain the **Quarter** and **Year** columns from the related record in the **Available Date** table, concatenated, as shown in *Figure 3-21*:

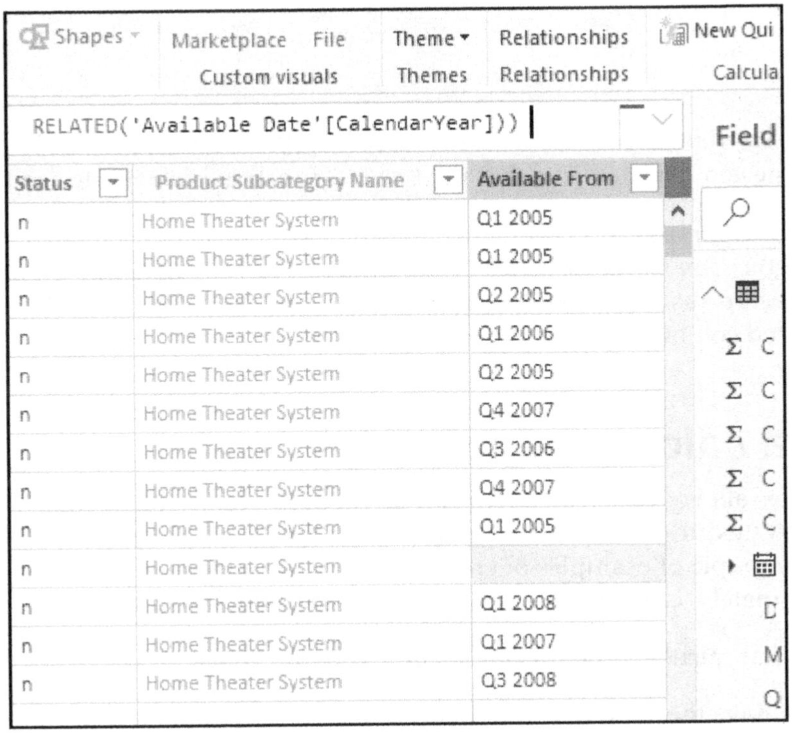

Figure 3-21: The new Available From column added to Product table

7. As you can see, there are blank values where the related **Available For Sale From** date is before January 1, 2005. This is because January 1, 2005 is the first date in the **Available Date** table. To handle situations where the date is before or after the dates in the related **Available Date** table, change the column definition to the following:

```
Available From =
SWITCH (
    // the value that the evaluated expression should equate to
    TRUE (),
    // is available for sale date before 01/01/2005?
    'Product'[Available For Sale Date]
        < DATE ( 2005, 01, 01 ), "Before Q1 2005",
    // is available for sale date after 31/12/2011?
```

```
'Product'[Available For Sale Date]
    > DATE ( 2011, 12, 31 ), "After Q4 2011",
// if we get here, available for sale date is in range
CONCATENATE (
    RELATED ( 'Available Date'[Quarter] ) & " ",
    RELATED ( 'Available Date'[CalendarYear] )
)
)
)
```

This final expression uses the `SWITCH` function to step through a number of options. We could also use nested IF statements, but the `SWITCH` function is clearer to read.

While calculated columns are a relatively easy way to expand your data model, you must remember that they are stored in memory with the rest of your data model. Each calculated column will take up space in memory, which can have a significant impact, especially when adding calculated columns to large tables.

Adding a calculated table

Calculated tables allow you to extend your data model by adding new tables. They are created by a DAX expression, which also creates the table's values. In this section, we will walk through a couple of examples of creating calculated tables to store intermediate results. Unfortunately, calculated tables are not available in Excel Power Pivot.

Let's go over what calculated tables can do and what they have:

- They have the ability to store intermediate results for querying.
- They have relationships with other tables, just like imported tables.
- They contain columns that have a definable data type and format.
- They can be used in report visualization, such as imported tables.
- They are recalculated when the base table's data is updated or refreshed.
- They are in-memory tables that use RAM.

To create a calculated table through Power BI Desktop, follow these steps:

1. Switch to the **Report** or **Data** view.
2. From the **Calculations** section of the **Modeling** ribbon, select **Create New Table**. This will bring up the DAX editor, as shown in *Figure 3-22*. Here, you can name the table and add the DAX expression that defines it:

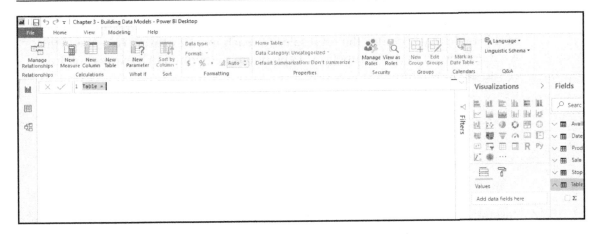

Figure 3-22: Adding a calculated table using the DAX editor

3. In this first example, we're going to create a table that contains a list of manufacturers that have been extracted from the **Product** table. To do this, enter the following DAX expression:

```
Manufacturer =
DISTINCT ( 'Product'[Manufacturer] )
```

4. Now, we have a new table called **Manufacturer** that acts like a normal table. It can be used in relationships and reporting visualization. The screenshot in *Figure 3-23* shows that the table can be related to the **Product** table:

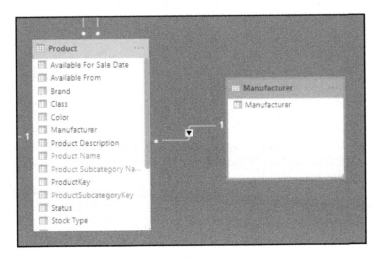

Figure 3-23: Creating a relationship with a calculated table

5. In the following example, we're going to create a slightly more complex version of this table that includes the total sales for each manufacturer. To achieve this, we'll use the SUMMARIZE function. Type in the following DAX expression to create the new table:

```
Manufacturer Sales =
SUMMARIZE (
    Sales,
    'Product'[Manufacturer],
    "Total Sales",
    SUM ( 'Sales'[Sales Amount] )
)
```

6. Finally, we're going to create a table that contains the top 10 products, based on the quantity of products that have been sold in the **Sales** table. To do this, we will create a table called **Product Sales**. This is very similar to the table we created in step 5. The DAX expression to use for this is as follows:

```
Product Sales =
SUMMARIZE (
    Sales,
    'Product'[ProductKey],
    "Total Sales",
    SUM ( 'Sales'[Sales Quantity] )
)
```

7. Then, we will use the DAX TOPN function to create a table that contains the top 10 products. The DAX expression for this is as follows:

```
Top 10 Products =
TOPN (
    10,
    'Product Sales',
    'Product Sales'[Total Sales],
    DESC
)
```

8. To complete our expanded data model, we need to create relationships between these new tables and the **Product** table. Once completed, the expanded data model should look like the one shown in *Figure 3-24*:

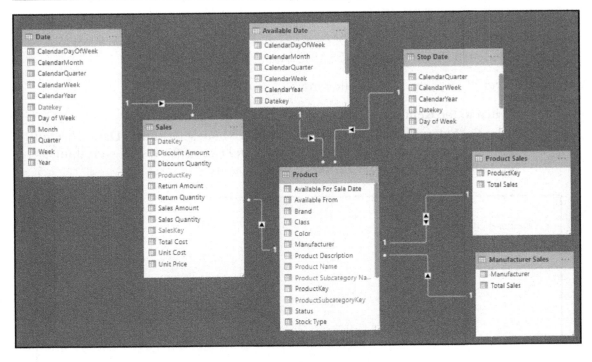

Figure 3-24: The expanded data model with calculated tables

Other DAX functions that can be useful when creating calculated tables include CROSSJOIN, UNION, NATURALINNERJOIN, NATURALLEFTOUTERJOIN, INTERSECT, CALENDAR, and CALENDARAUTO.

We will be looking at some examples of using the CALENDAR and CALENDARAUTO functions in the next section, where we will create a custom date table.

Calculated tables can also be expanded by the addition of calculated columns, just like imported tables. However, just like calculated columns, calculated tables are stored in memory, so you will need to keep the table size in mind to ensure optimal performance.

Adding a measure

As we saw in Chapter 1, *What is DAX?*, measures are a way of creating aggregations of data using a DAX expression. A measure always involves some form of aggregation, such as calculating the sum of a numeric column, for example, the sales amount. Measures invariably involve more complex DAX expressions than a calculated column or calculated table. You also need to take the evaluation context into account.

Before we start creating any measures, we will create a **measures** table to store them. Again, this is something we can do in Power BI Desktop, but not Excel Power Pivot. We'll look at creating measures in Power Pivot and SSAS Tabular in the next chapter.

From the Power BI Desktop, do the following:

1. Switch to the **Report** or **Data** view.
2. From the **External** data section of the **Home** ribbon, select **Enter Data**. This will bring up the **Create Table** editor, as shown in *Figure 3-25*. Leave everything as is but rename the table from **Table1** to **Key Measures**:

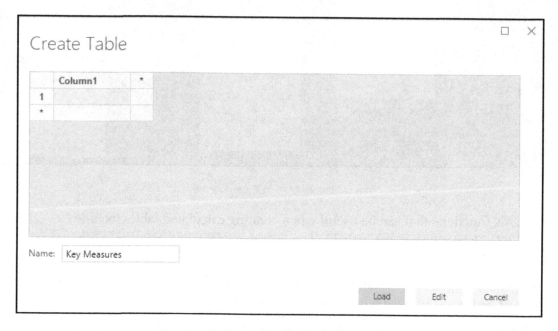

Figure 3-25: The Create Table dialog in Power BI Desktop

3. Click **Load**. A new table called **Key Measures** will be created with just one empty field called **Column1**. For now, do not delete this field or Power BI will think the table is redundant and automatically delete it.
4. Once you have created a measure in the table, you can delete **Column1**. The next time you open the Power BI file, the table will have been converted into a special measure table.

Having created our **Key Measures** table, we can add a few example measures to our data model.

From the Power BI Desktop, we will do the following:

1. Switch to the **Report** or **Data** view.
2. Right-click on the **Key Measures** table on the **Fields** pane and select **New measure**. This will bring up the DAX editor, where you can name the measure and add the DAX expression that defines it.
3. For our first measure, we will keep things simple by creating a measure that calculates the sum of the **Sales Amount** column in the **Sales** table. To do this, use the following DAX expression:

```
Sum Of Sales Amount = SUM ( Sales[Sales Amount] )
```

4. Once created, this new measure can be used in report visuals, where it will work within the evaluation contexts created by other columns that are used within the visual. In *Figure 3-26*, the new measure has been added to a table to show the sum of sales by product subcategory. It also includes the **Sales Amount** field that this measure is built upon. You will see that it gives the same result. While we have created the measure explicitly by including the **Sales Amount** field in this table, DAX is creating the same measure implicitly to give the desired result:

Product Subcategory Name	Sales Amount	Sum Of Sales Amount
Bluetooth Headphones	£41,907,488.9135	£41,907,488.9135
Camcorders	£1,335,302,769.92	£1,335,302,769.92
Cameras & Camcorders Accessories	£51,643,775.8286	£51,643,775.8286
Car Video	£306,818,844.52	£306,818,844.52
Cell phones Accessories	£120,017,198.2572	£120,017,198.2572
Computers Accessories	£111,023,802.1072	£111,023,802.1072
Desktops	£508,196,937.084	£508,196,937.084
Digital Cameras	£365,082,489.926	£365,082,489.926
Digital SLR Cameras	£809,994,738.386	£809,994,738.386
Home & Office Phones	£48,333,160.9812	£48,333,160.9812
Home Theater System	£709,120,510.209	£709,120,510.209
Laptops	£933,130,593.776	£933,130,593.776
Monitors	£268,114,052.77	£268,114,052.77
Movie DVD	£165,804,705.9811	£165,804,705.9811
MP4&MP3	£65,190,616.3964	£65,190,616.3964
Printers, Scanners & Fax	£281,762,342.2	£281,762,342.2
Projectors & Screens	£1,107,199,413.48	£1,107,199,413.48
Recording Pen	£44,516,259.001	£44,516,259.001
Smart phones & PDAs	£423,389,457.48	£423,389,457.48
Televisions	£307,373,914.4742	£307,373,914.4742
Touch Screen Phones	£300,493,447.58	£300,493,447.58
VCD & DVD	£36,807,845.561	£36,807,845.561
Total	£8,341,224,364.8324	£8,341,224,364.8324

Figure 3-26: Adding a measure to a report visual in Power BI Desktop

5. For the following example, we will create a measure that is a little more complex. For this measure, we will use one of the DAX `AggregateX` functions. These functions are much like the normal versions of their equivalent function. However, instead of just working on the values in a single column, they iterate through the rows for the current filter context and apply a DAX expression, before carrying out the operation of the function.

6. Let's illustrate this. Once again, from the **Key Measures** table, create a new measure. In the DAX editor, enter the following DAX expression:

```
Sum Of Sales Less Returns =
SUMX (
    Sales,
    Sales[Sales Quantity] - Sales[Return Quantity]
)
```

7. In this example, we have created a measure that iterates through the rows in the **Sales** table for the current filter context. For each row, it calculates the sales quantity minus the return quantity, almost as if we had added this as a calculated column. Then, it calculates the sum of all of these resulting values, much like the `SUM` function would, had this been a calculated column.

8. For the final example of a measure, we will add a ratio to our data model to give us a percentage of returns over sales. Again, from the **Key Measures** table, create a new measure. In the DAX editor, enter the following DAX expression:

```
% Returns Over Sales =
DIVIDE (
    SUM ( Sales[Return Quantity] ),
    SUM ( Sales[Sales Quantity] )
)
```

9. Since we are dealing with a percentage here, we can finish off the measure by making sure it has the correct data type of **Percentage** and that it is formatted to have one decimal place displayed. We can do this from the **Formatting** section of the **Modeling** ribbon, as shown in *Figure 3-27*:

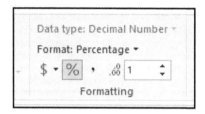

Figure 3-27: Formatting a measure from the modeling ribbon in Power BI Desktop

As we have seen, measures allow you to extend your data model without increasing memory usage. In many cases, a measure can be used in place of a calculated column. In fact, wherever possible, you would be wise to use measures over calculated columns. Although measures can have an impact on the performance of your report, the advantages of reducing the size of your data model outweigh the disadvantages.

The downside to using measures is that the DAX required to produce them can be quite complex. In addition, you need to be aware of the evaluation context. However, measures are perhaps the most powerful way DAX can extend your data model and give you deeper insights into your data.

It's a date

In this section, we will look at how you can use DAX, with the create table function, to create a custom date table.

In our data model, we already have some date tables. However, as we have seen, there are no dates prior to December 1, 2011. In the **Product** table, we have products that have values in the **Available For Sale Date** field that are before this date. To get around this issue, we are going to create a custom date table that covers all of the dates referenced in the **Product** table.

To start, we will need to create a calculated table. From Power BI Desktop, follow these steps:

1. Switch to the **Report** or **Data** view.
2. From the **Calculations** section of the **Modeling** ribbon, select **Create New Table**. This will bring up the DAX editor, where we can name the table and add the DAX expression to define it. In the DAX editor, enter the following expression to create the new base date table:

   ```
   Available Date New =
   CALENDAR (
       FIRSTDATE ( 'Product'[Available For Sale Date] ),
       LASTDATE ( 'Product'[Available For Sale Date] )
   )
   ```

3. This will create a basic date table with a single column called **Date**. Check that this column is correctly formatted as a date and rename it to **DateKey**.

4. Next, mark the new table as a date table. To do this, right-click on the new date table in the **Fields** pane and select **Mark as date table**. This will bring up the dialog shown in *Figure 3-28*. Change the **Date** column to **DateKey** and click **OK**:

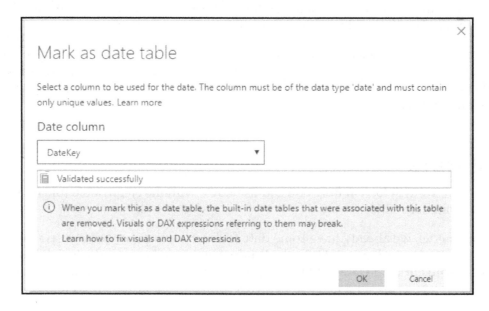

Figure 3-28: Marking a table as a date table in Power BI Desktop

5. Now, we will replicate the columns from the original **Available Date** table using DAX expressions. We'll start by adding the **CalendarYear** column. Create a new column and enter the following DAX expression:

```
CalendarYear =
YEAR ( [DateKey] )
```

6. Next, create the **CalendarQuarter** column using the following DAX expression:

```
CalendarQuarter =
INT ( YEAR ( [DateKey] ) &
    IF ( MONTH ( [DateKey] ) < 4, 1,
        IF ( MONTH ( [DateKey] ) < 7, 2,
            IF ( MONTH ( [DateKey] ) < 10, 3,
                4
                )
            )
        )
    )
```

7. Create the **CalendarMonth** column using the following DAX expression:

```
CalendarMonth =
INT ( YEAR( [DateKey] ) & FORMAT( MONTH ( [DateKey] ), "00" ) )
```

8. Create the **CalendarWeek** column using the following DAX expression:

```
CalendarWeek =
INT ( YEAR( [DateKey] ) & FORMAT( WEEKNUM( [DateKey] ), "00" ) )
```

9. Create the **CalendarDayOfWeek** column using the following DAX expression:

```
CalendarDayOfWeek =
INT ( YEAR( [DateKey] ) & FORMAT( WEEKNUM( [DateKey] ), "00" ) &
WEEKDAY( [DateKey] ) )
```

10. Create the **Year** column using the following DAX expression:

```
Year =
"Year " & [CalendarYear]
```

11. Create the **Quarter** column using the following DAX expression:

```
Quarter =
IF( MONTH ( [DateKey] ) < 4, "Q1",
    IF( MONTH ( [DateKey] ) < 7, "Q2",
        IF( MONTH ( [CalendarMonth] ) < 10, "Q3",
            "Q4"
        )
    )
)
```

12. Create the **Month** column using the following DAX expression:

```
Month =
FORMAT ( [DateKey], "MMMM" )
```

13. Create the **Week** column using the following DAX expression:

```
Week =
"Week " & WEEKNUM( [DateKey] )
```

14. Finally, create the **Day Of Week** column using the following DAX expression:

```
Day Of Week =
FORMAT ( [DateKey], "DDDD" )
```

Now that we have created our custom date table to replace the original **Available Date** table, all we need to do is delete the original table, rename our new table to **Available Date**, and recreate the relationship with the **Product** table.

You will also need to amend the DAX code for the calculated column, **Available From**, in the **Product** table so that it no longer checks for out of range dates. To do this, use the following DAX expression:

```
Available From =
CONCATENATE (
    RELATED ( 'Available Date'[Quarter] ) & " ",
    RELATED ( 'Available Date'[CalendarYear] )
)
```

In addition to the CALENDATE function, there is another DAX function called CALENDARAUTO. This function looks through your data model and creates a date table that covers all of the years referenced in the model.

Internally, the CALENDARAUTO function uses the CALENDAR function and provides a date range that includes the earliest date in the model that is not in a calculated column and the latest date in the model that is not in a calculated column.

The CALENDARAUTO function can also take a parameter that is an integer from 1 to 12, which represents the end month of the fiscal year. The date range that's returned includes all dates between the beginning of the fiscal year for the start date and the end of the fiscal year for the end date.

One thing to note when using the CALENDARAUTO function over the CALENDAR function is that it scans all of the dates in a data model to establish the start and end dates. There is a risk with this approach that it will use dates that don't need to be included and you end up with a table that covers a much wider range than necessary.

Summary

In this chapter, you learned about why it is important to build a well-defined data model. Not only does it make it easier to understand and report from as an end user, but it also makes it easier to work with as a BI professional by making the execution of DAX code easier to understand. From here, you learned about a couple of different schema designs with the star and snowflake shaped schemas. You also learned about some important data modeling concepts that you then put into practice by building a simple data model using hands-on examples.

Then, you looked at how to load data and create relationships and how to use DAX functions to extend your data model by creating calculated columns, calculated tables, and measures. Finally, you learned how to extend your data model further by adding a custom date table to it using the CALENDAR function.

In the next chapter, we'll build on this knowledge by looking at how to import data and create data models using Excel Power Pivot and SSAS Tabular.

Working with DAX in Power BI, Excel, and SSAS

4

In this chapter, we will look at the three different platforms that support DAX – Power BI Desktop, Excel Power Pivot, and **SQL Server Analysis Services (SSAS)** Tabular. By the end of this chapter, you will be familiar with using the DAX formula editor in Power BI Desktop. You will also have learned how to load data into an Excel Power Pivot data model and expand it using DAX formulas. Finally, you will learn how to use DAX with SSAS Tabular, import the data model from Excel Power Pivot, and use DAX to query the data in SSAS.

The chapter is broken down into the following sections:

- Working with DAX in Power BI Desktop
- Working with DAX in Excel Power Pivot
- Working with DAX in SSAS Tabular

Working with DAX in Power BI Desktop

In the previous chapter, we created a data model using Power BI Desktop. As part of that, we used DAX to add tables, columns, and measures to our data model.

With Power BI Desktop, you enter DAX code using the DAX formula editor. In this chapter, we will look at the DAX formula editor in more detail. We'll look at how you can speed up the process of entering code using some of the shortcut keys that are available in the editor. We'll then look at how the built-in IntelliSense helps to reduce errors when entering code. We'll also look at how to use the editor so that your code is indented correctly, helping to maintain an easy-to-read layout.

The DAX formula editor

Figure 4-1 shows the DAX formula editor being used to enter some DAX code in Power BI Desktop:

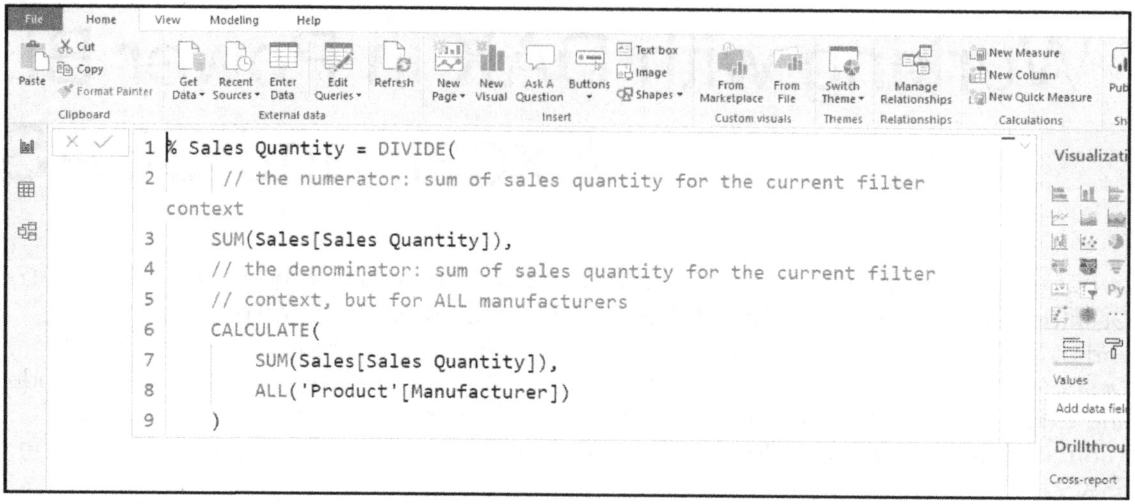

Figure 4-1: Entering DAX code in the formula editor in Power BI Desktop

By default, when you start to enter your DAX code, the editor will resize as you type in text. If you want to expand the editor screen to make use of the whole screen's height, click on the down arrow on the right-hand side of the editor. Likewise, you can shrink the editor screen back down again by clicking on the up arrow.

You can alter the size of the font by holding down the *Ctrl* key and either rolling the scroll wheel on your mouse or by pressing the plus and minus keys.

In addition to these shortcut keys, there are other shortcut key combinations that you can use, and these are given in the following table:

Shortcut Result	Key Combination
Column selection page down	*Ctrl + Shift + Alt + PgDn*
Column selection page up	*Ctrl + Shift + Alt + PgUp*
Comment lines	*Ctrl + KC*
Copy line	*Ctrl + C*
Copy line down	*Shift + Alt + Down Arrow*
Copy line up	*Shift + Alt + Up Arrow*

Cut line	*Ctrl + X*
Delete a word	*Ctrl + Delete*
Delete line	*Ctrl + Shift + K*
Find and replace a word	*Ctrl + D*
Go to beginning of file	*Ctrl + Home*
Go to beginning of line	*Home*
Go to end of file	*Ctrl + End*
Go to end of line	*End*
Go to selected line number	*Ctrl + G*
Indent line left	*Ctrl + [*
Indent line right	*Ctrl +]*
Insert cursor	*Alt + Click*
Insert cursor above	*Ctrl + Alt + Up Arrow*
Insert cursor below	*Ctrl + Alt + Down Arrow*
Insert new line above	*Ctrl + Shift + Enter*
Insert new line below	*Ctrl + Enter*
Jump to matching bracket	*Ctrl + Shift + *
Move the line down	*Alt + Down Arrow*
Move the line up	*Alt + Up Arrow*
New line above	*Ctrl + Shift + Enter*
New line with indent	*Shift + Enter*
New line without indentation	*Alt + Enter*
Redo DAX code	*Ctrl + Y*
Scroll line down	*Ctrl + Down Arrow*
Scroll line up	*Ctrl + Up Arrow*
Scroll page down	*Alt + PgDn*
Scroll page up	*Alt + PgUp*
Select all occurrences of current selection	*Ctrl + Shift + L*
Select all occurrences of current word	*Ctrl + F2*
Select current line	*Ctrl + I*
Toggle the 'Tab moves focus' feature	*Ctrl + M*
Uncomment lines	*Ctrl + KU*
Undo DAX code	*Ctrl + Z*
Undo last cursor operation	*Ctrl + U*

It is important to remember to use the combination of *Shift + Enter* or *Alt + Enter* when you want to move to a new line. If you just hit the *Enter* key, then the editor will think you have finished entering your DAX expression. Unless you have finished, this will invariably result in an error.

> Using the *Alt* and *Enter* key combination will give you an indented new line, which will help you to follow the formatting rules we looked at in Chapter 2, *Using DAX Variables and Formatting*.

The DAX formula editor is IntelliSense enabled. This means that it will give you information about the DAX function you are typing in, along with some suggestions for the parameter values. *Figure 4-2* shows an example of IntelliSense in action:

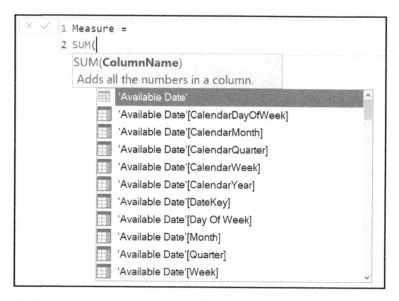

Figure 4-2: IntelliSense in action in the DAX formula editor

The following are some additional points on using the DAX formula editor in Power BI Desktop:

- The IntelliSense feature helps you to create syntactically correct DAX expressions by giving you a list of suggestions on what to type next, as you type in your expression.
- If you are partway through entering some DAX and decide to cancel what you're entering, click on the **X** in the top left-hand corner to close the editor and discard its content.

- If you have finished entering the DAX code, click on the tick symbol to save your work and close the editor.
- Clicking on any bracket within your DAX code brings up another helpful feature. The editor will automatically highlight the opposing start or end bracket, which is especially helpful if you are using nested expressions.

Along with the work that we did on creating and expanding our data model in Chapter 3, *Building Data Models*, this concludes our look at using DAX with Power BI Desktop. In the next section, we will look at a similar exercise using the Excel Power Pivot add-in to import data and create a data model.

Working with DAX in Excel Power Pivot

Power Pivot is an add-in for Excel that originally became available with Excel 2010. It essentially gives you SQL Server Analysis Services running directly within your copy of Excel. What this allows you to do is create an in-memory data model using data imported from external sources as well as from worksheets within the Excel file itself.

Just like the data model we created in Chapter 3, *Building Data Models*, it is a collection of tables and relationships that can be expanded using DAX to create new columns and measures. However, unlike Power BI Desktop, you cannot use DAX to create new tables in Excel.

Installing and enabling the Power Pivot add-in

While Power Pivot is included as an integral part of certain versions of Excel 2013 and beyond, Excel 2010 requires a separate component to be downloaded and installed.

> The following link provides further details of what versions of Office include Power Pivot and where to find the download for Excel 2010: https://support.office.com/en-us/article/where-is-power-pivot-aa64e217-4b6e-410b-8337-20b87e1c2a4b.

If you have a version of Excel that includes the Power Pivot add-in, you may also need to enable it. To do this, follow these steps:

1. Go to **File**, click on **Options**, and then click on **Add-Ins**.
2. In the **Manage** dialog, select **COM Add-ins** from the drop-down list, and then click on **Go**.

3. This will bring up the **COM Add-Ins** dialog shown in *Figure 4-3*:

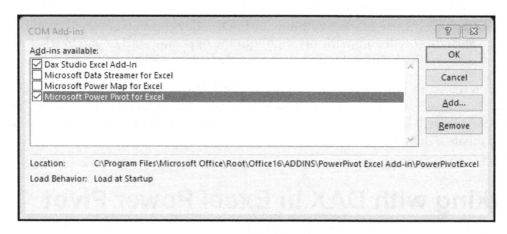

Figure 4-3: The COM Add-ins dialog in Excel

4. Check the **Microsoft Power Pivot for Excel** box (some versions will have a slightly different name) and click on **OK**.

5. With Power Pivot enabled, you will have a new tab available that will give you the **Power Pivot** ribbon, as shown in *Figure 4-4*:

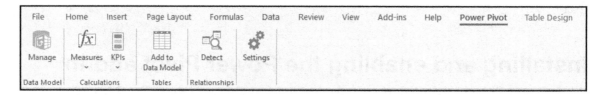

Figure 4-4: The Power Pivot ribbon in Excel

The Power Pivot ribbon contains some options required to start building your data model. The most important of these is the **Manage** icon in the **Data Model** section. This opens the Power Pivot window where you load and prepare data, or work on the data already imported into your data model. We will look at this and a couple of the other icons in more detail as we go through the process of building our data model.

Adding data to an Excel data model

When dealing with data sources for an Excel data model, they can either be external or they can be Excel tables from the current workbook.

Much like we did when building a data model with Power BI Desktop in Chapter 3, *Building Data Models*, we'll start by importing some data from an Access database. Once we have done this and made sure the relationships between tables are correct, we'll add data from a table to the current workbook:

1. To start, click on the **Manage** icon in the **Data Model** section of the **Power Pivot** ribbon. This will open the Power Pivot window, as shown in *Figure 4-5*:

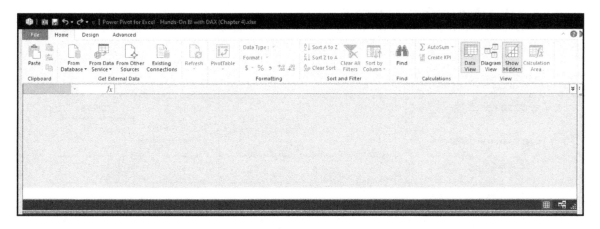

Figure 4-5: The Excel Power Pivot window

2. Next, we'll import data from an Access database. From the Power Pivot window, click on **From Database** in the **Get External Data** section of the **Home** ribbon, and then select **From Access** from the drop-down menu, as shown in *Figure 4-6*:

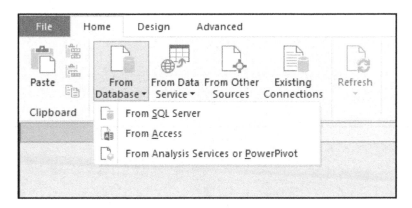

Figure 4.6: Getting data from an Access database

This will open the first screen of the **Table Import Wizard,** as shown in *Figure 4-7.* From here, we can add the path to the Access database file and, if necessary, enter details of the username and password required to connect to the database. In this example, we only need to give the file path:

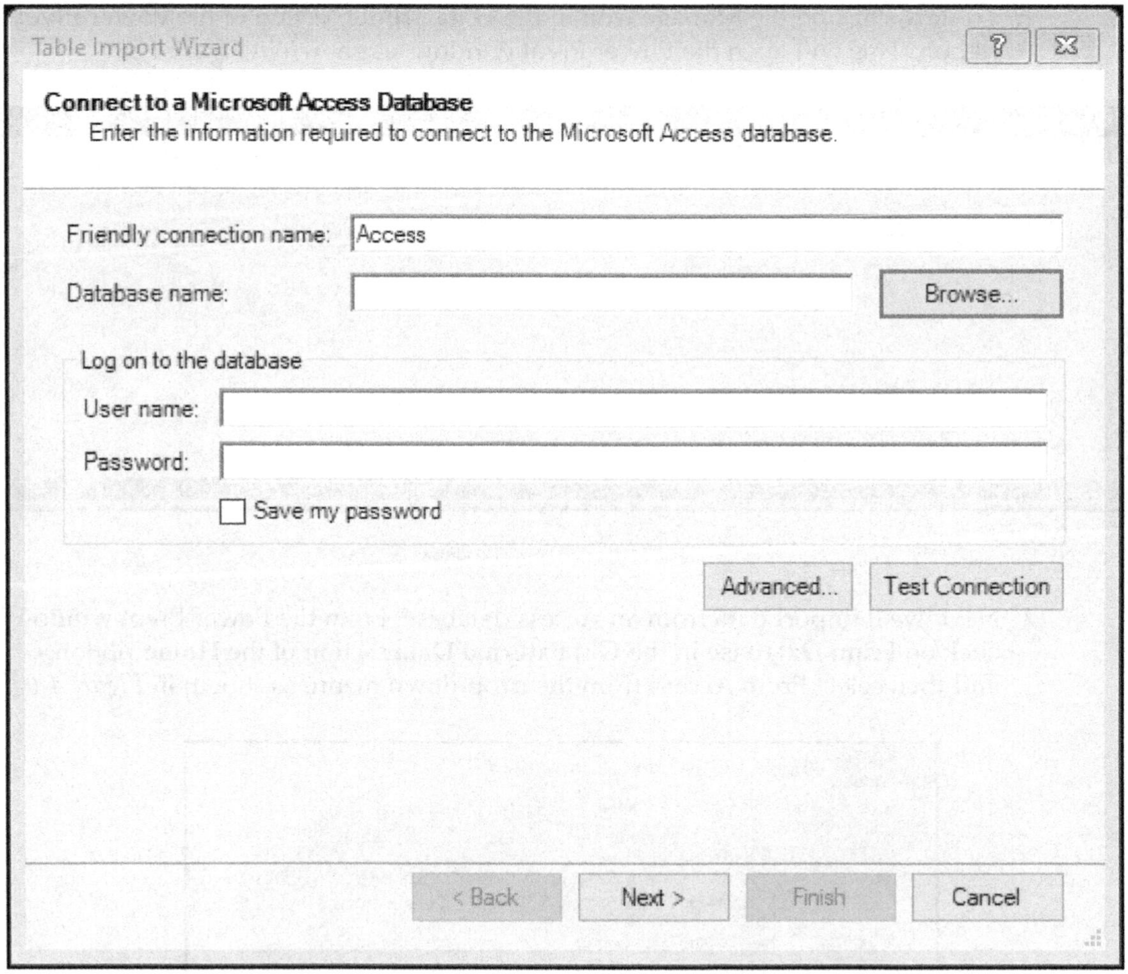

Figure 4-7: Entering details of the Access database with the table import wizard

3. Click on **Browse** to open the **Open** file dialog, as shown in *Figure 4-8*, from where we can select the Access database to open:

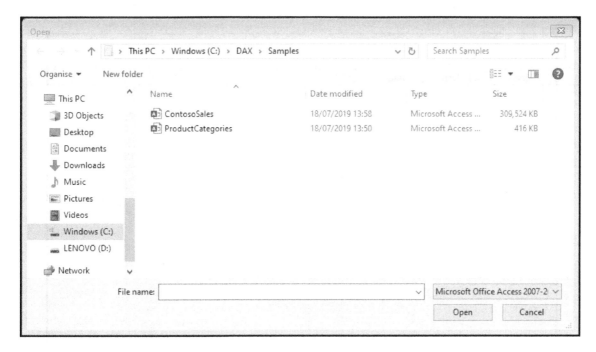

Figure 4-8: Selecting the Access database with the file explorer dialog

In this exercise, we're going to import some data from the **ContosoSales** Access database.

4. Select that file and click on **Open**. This will open a new dialog, as shown in *Figure 4-9*, asking us whether we want to select data from a list or import data based on the results of a query:

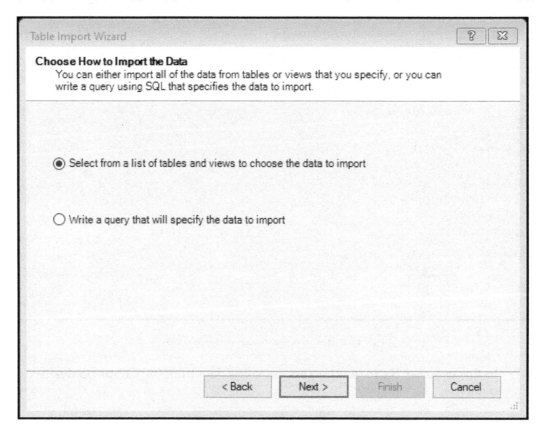

Figure 4-9: Selecting the method to use to import data from an Access database

For now, we'll go with the option to select from a list of tables.

5. Click on **Next** to open the **Select Tables and View** dialog, as shown *Figure 4-10*. Here, we can select which tables we want to add to our data model. Using this dialog, we can also give them more business user-friendly names.

6. Click on **Finish** to start the data import process:

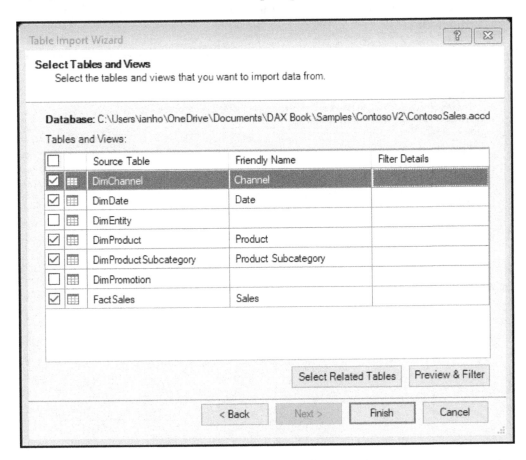

Figure 4-10: Selecting the tables and views to import from an Access database

Our data model will now be created and data from the selected Access database tables will be imported. Progress will be displayed on the **Import** dialog, as shown in the following screenshot.

7. If there are any errors, click on the **Details** link in the appropriate message column; as shown in *Figure 4-11*, otherwise click on **Close** when the import has completed:

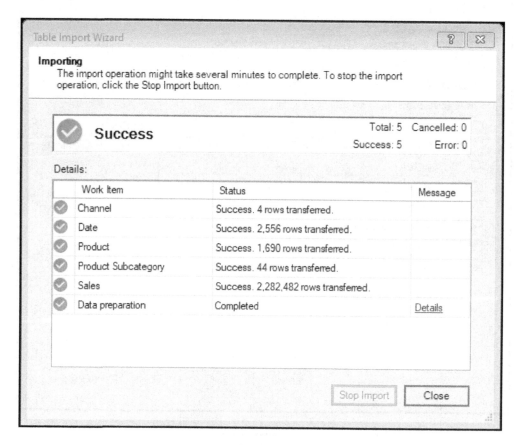

Figure 4-11: Clicking on the details link will show more information

You will now be returned to the Power Pivot window where you will have a tab for each of the tables you've just imported. Each table will look much like a worksheet. However, a Power Pivot table can contain far more rows of data than a worksheet. The screen is split into two sections, with the top being the Data View and the bottom section being the Calculation Area. This is where you can create measures using DAX.

The screenshot in *Figure 4-12* shows the Power Pivot window with tabs for each of the tables we chose to import from the Access database:

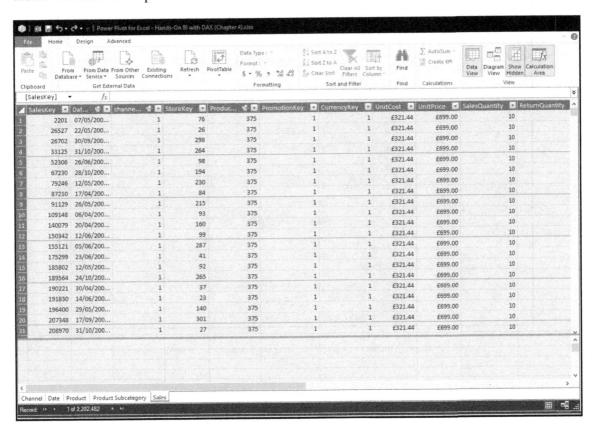

Figure 4-12: The Power Pivot window with tabs added for each table

If you want to rename or delete a column from your data model, right-click on a column heading and select the appropriate option from the drop-down menu, as shown in *Figure 4-13*:

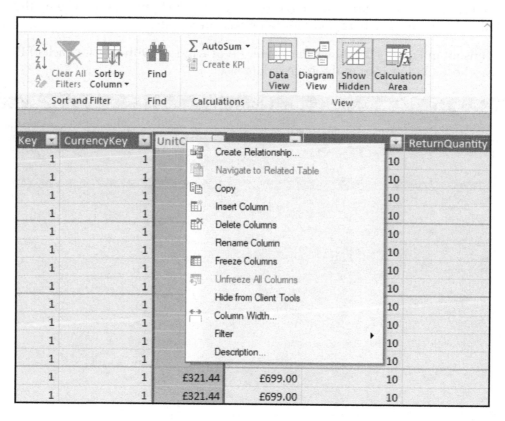

Figure 4-13: The column heading context menu where you can rename or delete a column from the data model

For now, close the Power Pivot window and return to the worksheet. This worksheet contains an Excel table called **Stores**, which contains a list of store names. To add this table to our data model, select a cell in the table and click on the **Add to Data Model** icon in the **Tables** section of the Power Pivot ribbon, as shown in *Figure 4-14*:

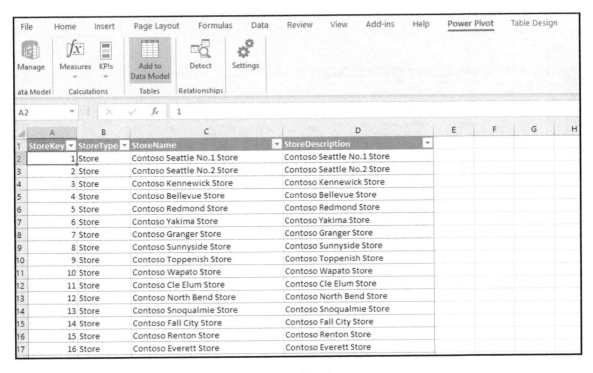

Figure 4-14: Adding a worksheet table to an Excel data model

This will reopen the Power Pivot window and you will see the Excel table has been imported and a new tab added, as shown in *Figure 4-15*:

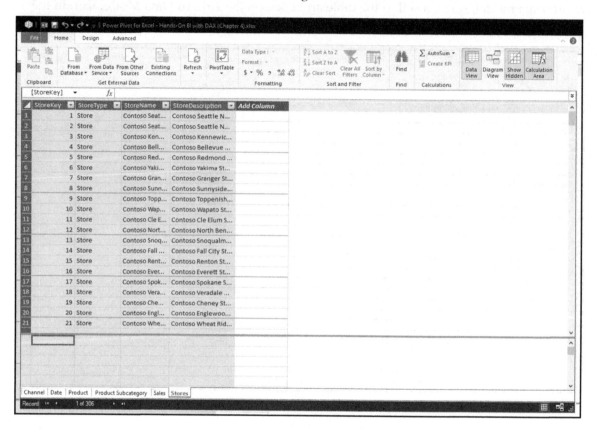

Figure 4-15: Power Pivot window showing imported Excel table

When we imported the tables from the Access database, they were imported with the existing relationships that were already defined there. However, as there are no relationships defined with the Excel table, we will need to manually add a relationship. To do this, switch from the **Data View** to the **Diagram View**, on the **View** section of the **Home** ribbon. *Figure 4-16* shows the **Stores** table without a relationship to any other tables:

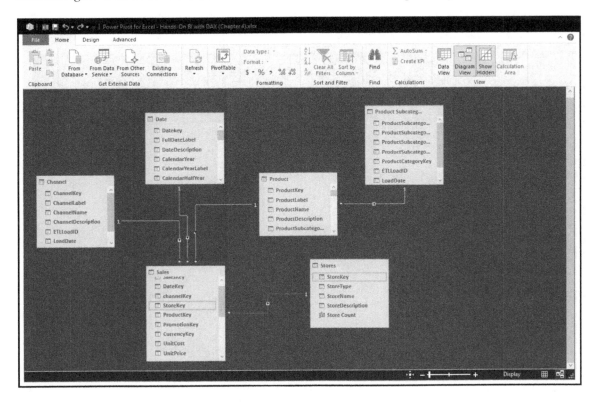

Figure 4-16: The imported table without a relationship

To create a relationship, drag a line between the **StoreKey** in the **Sales** table to the **StoreKey** in the **Stores** table. This will create a relationship between the two tables, as shown in *Figure 4-17*:

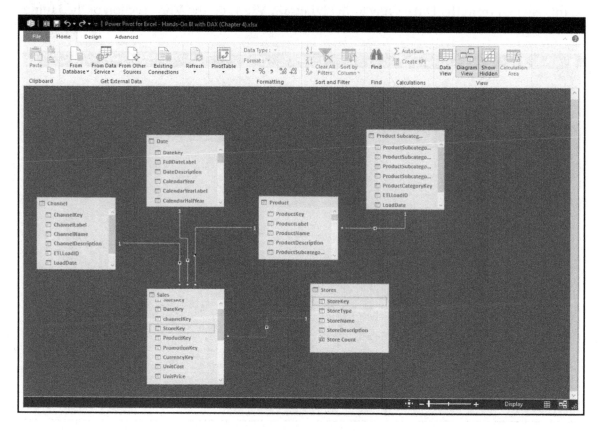

Figure 4-17: The imported table with the relationship created

We are now in a position to start expanding our data model using DAX. We'll start by creating a new measure. For now, close the Power Pivot window and return to the worksheet.

Extending an Excel data model

On the Power Pivot ribbon, do the following:

1. Click on **Measures** in the **Calculations** section.
2. Select **New Measure** from the drop-down menu. This will open the **Measure** dialog shown in *Figure 4-18*.

Here, we can, do the following:

- Create a new measure, defining the table it will be stored with, its name, and of course the DAX code used to define it.
- We can also specify the category and format:

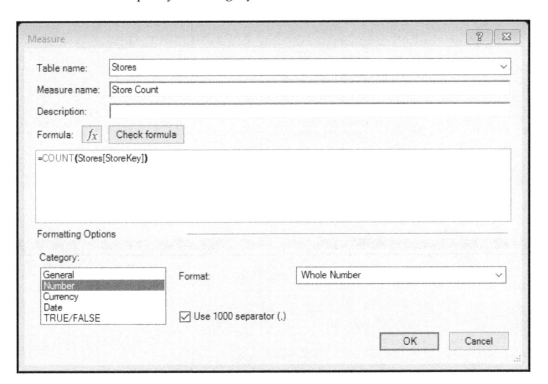

Figure 4-18: The Measure dialog in Excel Power Pivot

- We can define measures in the calculation area of a table in the Power Pivot window.

The screenshot in *Figure 4-19* shows the measure we created for the **Stores** table. In the calculation area, we can see the value that was returned for the measure, while the DAX used to define it is shown in the DAX formula editor:

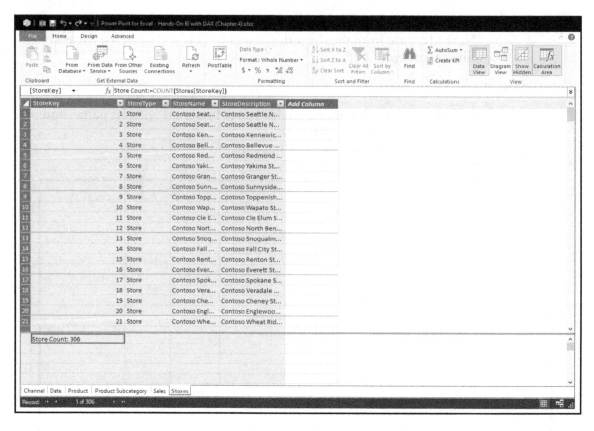

Figure 4-19: Showing a measure in the calculation area with the DAX for it shown in the formula editor

Now, let's define a new measure in the **Sales** table:

1. Switch to the **Sales** tab and then select any cell in the calculation area.
2. Enter the following code into the DAX formula editor:

```
Sum of Sales Amount := SUM ( Sales[SalesAmount] )
```

The result of the new DAX measure will be displayed in the calculation area, as shown in *Figure 4-20*:

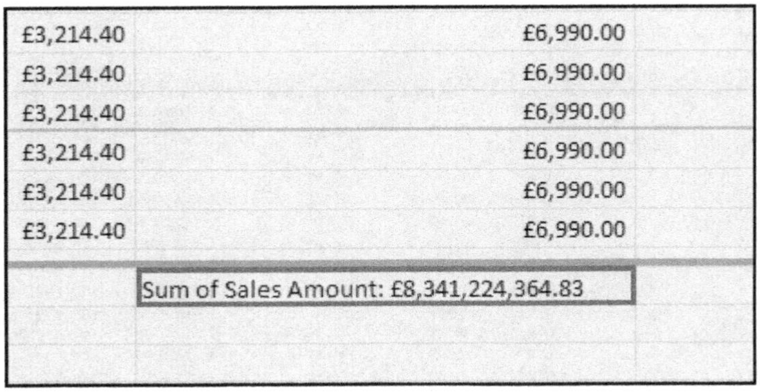

£3,214.40	£6,990.00
£3,214.40	£6,990.00
£3,214.40	£6,990.00
£3,214.40	£6,990.00
£3,214.40	£6,990.00
£3,214.40	£6,990.00
Sum of Sales Amount: £8,341,224,364.83	

Figure 4-20: The result of the sum of sales amount measure shown in the calculation area

We can extend the data model further by using DAX to define calculated columns for a table. To add a new column, do the following:

1. Click on the column heading of the end column, where it says **Add Column.**
2. Then, in the DAX formula editor, enter the DAX that will define the new column.
3. In our data model, in the **Sales** table, add a new column using the following DAX code:

```
Sales Less Returns :=
    Sales[SalesAmount] –
    Sales[ReturnAmount]
```

The screenshot in *Figure 4-21* shows the **Sales** table with the new calculated column added and the values calculated for the new column. Remember, as with Power BI Desktop, calculated columns will add to the overall memory footprint of your data model, so they should be used sparingly:

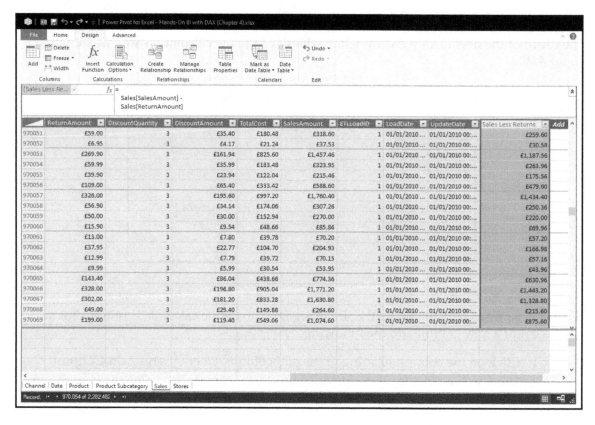

Figure 4-21: Adding the sales less returns calculated column to the sales table

That concludes our look at building a data model with Excel. However, in the next section, we will look at how this data model can be used as the basis of building a data model using SSAS Tabular.

Working with DAX in SSAS Tabular

Microsoft added the tabular model to SQL Server Analysis Services with the release of SQL Server 2012. As with Power BI Desktop and Excel Power Pivot, it is an in-memory database that utilizes compression algorithms to store large amounts in memory instead of storing it on disk. This means that, unlike the multidimensional version of SSAS, the tabular model does not require aggregations to be pre-calculated and stored to offer fast, summarized data.

So far, we've looked at how to import data and build data models using Power BI Desktop and Excel Power Pivot. In each case, the data is imported and stored in the host file. While this is fine for limited use, it does make it difficult to share and reuse the data model. With Power BI Desktop, it is at least possible to publish the data model to the Power BI online service. For Excel Power Pivot, you could copy and share an Excel file. However, in addition to obvious security risks involved with this, it also makes it difficult to keep changes to the data model in sync as it will end up residing on multiple copies of the original file.

To get around this issue, it is possible to import an Excel Power Pivot model into a **SQL Server Data Tools (SSDT)** project and then deploy it to an instance of SSAS Tabular. Once we have created the project, it is possible to make changes to the data model, including adding additional calculated columns and measures. In fact, it is also possible to create a data model from scratch using SSDT, much like we did when we built the model using Excel Power Pivot.

The important point with deploying a data model to an instance of SSAS Tabular is that, once deployed, it can be used by multiple users in multiple files. Whenever an updated model is deployed, the changes will be propagated whenever the data is refreshed in the destination file.

Importing the Excel Power Pivot data model into the SSDT project

SQL Server Data Tools is a development environment built on top of Microsoft Visual Studio. In addition to being used to create SQL Server databases, it can be used to create and maintain an SSAS Tabular data model. As part of this, it is possible to import an existing Excel Power Pivot workbook.

For this exercise, we'll be using SSDT with Visual Studio 2019. The steps we'll follow will be very similar to when we used SSDT with previous versions of Visual Studio. We will be deploying the resulting data model to an instance of SSAS running on a copy of SQL Server 2017.

In addition to installing a version of Visual Studio 2019, you will also need to install the Visual Studio extension for Microsoft Analysis Services Projects, before you can follow along with this example. For more information, see the Microsoft documentation for SSDT at: `https://docs.microsoft.com/en-us/sql/ssdt/download-sql-server-data-tools-ssdt`

We'll start by creating a new project:

1. Open Visual Studio and select **File > New > Project** from the menu.
2. This will open a dialog for Create a new project, as shown in *Figure 4-22*.
3. This screen will look somewhat different on earlier versions of Visual Studio. However, whatever version it is, select the option to **Import from PowerPivot**:

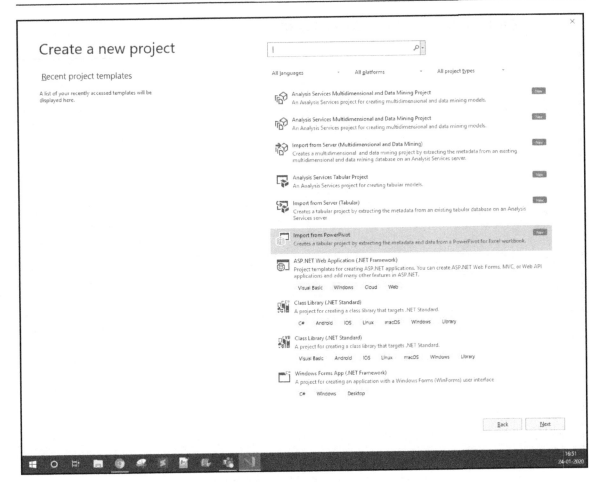

Figure 4-22: Creating a new Excel Power Pivot import project in Visual Studio

4. Next, give the new project a name, as shown in *Figure 4-23*. For this project, we'll call it **ContosoSales Tabular**.

5. Click on **Create** to create the project files:

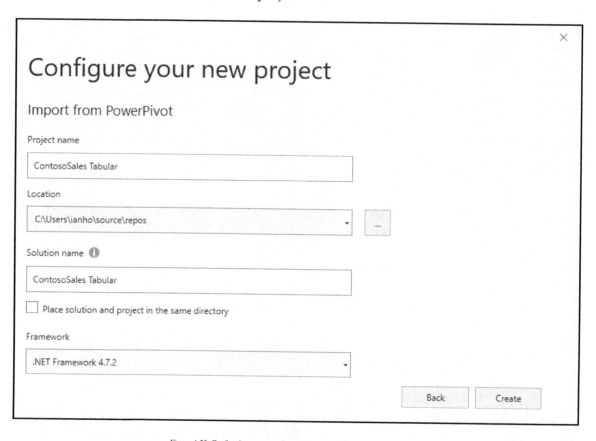

Figure 4-23: Configuring a new project to import data from Excel Power Pivot

6. The next screen, shown in *Figure 4-24*, will ask whether you want to use an **Integrated workspace** or a **Workspace server**. If you use an integrated workspace, then you do not need an instance of SSAS at this stage. However, you will still need an instance of SSAS to deploy your data model to when it is built. For this exercise, I have a local instance of SSAS running on my machine, so I will use **localhost** for my workspace, as shown in the following screenshot:

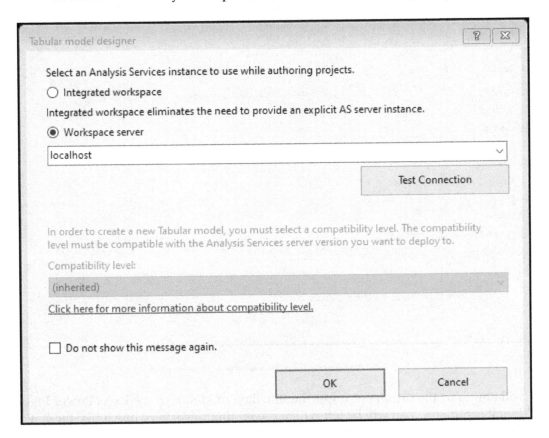

Figure 4-24: Choosing whether to use an integrated workspace or a workspace server

7. We now need to point to the Excel Power Pivot workbook we want to import into our SSDT project. At this point, we'll point to the Excel file we created in the previous exercise. Click on **Open**, as shown in *Figure 4-25*, to start the import process:

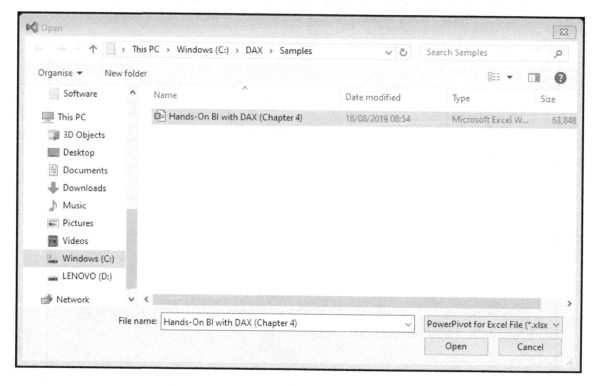

Figure 4-25: Selecting the Excel Power Pivot workbook to use for the data import

SSDT will now start the process of importing the data model from the Excel Power Pivot file. When it completes, you will be left with a screen that looks very much like the Power Pivot window that we were working with in the previous Excel exercise.

We will start off with the data view, with tabs for each of the tables imported from the data model. As with Power Pivot in Excel, it is here that you can add calculated columns to tables, and create measures, using DAX entered with the DAX formula editor. *Figure 4-26* shows this screen, along with the column and measure we created:

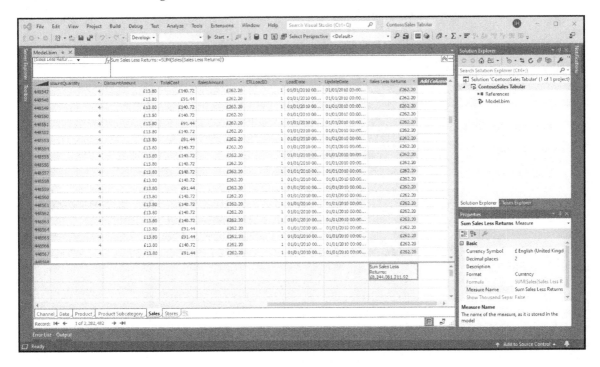

Figure 4-26: The data view in SSDT

You can also switch to the model view, which again looks very much like the model view you get with the Excel Power Pivot window. *Figure 4-27* shows the data model as it was imported from the Excel file. From here, you can manage relationships and create hierarchies. You can also delete, hide, and rename objects in the model:

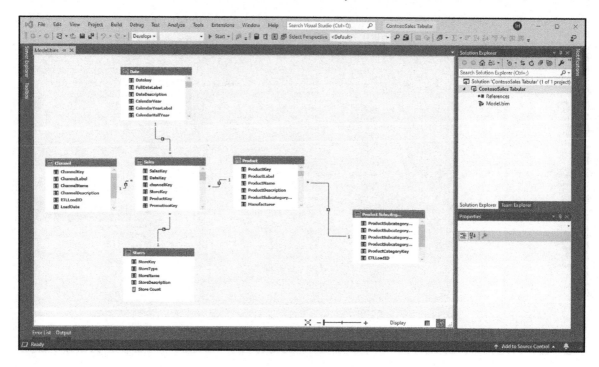

Figure 4-27: The Excel Power Pivot data model after being imported

With the Power Pivot data model successfully imported, and any additions or amendments completed, we are ready to make it available to a wider audience. To do this, we need to deploy it to an instance of SSAS Tabular.

Deploying your data model to an instance of SSAS Tabular

Before we deploy our data model to SSAS, we need to check the project's properties to ensure it is configured to the correct instance of SSAS.

In the Solution Explorer window, do the following:

1. Right-click on the project name, **ContosoSales Tabular**, and click on **Properties** from the context menu.

   This will bring up the properties for the project, as shown in *Figure 4-28*. Ensure you are happy with the server and the database name. In this example, it is pointing to an instance of SSAS Tabular running on a local machine. However, in reality, this should be a server that is accessible to the business intelligence users:

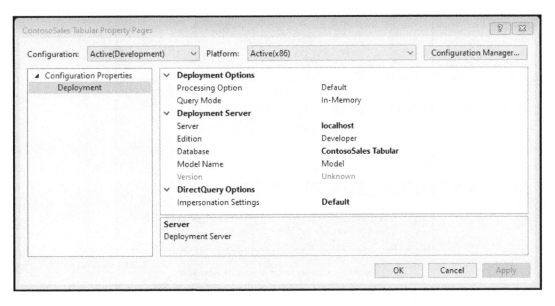

Figure 4-28: The properties dialog for the SSDT Excel Power Pivot project

2. Click on **OK** and, once again, right-click on the project name. This time, select **Deploy** from the context menu, as shown in the *Figure 4-29*:

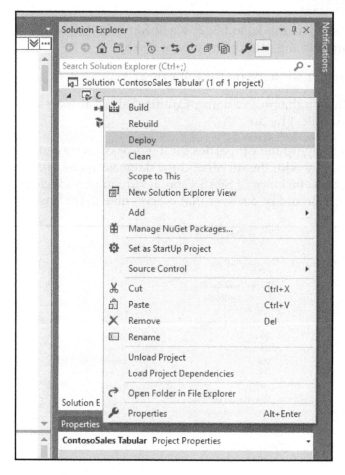

Figure 4-29: Deploying a data model from the context menu

The deployment of the data model will now begin and you will see a window showing the progress of the deployment. *Figure 4-30* shows this window for the completed deployment, giving the final status of each table and the number of rows transferred:

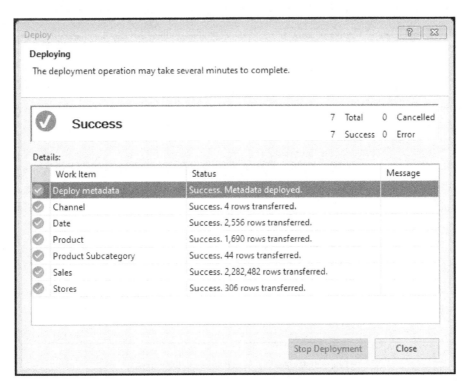

Figure 4-30: Final status of tables after deployment of the data model completes

With the data model deployed, we now need to move from using SSDT to **SQL Server Management Studio (SSMS)**. If you want to make further changes to the data model, then you will need to return to SSDT and make the changes there before redeploying.

Working with the tabular database in SSMS

Now that our data model has been deployed to a tabular database in SSAS, we can use SSMS to carry out some basic management tasks, albeit in a limited way. We can also use it to query data in the database using the browse option, or by using DAX expressions.

The screenshot in *Figure 4-31* shows the Object Explorer, where we can see the database where our data model has been deployed. There is also a second database, with the same name plus a long suffix, which is the workspace database. If you used an integrated workspace for your project in SSDT, then you will not see this second database:

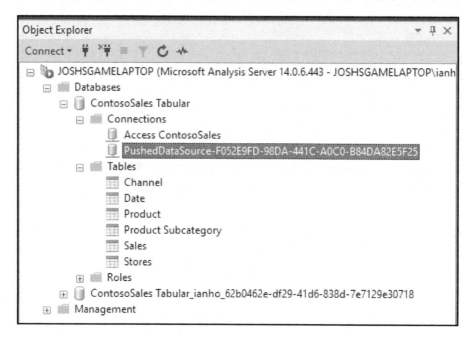

Figure 4-31: The Object Explorer in SSMS showing deployed tables

Looking at the database, there are three nodes:

- **Connections**: This contains the connections to the data sources. Under the properties for each connection, you can modify the connection string along with a few other property settings. You cannot add or delete connections in SSMS. This must be done in SSDT, with the data model then being redeployed to SSAS.
- **Tables**: This contains a list of the tables in the database. You can right-click on a table to view the table's properties, which are view-only and cannot be amended.
- **Roles**: From here, you can assign permissions to users accessing the database. When users are assigned to a role, they are granted the permissions that have been granted to that role. You can add, delete, and configure roles, and add and remove users from a role.

You can create row filters on a role. This specifies which rows in a table can be queried by members of that role. These filters are created using DAX formulas that will evaluate to true or false to determine what a user can access.

Unlike with a relational database, you are limited with what you can do with objects using Object Explorer. Instead, you need to right-click on the database name in Object Explorer and click on **Browse**. This will open a window, as shown in *Figure 4-32*, where you can browse the objects and their related data:

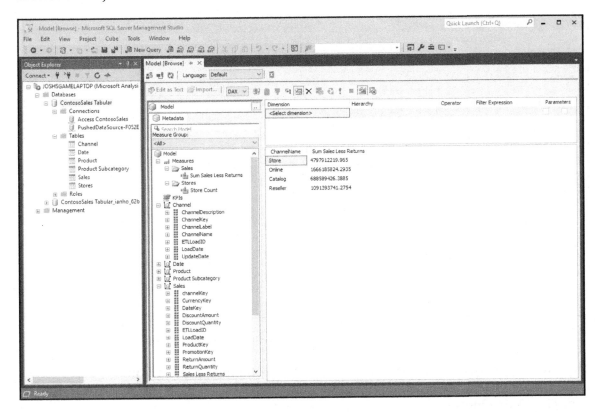

Figure 4-32: Opening a window to browse objects and related data

To view some data, drag columns or measures from the list on the left-hand pane to the bottom pane on the right. Here, we've dragged across the **ChannelName** column from the **Channel** table, and the **Sum Sales Less Returns** measure.

If you want to limit the data being returned, then you can do so by defining filters in the top pane.

If you want to do some analysis on your data in a more familiar environment, you can click on the **Analyze in Excel** icon on the top toolbar. Clicking on this icon opens a new Excel file, with a connection through to the data model already configured and a pivot table ready to use. *Figure 4-33* shows an Excel workbook ready to start work on some tabular data:

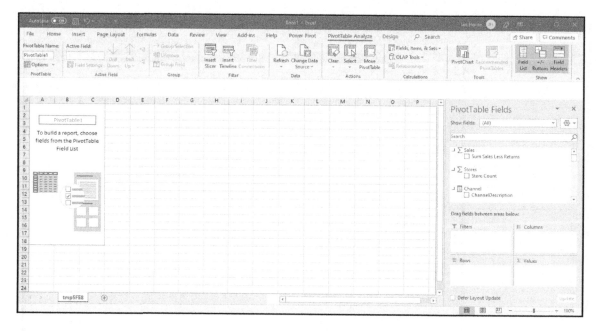

Figure 4-33: Starting work with tabular data in an Excel worksheet

The other way to query data in the tabular database is through a query window using DAX. To open a new query window, right-click on the database name in Object Explorer and select **New Query**.

Querying SSAS Tabular data using DAX

Unlike the DAX expressions we've used so far, DAX expressions in SSAS Tabular always begin with the EVALUATE keyword. This keyword is followed by a DAX expression that returns a table. This table expression defines the query, much like SQL expression does in a relational SQL database, with the EVALUATE keyword acting like the SELECT statement.

The simplest DAX expression is the EVALUATE keyword followed by the name of a table. This will act like SELECT *, returning all columns of all rows in a table.

Again, similar to SQL, you can specify an additional ORDER BY clause to the DAX expression to set the order of the returned rows.

The following expression will return all columns and rows from the **Channel** table, sorted in ascending order of the values in the **ChannelName** column:

```
EVALUATE
    'Channel'
ORDER BY
    'Channel'[ChannelName]
```

If you want to specify more than one column after the ORDER BY clause, then you can, but they must be separated by commas.

The result of running this DAX expression can be seen in *Figure 4-34*:

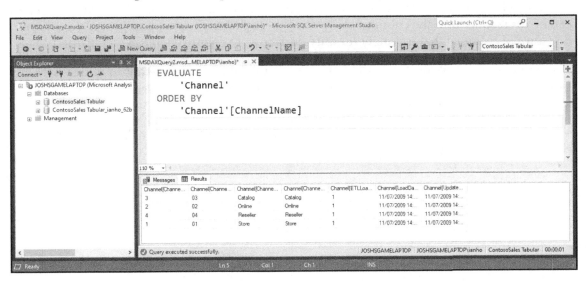

Figure 4-34: Querying data in a table using DAX

At the moment, we are retrieving all of the rows in a table. That's fine for a small table such as the **Channel** table, but for something larger, we will probably want to limit the number of rows being returned. To do this, we need to use the FILTER function.

The FILTER function takes two parameters. The first is a table expression and the second is a Boolean expression. The Boolean expression is evaluated against each row returned by the table expression, and rows that result in true are returned in the function's result set.

The following is an example that would return the rows in the **Sales** table, where the number of returns is greater than **3**:

```
EVALUATE
FILTER (
    'Sales',
    'Sales'[ReturnQuantity] > 3
)
ORDER BY 'Sales'[SalesKey]
```

While this example will limit the number of rows being returned, it is still returning all of the columns in the **Sales** table.

To limit the number of columns, we need to turn to the SUMMARIZE function. This function is designed for grouping rows together and summarizing but, because it returns a table, it can be utilized to limit the columns. However, to do this, we do need to provide a column or group of columns that uniquely identify each row, to ensure each row is returned.

The first parameter of the SUMMARIZE function is the table that you want to return data from. The subsequent parameters are the columns that we want to include in our query, including the columns that uniquely identify each row.

The following example will return six columns from the **Sales** table, including the **SalesKey** column, which acts as the unique row identifier:

```
EVALUATE
 SUMMARIZE (
    'Sales',
    'Sales'[SalesKey],
    'Sales'[DateKey],
    'Sales'[ProductKey],
    'Sales'[SalesAmount],
    'Sales'[ReturnQuantity],
    'Sales'[ReturnAmount]
 )
 ORDER BY Sales[SalesKey]
```

In the following example, we will combine these two examples to give us a filtered list, but only include the columns we need:

```
EVALUATE
SUMMARIZE (
    FILTER (
        'Sales',
        'Sales'[ReturnQuantity] > 3
    ),
    'Sales'[SalesKey],
    'Sales'[DateKey],
    'Sales'[ProductKey],
    'Sales'[SalesAmount],
    'Sales'[ReturnQuantity],
    'Sales'[ReturnAmount]
)
ORDER BY Sales[SalesKey]
```

Here, instead of specifying the **Sales** table as the first parameter, we are using a table expression using the FILTER function to filter the **Sales** table to just those rows where **ReturnQuantity** has a value greater than **3**.

Although we have only touched on what is possible to do with DAX and SSAS Tabular, there are a number of methods that can be used to retrieve and aggregate data. However, what we have covered will help to get you started on building data models with Excel Power Pivot and distributing them for wider access using SSAS Tabular.

Summary

In this chapter, we looked at the DAX formula editor in Power BI Desktop, including a look at some of the shortcut key combinations you can use to help when typing in DAX expressions. We looked at Excel Power Pivot and learned how to use it to build a data model inside an Excel workbook, much like we did using Power BI Desktop. We then learned how to import that data model into an SSDT project and how to extend it using DAX. We then deployed the data model to an instance of SSAS Tabular. Finally, we learned how to query the data once it was in the SSAS Tabular database, using SSMS.

In the next chapter, we will return to the subject of the evaluation context, moving beyond what we learned in Chapter 1, *What is DAX?* We will take a more in-depth look at the difference between the row context and the filter context, and how these affect DAX functions.

Getting It into Context **5**

In this chapter, we will move beyond the basics, and build upon what you learned about evaluation contexts in Chapter 1, *What is DAX?*.

We'll learn about evaluation contexts in more depth, including how **Data Analysis Expressions (DAX)** are evaluated inside a context. We'll learn about the difference between the row context and the filter context, and how these affect different DAX functions. We'll also look at how changing filters impact the evaluation of DAX functions. Finally, we'll look at some DAX functions that can change the context under which an expression is evaluated. These include the CALCULATE function, the ALL function, and the KEEPFILTERS function.

The chapter is broken up into the following sections:

- Introducing evaluation contexts—part 2
- Deep diving into row context
- Deep diving into filter context
- Changing context using DAX functions

Introducing evaluation contexts – part 2

The word *context* is derived from the Latin word *contextus*, which means closely connected or interwoven. In modern language, context is the setting or the set of circumstances around an event.

In DAX, when we talk about the evaluation context, we're talking about the set of circumstances under which a DAX expression is evaluated, brought about by the state of filters, slicers, interactions with visuals, and row and column selections.

In Chapter 1, *What is DAX?*, we took a brief look at the two types of evaluation context that exist in DAX, which are the following:

- The row context
- The filter context

In this chapter, we'll look at these in more detail. We will use examples to help us understand how changes in context change the results that we get back from DAX expressions when they are evaluated within that context.

Strictly speaking, there is also a third context: the query context. The Microsoft documentation describes this as *the filters applied by the user interface of a pivot table*, while the same documentation describes the filter context as *the filters applied by DAX expressions written in a measure*. However, these filters are almost identical in their effects, so we will not cover them separately.

A thorough understanding of how DAX expressions are evaluated within these contexts is essential if you are to truly master using DAX as a **business intelligence (BI)** professional, especially as you move on to more complex DAX expressions. While the theory may appear simple, there are some subtle considerations you will need to be aware of if you are to fully understand how your DAX expressions are being evaluated.

Let's start with just about the simplest measure we can create, shown here:

```
Sum of Sales Amount Measure = SUM ( Sales[Sales Amount] )
```

As you might expect, this will create a measure that returns the sum of all values in the **Sales Amount** column of the **Sales** table. If we now drag this onto the report designer in Power BI Desktop or a pivot table in Excel, it will give a single numeric value, as can be seen in *Figure 5-1*:

Sum of Sales Amount Measure
£8,341,224,364.83

Figure 5-1: Returning the sum of sales with a measure

If we expand our pivot table by adding the **Manufacturer** field from the **Products** table, we will get result shown in *Figure 5-2*:

Manufacturer	Sum of Sales Amount Measure
A. Datum Corporation	£619,803,753.56
Adventure Works	£1,089,734,248.74
Contoso, Ltd	£1,497,920,768.36
Fabrikam, Inc.	£1,874,455,854.35
Litware, Inc.	£327,894,810.44
Northwind Traders	£20,163,003.97
Proseware, Inc.	£954,540,220.53
Southridge Video	£471,653,445.03
The Phone Company	£673,525,407.96
Wide World Importers	£811,532,851.91
Total	**£8,341,224,364.83**

Figure 5-2: Adding a measure to a pivot table

Again, this may well be what you expect to see, especially if you already have some experience of using pivot tables in Excel. But how is this achieved, without the need to change the definition of the measure? In fact, this is an example of the filter context in action. In this case, it is an implicit filter context that is automatically created by adding a field to the pivot table.

With each cell in the **Total Sales Amount** column, our **Sum of Sales Amount Measure** is being calculated within a context. In this case, it is a filter being applied that is equal to the value in the corresponding **Manufacturer** row. It should also be noted that the **Total** row is not adding up the values of each manufacturer; instead, it is evaluating our measure in the context of all **Manufacturer** values.

If we were to add the **Class** column from the **Product** table to the columns of our pivot table, we would be adding another element to the filter context. This means that with each cell, our measure is now being filtered, based on the value of the corresponding **Manufacturer** and **Class**, as can be seen in *Figure 5-3*:

Manufacturer	Deluxe	Economy	Regular	Total
A. Datum Corporation	£71,882,480.30	£97,045,726.08	£450,875,547.18	**£619,803,753.56**
Adventure Works	£227,126,317.70	£148,905,083.74	£713,702,847.29	**£1,089,734,248.74**
Contoso, Ltd	£379,160,840.05	£277,868,875.39	£840,891,052.92	**£1,497,920,768.36**
Fabrikam, Inc.	£420,114,104.80	£150,969,141.35	£1,303,372,608.20	**£1,874,455,854.35**
Litware, Inc.	£6,606,812.05	£51,517,141.64	£269,770,856.75	**£327,894,810.44**
Northwind Traders		£11,551,306.53	£8,611,697.44	**£20,163,003.97**
Proseware, Inc.	£375,496,320.92	£101,011,593.31	£478,032,306.30	**£954,540,220.53**
Southridge Video	£79,416,013.42	£129,786,863.57	£262,450,568.03	**£471,653,445.03**
The Phone Company	£197,094,815.33	£48,025,341.10	£428,405,251.53	**£673,525,407.96**
Wide World Importers	£201,039,835.86	£191,553,277.11	£418,939,738.94	**£811,532,851.91**
Total	**£1,957,937,540.43**	**£1,208,234,349.82**	**£5,175,052,474.58**	**£8,341,224,364.83**

Figure 5-3: Adding a measure to a pivot table with multiple columns

If we look at the totals, the totals for each **Class** column will be evaluated within the context of the corresponding **Class** value, and for all manufacturers.

Next, we are going to use the same expression to create a calculated column in the **Sales** table. This time, we'll call it **Sum of Sales Amount Column**, to differentiate it from our measure, like this:

```
Sum of Sales Amount Column = SUM ( Sales[Sales Amount] )
```

As before, we'll create a pivot table that includes **Manufacturer**. However, we now get a very different result, as can be seen in *Figure 5-4*:

Manufacturer	Sum of Sales Amount Column
A. Datum Corporation	£1,660,245,638,800,605
Adventure Works	£1,422,370,602,364,314.5
Contoso, Ltd	£6,191,540,703,976,528
Fabrikam, Inc.	£2,036,901,966,218,975.3
Litware, Inc.	£429,623,102,135,057.63
Northwind Traders	£255,399,948,826,803.16
Proseware, Inc.	£2,114,642,177,299,217.3
Southridge Video	£1,953,247,827,064,072.3
The Phone Company	£1,699,816,407,187,370.8
Wide World Importers	£1,274,906,096,818,442.3
Total	**£19,038,694,470,691,388**

Figure 5-4: Getting a unexpected result with a measure

Why is this? Well, if we look at *Figure 5-5*, we can see that for every record in the **Sales** table, the value in the new calculated column is the total sum of all the values in the **Sales Amount** column:

Amount	Discount Quantity	Discount Amount	Total Cost	Sales Amount	Sum of Sales Amount Column
£0	0	£0.0	£3,214.4	£6,990.00	£8,341,224,364.83
£0	0	£0.0	£3,214.4	£6,990.00	£8,341,224,364.83
£0	0	£0.0	£3,214.4	£6,990.00	£8,341,224,364.83
£0	0	£0.0	£3,214.4	£6,990.00	£8,341,224,364.83
£0	0	£0.0	£3,214.4	£6,990.00	£8,341,224,364.83
£0	0	£0.0	£3,214.4	£6,990.00	£8,341,224,364.83
£0	0	£0.0	£3,214.4	£6,990.00	£8,341,224,364.83
£0	0	£0.0	£3,214.4	£6,990.00	£8,341,224,364.83
£0	0	£0.0	£3,214.4	£6,990.00	£8,341,224,364.83
£0	0	£0.0	£3,214.4	£6,990.00	£8,341,224,364.83
£0	0	£0.0	£3,214.4	£6,990.00	£8,341,224,364.83
£0	0	£0.0	£3,214.4	£6,990.00	£8,341,224,364.83
£0	0	£0.0	£3,214.4	£6,990.00	£8,341,224,364.83
£0	0	£0.0	£3,214.4	£6,990.00	£8,341,224,364.83
£0	0	£0.0	£3,214.4	£6,990.00	£8,341,224,364.83
£0	0	£0.0	£3,214.4	£6,990.00	£8,341,224,364.83

Figure 5-5: Adding a measure that gives a sum total to a table

This time, this might not have been what you expected. This is because calculated columns do not use the filter context. Instead, they are evaluated using the row context, or, in other words, within the context of each row. Later in this chapter, we will look at a way you can change this behavior, using something called context transition.

Deep diving into row context

The simplest way to explain row context is by adding a calculated column to a table. Whenever we create a calculated column, the DAX expression behind it will be evaluated using the row context. Each row in a table will have its own row context that consists of the values in each of the columns for that row.

Let's show this by adding a calculated column to the **Sales** table. In this instance, we'll add a column that calculates the **Sales Amount**, plus an additional 20 percent to represent sales tax. We can do this using the following DAX expression:

```
Sales Amount with Tax = Sales[Sales Amount] * 1.2
```

Once created, DAX will iterate through all the rows in the **Sales** table, evaluating the expression using the value of the **Sales Amount** column of the current row. It will work its way through the table row by row, with each row providing the row context needed to evaluate the expression.

If we look at the **Sales** table, with our new calculated column, we will see the result will be different for each row and will depend on the value held in the **Sales Amount** column:

Amount	Discount Quantity	Discount Amount	Total Cost	Sales Amount	Sales Amount with Tax
£0	3	£10.7	£54.78	£96.66	£115.99
£0	3	£52.1	£493.02	£1,435.92	£1,723.10
£0	3	£53.4	£544.5	£1,014.60	£1,217.52
£0	3	£186.0	£855.36	£1,674.00	£2,008.80
£0	3	£948.0	£3,140.94	£8,532.00	£10,238.40
£0	3	£948.0	£3,140.94	£8,532.00	£10,238.40
£0	3	£53.9	£274.98	£485.46	£582.55
£0	3	£16.5	£168.24	£313.50	£376.20
£0	3	£21.1	£93.42	£260.79	£312.95
£0	3	£74.4	£493.02	£1,413.60	£1,696.32
£0	3	£4.7	£47.4	£88.35	£106.02
£0	3	£23.4	£238.62	£444.60	£533.52

Figure 5-6: Adding a calculated column to a table

So, as can be seen in the preceding screenshot:

- The value for the first row is **£115.99**, which equates to the value held in the **Sales Amount** column of **£96.66**, multiplied by 1.2.
- For the second row, it is **£1,723.10**, which again equates to the value held in the **Sales Amount** column, multiplied by 1.2.
- This will continue for every row in the table, each row using its own row context.

At the point when our DAX expression for the calculated column is evaluated, it only knows about the values of the columns in the current row. Unlike the filter context, it does not follow relationships, so it does not know about the values in the related row of a table on the *one* side of a one-to-many relationship. It also doesn't know about the values in other rows of the table.

If we look at the data model we're using for the examples in this chapter, we will see that the **Sales** table is a fact table. It is on the *many* side of a one-to-many relationship, with the **Date** and **Product** tables, as can be seen in *Figure 5-7*:

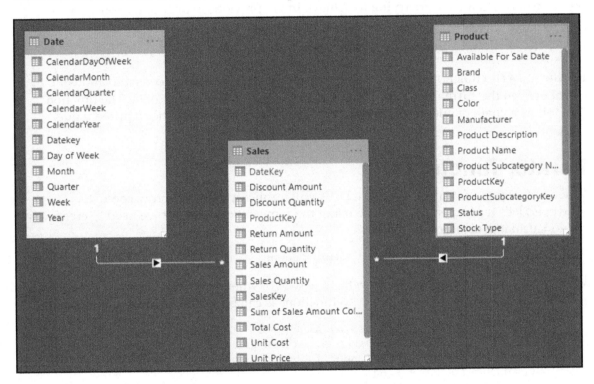

Figure 5-7: One-to-many relationships in a data model

If we try to create a calculated column that uses an expression referencing a column in a related table, we will see that it generates an error. Let's do this, using the following expression:

```
Sales Unit Cost = Sales[Sales Quantity] * Product[Unit Cost]
```

This results in the following error:

```
"A single value for column 'Unit Cost' in table 'Product' cannot be
determined. This can happen when a measure formula refers to a column that
contains many values without specifying an aggregation such as min, max,
count, or sum to get a single result."
```

However, there is a way to fetch the value of a specified column in a related table on the one side of a one-to-many relationship. To do this, we use the RELATED function.

So, to achieve what we were trying to achieve in the previous expression, we need to modify it, as follows:

```
Sales Unit Cost = Sales[Sales Quantity] * RELATED ( Product[Unit Cost] )
```

For the RELATED function to work, it requires a row context. It also needs a relationship to exist between the current table and the table that contains the related data. The function will follow a chain of one or more many-to-one relationships to get the required value.

Iterator functions

When you create a calculated column, DAX will implicitly create the row context. However, let's try to create a measure using the same expression that we used to create one of our calculated columns, as follows:

```
Sales Amount with Tax = Sales[Sales Amount] * 1.2
```

We will get a similar error message to the one we got when we tried to reference a row in a related table without using the RELATED function, as can be seen in the following code:

```
"A single value for column 'Sales Amount' in table 'Sales' cannot be
determined. This can happen when a measure formula refers to a column that
contains many values without specifying an aggregation such as min, max,
count, or sum to get a single result."
```

What this is saying is that it doesn't know which row in the **Sales** table to refer to. When creating a measure, we can only refer directly to a column in a table if we use it with an aggregation function, such as the SUM function. However, we can only use this method to aggregate the values in a column. It cannot be used to evaluate an expression against the column.

In order to be able to create a measure that evaluates an expression against a column in a table, we need to be able to explicitly create a row context. Fortunately, we can do this using one of the iterator functions. An iterator function will iterate over the rows in a specified table and will either apply a filter or evaluate an expression.

In addition to the `FILTER` function, which applies a set of filter rules to return a filtered table, there are several X functions. These are so-called because they have an X as the last character of their name.

These X functions will iterate over a specified table, evaluating a given expression against each row in that table, before applying some form of aggregation. Examples of X functions include `AVERAGEX`, `COUNTX`, `MAXX`, `MINX`, `RANKX`, and `SUMX`. In effect, they create a temporary calculated column that is then used to perform the aggregation, before being dropped.

All these X functions have a corresponding non-iterating aggregation function. Each of the non-iterating aggregation functions uses the X version of their function behind the scenes, in a process known as **syntax sugar**.

 Syntax sugar is a process whereby the language contains simplified versions of more complex functionality, making it easier for people to read and write. There are many examples of this in the DAX language.

For example, previously, we used the `SUM` function to find the total of all the values in the **Sales Amount** column of the **Sales** table. To define that measure, we used the following expression:

```
Sum of Sales Amount Measure = SUM ( Sales[Sales Amount] )
```

To achieve this result, DAX will use the `SUMX` function. In reality, the expression that is actually being evaluated is the following:

```
SUMX ( Sales, Sales[Sales Amount] )
```

While this example might not look particularly interesting, it means that we can use iterator functions to help us reduce the number of calculated columns we need. Remember the calculated column we created, at the start of this section, to calculate the sales amount plus sales tax? For that, we used the following expression:

```
Sales Amount with Tax = Sales[Sales Amount] * 1.2
```

However, using the SUMX iterator function, we can replace this calculated column with a measure, using the following expression:

```
Sales Amount with Tax = SUMX ( Sales, Sales[Sales Amount] * 1.2 )
```

You may remember that this is the preferred approach as it reduces the overall memory footprint of your data model. Wherever possible, you should always create a measure unless there is a specific requirement for a new column in a table, or there is no way of creating the same functionality without using a calculated column.

Iterator functions can also be nested, with each iterator retaining its own row context. The following is a typical example of using nested iterators:

```
Sales Amount with Tax (Deluxe Products) =
SUMX (
    FILTER (
        Sales,
        RELATED ( 'Product'[Class] ) = "Deluxe"
    ),
    Sales[Sales Amount] * 1.2
)
```

In this example, we can see the following:

- The FILTER function is the inner iterator and is being used to filter rows in the **Sales** table to those relating to products in the **Product** table with a **Class** equal to **Deluxe**.
- The outer iterator is the SUMX function, which is used to calculate the total of product sales, with a sales tax of 20% added.

Deep diving into filter context

As we have seen already in Chapter 1, *What is DAX?*, the filter context can be defined as a set of filters that are applied over the tables in a data model before a DAX expression is evaluated. The context in which a DAX expression is evaluated directly affects the result that is returned. This means that the same DAX expression can return different results, depending upon the context.

Filter context exists in the following:

- All visuals in Power BI
- A pivot table in Excel

Filter context can be applied through use of the following:

- Rows and columns in a visual or a pivot table
- Slicers
- Filters
- Interaction with visuals (acting as filters)
- The CALCULATE function

A DAX expression is only evaluated when all the filters coming from the context just listed have been applied to the tables in the data model. In the case of a matrix visual in Power BI or a pivot table in Excel, this means that for every cell, including totals, a DAX expression is evaluated only when the context of the cell has been applied.

Let's look at through an example. Start by creating a new measure called **Sales Count**, using the following expression:

```
Sales Count = COUNTROWS ( Sales )
```

As you might expect, this will return the number of rows in the **Sales** table. If we now add this to a pivot table, along with the **Manufacturer** field from the **Product** table, we will get the result shown in *Figure 5-8*:

Manufacturer	Sales Count
A. Datum Corporation	199,041
Adventure Works	170,523
Contoso, Ltd	742,282
Fabrikam, Inc.	244,197
Litware, Inc.	51,506
Northwind Traders	30,619
Proseware, Inc.	253,517
Southridge Video	234,168
The Phone Company	203,785
Wide World Importers	152,844
Total	**2,282,482**

Figure 5-8: Adding a count of sales to a pivot table

If we take, for example, the cell that is selected in *Figure 5-8*, then we would say the initial filter context for this cell is coming from the row, which in this case is where Product[Manufacturer] equals **Contoso, Ltd**.

The initial filter context is the filter context that is applied to tables in the data model before any changes, if any, are made using the CALCULATE function.

If we were to add a slicer based on the **Year** field in the **Date** table, then the initial filter context would include **Year** from the slicer, in addition to the **Manufacturer** coming from the row of the pivot table.

For example, let's look at the screenshot shown in *Figure 5-9*:

Manufacturer	Q1	Q2	Q3	Q4	Total	Year
A. Datum Corporation	10,861	11,293	11,390	11,447	**44,991**	☐ Year 2005
Adventure Works	13,537	15,057	13,785	14,242	**56,621**	☐ Year 2006
Contoso, Ltd	43,661	46,998	48,988	49,181	**188,828**	☐ Year 2007
Fabrikam, Inc.	16,092	16,852	15,882	16,424	**65,250**	☐ Year 2008
Litware, Inc.	3,624	3,961	4,231	4,206	**16,022**	■ Year 2009
Northwind Traders	2,371	2,320	2,323	2,338	**9,352**	☐ Year 2010
Proseware, Inc.	15,179	16,287	16,116	16,165	**63,747**	☐ Year 2011
Southridge Video	13,644	14,252	14,764	14,944	**57,604**	
The Phone Company	11,598	12,823	13,241	13,402	**51,064**	
Wide World Importers	11,005	13,676	13,099	13,555	**51,335**	
Total	**141,572**	**153,519**	**153,819**	**155,904**	**604,814**	

Figure 5-9: Initial filter context

Here, the initial filter context for the highlighted cell is as follows:

- Date[Year] = **Year 2009** (from the slicer)
- Date[Quarter] = **Q3** (from the pivot column)
- Product[Manufacturer] = **The Phone Company** (from the pivot row)

In order to follow through what is happening here in detail, we need to remember that filters propagate down through relationships, from the one side to the many side of a one-to-many relationship. In this instance, the following steps take place prior to our DAX measure being evaluated:

1. All rows in the **Date** table are filtered to only include those where the year is **Year 2009** and the quarter is **Q3**.
2. The filtered rows are propagated down from the **Date** table to the **Sales** table.
3. All the rows in the **Product** table are filtered to only include those where the **Manufacturer** is **The Phone Company**.
4. The filtered rows are propagated down from the **Product** table to the **Sales** table.
5. The **Sales** table exists with only the rows that have been filtered by the propagated filters.

Only once these steps have been followed is our DAX expression for **Sales Count** evaluated. This is repeated for each row, including the **Total**, which does not include the filter coming from the **Product** table in the initial filter context. It is important to remember that each cell in a row or a column of a matrix visual or a pivot table is evaluated in its own context. It is not adding up values coming from other cells, as you might expect.

Expanded tables

Before we go any further, we are going to explore the concept of expanded tables. In DAX, each table in a data model has an expanded version that contains all the columns of the original table, plus all the columns of tables related to it through many-to-one and one-to-one relationships. This concept will help you to understand the filter context, by showing you which columns in a table will propagate their filters to a related table.

In Power BI, you can have bidirectional relationships, which will add columns to an expanded table through a many-to-one relationship. However, they will not add columns to a table on the one side of the relationship. Instead, the filter propagates through using filtering columns. Although internally they are different, expanded columns and filtering columns act in the same way.

To illustrate this, let's take a simplified version of the data model that we have been working with in this chapter, which is shown in *Figure 5-10*:

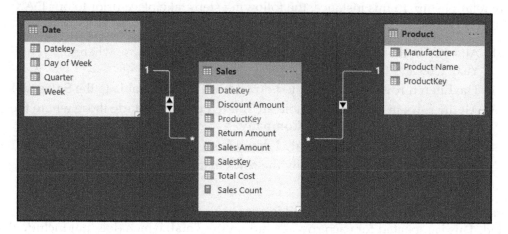

Figure 5-10: The simplified data model

In this case, the base table is the **Sales** table, and it is related to the **Date** table and the **Product** table through many-to-one relationships. For this example, the filter direction on the relationship between the **Sales** table and the **Date** table has been amended so that it's bidirectional.

Figure 5-11 illustrates how the relationships in the data model, shown in *Figure 5-10*, will create expanded versions of each table:

	Column Name	Sales	Product	Date	Key:	
Sales	SalesKey					Original Columns
	Discount Amount					Expanded Columns
	Return Amount					Filtering Columns
	Sales Amount					
	Total Cost					
	ProductKey					
	DateKey					
Product	ProductKey					
	Manufacturer					
	Product Name					
Date	DateKey					
	Day of Week					
	Quarter					
	Week					

Figure 5-11: Expanded tables

Looking at this chart, we can tell the following about the expanded tables for this data model:

- If we start with the **Sales** table, the many-to-one relationships it has with the **Product** and **Date** tables means that its expanded table contains all of the columns of the **Sales** table, plus all of the columns of the **Product** table, plus all of the columns of the **Date** table.
- The **Product** table has no many-to-one relationships. Therefore, its expanded table only contains the original columns.
- The **Date** table has no many-to-one relationships, so its expanded table only contains the original columns. However, as the filter direction on the relationship is bidirectional, filters on any of those columns will propagate through to the **Sales** and **Product** tables.

Using this chart, we can see which expanded tables will be affected by a filter context applied to a column. For example, if a filter were applied to the **Product Name** column in the **Product** table, it would filter the expanded **Sales** table. It would also filter the **Date** table, but, as this is a one-to-many relationship, this would not be through an expanded table. The expanded version of the **Date** table only contains the original columns of the **Date** table. It is the bidirectional nature of the relationship between the **Sales** and **Date** tables that causes it to be filtered by the **Product Name** column, through filtering columns.

When you have a bidirectional relationship in a Power BI data model, DAX will, behind the scenes, add the CROSSFILTER function to an expression to make the filtering work on the one-to-many side of the relationship. Only with a one-to-one relationship will the tables on both sides have expanded tables, and both expanded tables would have identical columns.

For this example, we have only used a very simple data model, so the benefit of understanding expanded tables may not be so obvious. However, as soon as you start working on larger and more complex data models, the importance of this concept will become apparent. This will be especially so when we start to look at DAX functions that allow us to change contexts, which we will look at in the next section.

Changing context using DAX functions

Having covered the evaluation contexts in some detail, we are now going to look at some ways in which we can use DAX functions to change the evaluation context. We'll start off by looking at how we can change the behavior of an expression that is evaluated using the row context.

Context transition

You may remember that, at the start of this chapter, we looked at how an expression we used for a measure did not work in the same way when used in the definition of a calculated column. This is because calculated columns are evaluated using row context, and not filter context. However, it is possible to convert an expression from using the row context into using the filter context by wrapping the expression with the CALCULATE function.

For example, we can define a column with the following expression:

```
Sum of Sales Amount Column = SUM ( Sales[Sales Amount] )
```

But this will give us the same figure for each row: the total of all the values in the **Sales Amount** column. Now, let's amend this expression using the CALCULATE function, as follows:

```
Sum of Sales Amount Column = CALCULATE ( SUM ( Sales[Sales Amount] ) )
```

We will see that our table now looks different. The values in our calculated column match the value in the **Sales Amount** column, as can be seen in *Figure 5-12*:

Quantity ▼	Discount Amount ▼	Total Cost ▼	Sales Amount ▼	Sum of Sales Amount Column ▼
0	£0.0	£3,214.4	£6,990.00	£6,990.00
0	£0.0	£3,214.4	£6,990.00	£6,990.00
0	£0.0	£3,214.4	£6,990.00	£6,990.00
0	£0.0	£3,214.4	£6,990.00	£6,990.00
0	£0.0	£3,214.4	£6,990.00	£6,990.00
0	£0.0	£3,214.4	£6,990.00	£6,990.00
0	£0.0	£3,214.4	£6,990.00	£6,990.00
0	£0.0	£3,214.4	£6,990.00	£6,990.00
0	£0.0	£3,214.4	£6,990.00	£6,990.00
0	£0.0	£3,214.4	£6,990.00	£6,990.00
0	£0.0	£3,214.4	£6,990.00	£6,990.00
0	£0.0	£3,214.4	£6,990.00	£6,990.00
0	£0.0	£3,214.4	£6,990.00	£6,990.00
0	£0.0	£3,214.4	£6,990.00	£6,990.00
0	£0.0	£3,214.4	£6,990.00	£6,990.00
0	£0.0	£3,214.4	£6,990.00	£6,990.00

Figure 5-12: Using context transition with a measure to give row context

By using the CALCULATE function, the following happens:

- We are using a feature called **context transition**.
- When used in the definition for a calculated column, the CALCULATE function converts the row context into a filter context.
- With each execution of the expression that defines our calculated column, it now uses the filter context, adding a filter that includes the current row of the **Sales** table.
- In fact, whenever you create a measure, it is evaluated internally, with a hidden CALCULATE function wrapped around it.

So, for example, we could create our column using the **Sum of Sales Amount Measure** we created earlier in this chapter, like this:

```
Sum of Sales Amount Column = [Sum of Sales Amount Measure]
```

In this case, there would be no need to wrap it with the CALCULATE function, as this is already being done by DAX behind the scenes. The measure would take any available row context and change it to a filter context, giving us the same results we saw in *Figure 5-12*.

Changing the filter context

In Chapter 1, *What is DAX?*, we looked at the CALCULATE and ALL functions, and how these could be used in combination to alter the filter context. It's worth reiterating that the CALCULATE function and its table variant, CALCULATETABLE, are the only functions in DAX that can change a filter context.

At this point, it might be worth rereading the section in Chapter 1, *What is DAX?*, that covers the CALCULATE function. The rest of this section will look at examples of the CALCULATE function being used to change the filter context.

Using the ALL function

The ALL function will return all the rows in a table and ignores the filter context. By itself, it does not change the filter context. Only when used as a filter with the CALCULATE function does it modify the filter context. You can specify either a table name or column names for the parameters of the ALL function. If you specify a table name, then it will ignore all the filters on that table. If you specify column names, then it will ignore only the filters on those columns. The ALL function is not used by itself; instead, is used with other functions such as CALCULATE, altering the results returned by those functions.

 There is a similar function called ALLEXCEPT that works in the same way as ALL, but it will ignore filters on all of the columns, except those specified as parameters for the function.

Let's return to the example that we used in Chapter 1, *What is DAX?*, where we were calculating the percentage of sales quantity by manufacturer. To do this, we created the following measure:

```
%SalesQuantity =
DIVIDE (
    // The sum of sales quantity - current filter context
    SUM ( Sales[Sales Quantity] ),
    // The sum of sales quantity - current filter context altered
    // to remove filter from Manufacturer field
    CALCULATE (
        SUM ( Sales[Sales Quantity] ),
        ALL ( 'Product'[Manufacturer] )
    )
)
```

In this case, we wanted to remove the filter from the **Manufacturer** column of the **Product** table, because this was the column we were splitting the data by on the pivot table.

Let's say we now want to add a couple of slicers to our report, to filter the **Class** and **Color** columns and show the percentage of those filtered products against the overall product sales. To do this, we would need to create a copy of our **%SalesQuantity** measure and change it, to remove all the filters from the filter context of the **Product** table.

To do this, we need to alter the second parameter of the DIVIDE function. We could include the **Class** and **Color** columns for the ALL function to remove these from the filter context. Alternatively, we could just specify the **Product** table to remove all the filters from the filter context. As we are looking to compare the filtered sales quantity against the sales quantity for all products, the second option seems to be the most sensible choice.

The code for the new measure should be as follows:

```
%OverallSalesQuantity =
DIVIDE (
    // The sum of sales quantity - current filter context
    SUM ( Sales[Sales Quantity] ),
    // The sum of sales quantity - current filter context altered
    // to remove all filters from Product table
    CALCULATE (
        SUM ( Sales[Sales Quantity] ),
        ALL ( 'Product' )
    )
)
```

Figure 5-13 shows the results the **%OverallSalesQuantity** measure, used with a pivot table showing the sales quantity for **Silver, Deluxe** products compared against the overall sales quantity:

Manufacturer	Sales Quantity	%SalesQuantity	%OverallSalesQuantity
Contoso, Ltd	159,179	32.76%	0.43%
The Phone Company	91,450	18.82%	0.25%
Southridge Video	88,852	18.29%	0.24%
Proseware, Inc.	41,259	8.49%	0.11%
Adventure Works	32,047	6.60%	0.09%
A. Datum Corporation	31,230	6.43%	0.08%
Fabrikam, Inc.	20,860	4.29%	0.06%
Wide World Importers	19,099	3.93%	0.05%
Litware, Inc.	1,905	0.39%	0.01%
Total	**485,881**	**100.00%**	**1.32%**

Class
- ■ Deluxe
- ☐ Economy
- ☐ Regular

Color
- ☐ Azure
- ☐ Black
- ☐ Blue
- ☐ Brown
- ☐ Gold
- ☐ Green
- ☐ Grey
- ☐ Orange
- ☐ Pink
- ☐ Red
- ■ Silver
- ☐ Silver Grey
- ☐ White
- ☐ Yellow

Figure 5-13: Pivot table with measures and slicers

In later releases of DAX, there is a new function called REMOVEFILTERS. This is effectively an alias for the ALL function, but it can only be used as a filter for the CALCULATE function, and not as a table expression.

Using filters with CALCULATE

Now, suppose that we only need our pivot table to show quantities for silver products. We'll start by creating a new measure for total sales quantity, but this time, we will only include products in the **Product** table where the **Color** column equals **Silver**. To do this, we can add a Boolean expression as the filter condition of the CALCULATE function. In this case, the following DAX expression will create the measure that we need:

```
Sum of Sales Quantity Measure - Silver =
CALCULATE (
    SUM ( Sales[Sales Quantity] ),
    'Product'[Color] = "Silver"
)
```

To fully understand what is going on with this expression, we need to be aware that this measure uses compact syntax. When evaluated, the DAX engine will automatically use an expanded version that uses the FILTER function and the ALL function. In reality, the code for the measure would be as shown here:

```
Sum of Sales Quantity Measure – Silver =
CALCULATE (
    SUM ( Sales[Sales Quantity] ),
    FILTER (
        ALL ('Product'[Color] ),
        'Product'[Color] = "Silver"
    )
)
```

The reason for this is to overwrite any existing filters on the column the with the explicit filter being applied by the Boolean expression. This may lead to undesired results, as can be seen in *Figure 5-14*:

Manufacturer	Sales Quantity	Sum of Sales Quantity Measure - Silver
A. Datum Corporation	**2,400,635**	**294,317**
Azure	251,937	294,317
Black	336,579	294,317
Blue	68,885	294,317
Gold	56,214	294,317
Green	260,301	294,317
Grey	292,625	294,317
Orange	370,619	294,317
Pink	343,623	294,317
Silver	294,317	294,317
Silver Grey	125,535	294,317
Adventure Works	**2,421,433**	**522,753**
Black	705,745	522,753
Blue	83,983	522,753
Brown	280,235	522,753
Red	136,635	522,753
Silver	522.753	522.753
Total	**36,900,410**	**6,534,597**

Figure 5-14: Getting undesired results from a measure with explicit filter

Here, the result of the expanded syntax is to remove the external filter context generated by the matrix visual. However, there is a way to resolve this, by using the KEEPFILTERS function.

We can amend our measure to use the KEEPFILTERS function, like this:

```
Sum of Sales Quantity Measure – Silver =
CALCULATE (
    SUM ( Sales[Sales Quantity] ),
    KEEPFILTERS ( 'Product'[Color] = "Silver" )
)
```

Using the amended measure in our matrix, we now get the desired results, as can be seen in *Figure 5-15*:

Manufacturer	Sales Quantity	Sum of Sales Quantity Measure - Silver
A. Datum Corporation	**2,400,635**	294,317
Azure	251,937	
Black	336,579	
Blue	68,885	
Gold	56,214	
Green	260,301	
Grey	292,625	
Orange	370,619	
Pink	343,623	
Silver	294,317	294,317
Silver Grey	125,535	
Adventure Works	**2,421,433**	522,753
Black	705,745	
Blue	83,983	
Brown	280,235	
Red	136,635	
Silver	522,753	522,753
Total	**36,900,410**	6,534,597

Figure 5-15: Keeping filters to get the expected results from a measure

As the name suggests, the KEEPFILTERS function will keep any existing filters, while applying the new filter being created by the Boolean expression. In this example, for each row, the measure is counting the **Sales Quantity** for those products where the **Color** is equal to the color coming from the visual and where the color is **Silver**. Obviously, this means that we now only get a figure where the color coming from the visual is equal to **Silver**. For all the others, there are no products that match the filter context.

Summary

In this chapter, we took a more in-depth look at evaluation contexts, focusing on the two different types of evaluation contexts: row context and filter context.

First, we took a detailed look at the row context, learning how this applies when you create a calculated column or use a function that iterates through the rows of a table. We followed this with a detailed look at the filter context, learning about the different sources of filters, and how these can affect the results coming back from a DAX expression. Then, we learned about the concept of expanded tables, and how these can help you to understand how filters can propagate through related tables. Finally, we looked at how you can change a context in DAX. We learned how you can change a row context into a filter context, and how you change filter context with the CALCULATE function.

In the next chapter, we will learn more about the structure of DAX syntax. We'll also look at the different groups of functions that are available in DAX, including aggregation functions and parent-child functions.

Section 2: Understanding DAX Functions and Syntax

2

This section comprises an in-depth look at some important DAX functions, specifically those related to tables, date and time, filtering, and statistics. In addition to describing the functions in detail, part 2 offers a more hands-on approach, walking you through some practical examples of the functions in use:

- Chapter 6, Progressive DAX Syntax and Functions
- Chapter 7, Table Functions
- Chapter 8, Date, Time, and Time Intelligence Functions
- Chapter 9, Filter Functions
- Chapter 10, Statistical Functions
- Chapter 11, Working with DAX Patterns

6
Progressive DAX Syntax and Functions

In this chapter, we'll start by taking a more in-depth look at the structure of DAX syntax, including naming requirements. We'll learn more about relationships, including how we deal with relationships between tables that involve multiple columns and how to create virtual relationships.

Next, we will learn about the different groups of functions that can be found in the DAX language. We'll then start to look at these groups in more detail, beginning with aggregation functions. We'll round off this chapter by learning about the functions that will help to deal with parent-child hierarchies.

This chapter is broken down into the following sections:

- Breaking down DAX syntax
- Dealing with relationships
- Looking at DAX functions
- Introduction to aggregation functions
- Functions for parent-child hierarchies

Breaking down DAX syntax

So far, we've looked at quite a few examples of DAX expressions, but we haven't looked in detail at the structure of a typical DAX expression.

Let's set that straight by breaking down a typical DAX expression. For this one, we will define a measure that will give us the total sum of values in the **Sales Quantity** column of the **Sales** table, for products in the **Deluxe** class:

```
1 Deluxe Sales Quantity
2 =
3 CALCULATE
4 (
5 [Sum of Sales Quantity Measure]
6 ,
7 'Product'[Class]
8 = "Deluxe"
9 )
```

This DAX expression can be broken down as follows:

1. We start with the name we want to give to the measure, which in this case is **Deluxe Sales Quantity**.
2. The equals sign operator (=) defines the start of the DAX formula. When writing DAX expressions with Excel Power Pivot and SSAS Tabular, the equals sign will have a colon before it (:=).
3. Our measure uses the CALCULATE function, which takes an expression or measure as the first argument and then modifies the filter context in which it is evaluated, using the filters given in the following parameters.
4. The opening parenthesis specifies the start of the arguments being passed to the CALCULATE function.
5. The measure **Sum of Sales Quantity Measure** calculates the total sum of values in the **Sales Quantity** column of the **Sales** table. It is defined using this expression:

    ```
    Sum of Sales Quantity Measure = SUM ( Sales[Sale Quantity] )
    ```

6. The comma separates the expression passed as the first argument from the filter argument.
7. This gives the table and column name that we will use to modify the initial filter context used to evaluate the measure or expression given in the first argument.
8. This specifies the value that we want to filter the given column for, which will then define the new filter context.

This DAX expression ensures that the **Sum of Sales Quantity Measure** only includes values for sales of products in the **Product** table where the **Class** column has the value of **Deluxe**.

A DAX expression will return either a scalar value or a table. Where a DAX expression returns a table, it must be used with another DAX function that will evaluate the table and return a scalar value. The only exception to this is where an expression returns a single row table consisting of a single column, in which case it will be treated as a scalar value.

Most DAX functions require at least one argument. These can consist of tables, columns, expressions, or values. Where a function doesn't require any arguments, it will still need to include an empty set of parentheses after the function name. For example, you must type BLANK() and not BLANK.

Naming requirements

Within a data model, all tables must be identified using unique names. Within each table, the names of the columns must be unique, including calculated columns. However, the same column name can be used in multiple tables.

All object names in DAX are case-insensitive, which means that you could use either **PRODUCT** or **Product** to refer to the same table.

Columns (including calculated columns) and measures need to belong to a table. This can be done implicitly when you create a column or measure within a table, or explicitly, by specifying the name of the table where a measure should be defined.

When writing DAX functions, you should always adhere to the following naming convention:

- A table name should be specified as it appears in the data model, for example, **Sales**.
- A column name should be specified as it appears in the data model with square brackets enclosing it. Although not strictly necessary, for good practice, it should always be fully qualified by prefixing it with the name of the table that contains the column, for example, 'Product'[Class].
- If a table name contains spaces or uses a reserved keyword, it must be enclosed within single quotes, for example, 'Product Categories'. You will also need to enclose it with single quotes if it contains characters outside of the ANSI alphanumeric character set.
- Measure names must be unique within the data model.
- Measure names must always be specified in square brackets, and they must never be prefixed by the table name.

A fully qualified column name is always required when you reference a column in the following situations:

- A column is used as an argument to the VALUES, ALL, ALLEXCEPT, and RELATEDTABLE functions, or any of the time intelligence functions.
- A column is used as the filter argument for the CALCULATE and CALCULATETABLE functions.

The following cannot be used in the names of tables, columns, or measures:

- Leading or trailing spaces; unless the spaces are enclosed by name delimiters, brackets, or single apostrophes
- Control characters
- Any of the following characters: .,;':/*|?&%$!+=()[]{}<>

In this section, we've learned about the DAX syntax. Now, let's proceed toward the next section, which talks about dealing with relationships.

Dealing with relationships

In Chapter 3, *Building Data Models*, we looked at creating physical relationships between tables as part of our look at data modeling. For example, in our data model, we have a physical relationship defined between the **Product** and **Sales** tables, as shown in *Figure 6-1*:

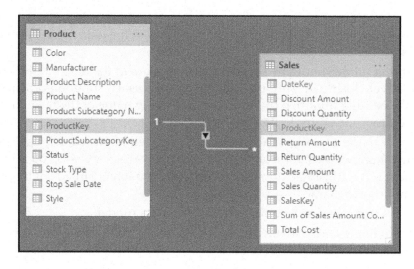

Figure 6-1: The one-to-many relationship between the Product and Sales tables

A physical relationship in a data model requires that at least one side of the relationship is linked to a column in a table that contains unique values. In the preceding example, we've built the relationship using the **ProductKey** column of the **Product** table linked to the **ProductKey** column of the **Sales** table, creating a one-to-many relationship.

With this relationship, any filters applied to columns of the **Product** table are propagated using a filter on the **Sales** table. The list of values filtered in the **ProductKey** column of the **Product** table is transferred to a filter that is applied to the **ProductKey** column of the **Sales** table.

However, there may be times when you may not be able to create a physical relationship between two tables. This could be because neither of the tables contains a column that consists of unique values, which is required by the one side of a one-to-many relationship (although it is now possible to create many-to-many relationships in Power BI Desktop). It may be the case that unique values involve two or more columns in a table, whereas relationships in a Tabular data model can only be created between tables using a single column on each side.

One way to deal with this situation is to combine the columns required in the relationship, using either the CONCATENATE function or the COMBINEVALUES function. The following gives the example where there is a need to create a relationship between two tables called **Dates** and **Sales**, using the columns **Year** and **DayOfYear**.

First, you would need to create a calculated column on the **Dates** table as shown:

```
Dates[SaleDate] = CONCATENATE ( Dates[Year], Dates[DayOfYear] )
```

Then, you would create another calculated column on the **Sales** table:

```
Sales[SaleDate] = CONCATENATE ( Sales[Year], Sales[DayOfYear] )
```

You would then complete the process by creating a physical relationship between the newly created **Dates[SalesDate]** and **Sales[SaleDate]** columns.

Dealing with multiple relationships

While it is possible to create multiple relationships between tables, only one of them can be active at a time. A classic example of this is where you have several dates in a data table, all of which are related to a single date in a date table. In the example shown in *Figure 6-2*, we have two date fields in the **Sales** table, both of which are joined to the **Date** table. The active relationship shown here is between the **Date[DateKey]** and **Sales[SalesDateKey]** columns:

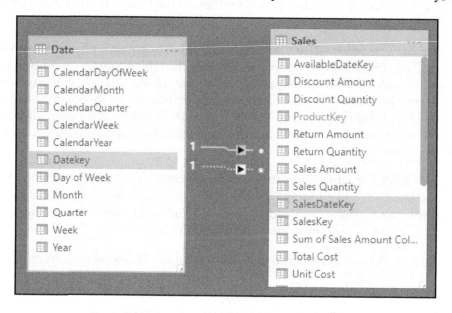

Figure 6-2: Multiple relationships between tables with active relationship highlighted

Figure 6-3 shows the second relationship between the **Date[DateKey]** and **Sales[DispatchedDateKey]** columns. This relationship is inactive, which is indicated by the dashed line:

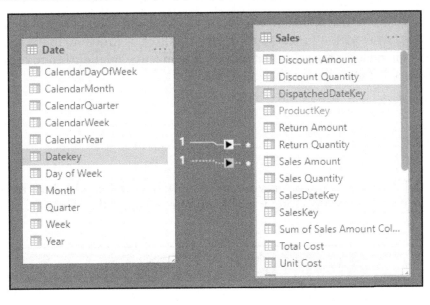

Figure 6-3: Multiple relationships between tables with inactive relationship highlighted

To make use of the active relationship, all you need to do is use an appropriate field from the **Sales** table, such as **SalesKey**, with a pivot table or matrix visual and aggregate it by a field from the **Date** table. *Figure 6-4* shows a count of sales by date:

Datekey	Count of SalesKey
01/01/2007	2453
02/01/2007	2461
03/01/2007	2365
04/01/2007	2378
05/01/2007	2287
06/01/2007	2369
07/01/2007	2490
08/01/2007	2231
Total	**2282482**

Figure 6-4: Making use of an active relationship to count sales by date

However, to be able to use an inactive relationship, you will need to create a measure that uses the USERELATIONSHIP function inside the CALCULATE function. In the following example, we will create a measure that will use the inactive relationship to calculate the number of sales dispatched on a particular date:

```
Orders Dispatched =
CALCULATE (
    COUNT ( Sales[SalesKey] ),
    USERELATIONSHIP ( 'Date'[Datekey], Sales[DispatchedDateKey] )
)
```

If we now add this measure to our pivot table or matrix visual, it will show us the number of sales made on a given date, along with the number of sales dispatched, as can be seen in *Figure 6-5*:

Datekey	Count of SalesKey	Orders Dispatched
01/01/2007	2453	
02/01/2007	2461	
03/01/2007	2365	2453
04/01/2007	2378	2461
05/01/2007	2287	2365
06/01/2007	2369	2378
07/01/2007	2490	2287
08/01/2007	2231	2369
Total	**2282482**	**2282482**

Figure 6-5: Using a measure with an inactive relationship to show orders dispatched by date

It is important to remember that the USERELATIONSHIP function will not work unless an inactive relationship has already been created in the data model.

An alternative to this method of dealing with multiple relationships would be to have multiple date tables. For example, you could have a date table called **SalesDate** and another called **DispatchDate**, each with an active relationship to the appropriate column in the Sales table. However, with this approach, it would be more complex to replicate the example given in the preceding screenshot. You would instead need to add a filter or slicer to pick a sales date and then you could use the pivot table or matrix visual to show the breakdown of sales made on that date, by the date of dispatch.

In the end, which method you choose to use will depend on the complexity of your data model, along with how you are intending to present your data.

Virtual relationships

Depending on the version of Excel Power Pivot, SSAS Tabular, or Power BI you are using, there are a couple of ways of achieving virtual relationships between tables.

If we return to our data model, we will start by removing all of the physical relationships between the **Date** table and the **Sales** table, as shown in *Figure 6-6*:

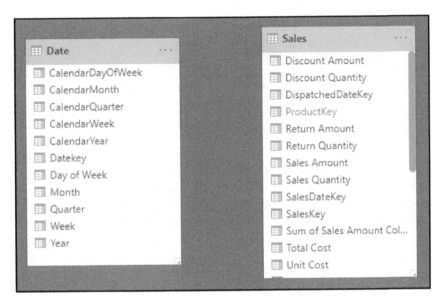

Figure 6-6: Removing relationships between tables

The first method we will look at will work with any version of the DAX language. To replicate the results we obtained in the previous section, we need to create two new measures. The first measure will create a virtual relationship between the **Date[DateKey]** and **Sales[SalesDateKey]** columns:

```
DateKey to SalesDateKey VR =
CALCULATE (
    COUNT ( Sales[SalesKey] ),
    FILTER (
        ALL ( Sales[SalesDateKey] ),
        CONTAINS (
            VALUES ( 'Date'[Datekey] ),
```

```
                       'Date'[Datekey], Sales[SalesDateKey]
            )
        )
    )
```

This measure is using the FILTER and CONTAINS functions to match rows in the **Sales** table with the selected date coming from the **Date** table, creating a virtual relationship between the **Date[DateKey]** and **Sales[SalesDateKey]** columns. Using the same logic, we can create a second measure that will create a virtual relationship between the **Date[DateKey]** and **Sales[DispatchDateKey]** columns:

```
DateKey to DispatchDateKey VR =
CALCULATE (
    COUNT ( Sales[SalesKey] ),
    FILTER (
        ALL ( Sales[DispatchedDateKey] ),
        CONTAINS (
            VALUES ( 'Date'[Datekey] ),
            'Date'[Datekey], Sales[DispatchedDateKey]
        )
    )
)
```

If you are working with DAX using more recent versions of Power BI Desktop or versions of Excel Power Pivot and Analysis Services from 2016 onward, you can make use of the INTERSECT function to achieve the same results as in the preceding. Here is the DAX expression to create the revised measure for the **Date[DateKey]** to **Sales[SalesDateKey]** virtual relationship:

```
DateKey to SalesDateKey VR2 =
CALCULATE (
    COUNT ( Sales[SalesKey] ),
    INTERSECT (
        ALL ( Sales[SalesDateKey] ),
        VALUES ( 'Date'[Datekey] )
    )
)
```

If we apply all three measures to a pivot table or matrix visual, we get the result shown in *Figure 6-7*:

Datekey ▲	DateKey to SalesDateKey VR	DateKey to DispatchDateKey VR	DateKey to SalesDateKey VR2
01/01/2007	2453		2453
02/01/2007	2461		2461
03/01/2007	2365	2453	2365
04/01/2007	2378	2461	2378
05/01/2007	2287	2365	2287
06/01/2007	2369	2378	2369
07/01/2007	2490	2287	2490
08/01/2007	2231	2369	2231
Total	2282482	2282482	2282482

Figure 6-7: Adding virtual relationship measures to a pivot table

As you can see, we get exactly the same result as we did with the physical relationship between these tables.

If you are using a version of Power BI Desktop released after February 2017, or a very recent version of Excel Power Pivot or SSAS Tabular, then there is a third way you can create a virtual relationship, by using the TREATAS function.

The TREATAS function will let you take filters from the current filter context and apply them to a table in your data model. Also, it will allow you to pass multiple filters from the source table to the target table.

The following is the DAX expression used to revise the measure for the **Date[DateKey]** to **Sales[SalesDateKey]** virtual relationship:

```
DateKey to SalesDateKey VR3 =
CALCULATE (
    COUNT ( Sales[SalesKey] ),
    TREATAS (
        VALUES ( 'Date'[Datekey] ),
        Sales[SalesDateKey]
    )
)
```

While a physical relationship will always give the best performance if you do need to create a virtual relationship, and you are working with the latest version of DAX, then you should consider using the TREATAS function as the best way to implement this. The TREATAS function gives the best performance, while the method using the FILTER function is the worst in terms of performance. It does, however, have the advantage that it works across all versions of DAX.

Let's move ahead toward the next section now, which talks about DAX functions.

Looking at DAX functions

The DAX language contains over 250 different functions. These functions are split into two different types, depending on the result returned. They can also be grouped depending on the functionality performed.

Function types

When evaluated, a DAX function will perform a specified action against the data in your data model and return a result. These functions fall into one of two categories depending on whether they return a single value or a table of data.

Those functions that return a single value are called scalar functions and form the majority of functions in the DAX language. They are typically used in expressions used for creating measures and calculated columns, which require a scalar value. These are then used as the input value to a pivot table or a Power BI visual. The following is an example of a scalar value being used to create a measure:

```
SumOfSalesQuantity = SUM ( Sales[SalesQuantity] )
```

Here, the SUM function will add together all the values in the **SalesQuantity** column of the **Sales** table and return a single total value.

Functions that return Boolean values, such as the IF function, can also be considered scalar as they return a single value of either TRUE or FALSE.

Functions that return a table of data are called table functions. These functions cannot be used directly in expressions that are used to define measures or calculated columns, but instead are used as the input for other DAX functions. Any function that iterates over a table, such as the SUMX function, requires a table for the first argument and is an ideal candidate for using with the output of a table function:

```
Very large sales amount =
SUMX (
    FILTER (
        Sales,
        Sales[Sales Quantity] >= 1000
    ),
    Sales[Sales Amount]
)
```

In the preceding example, the table function, FILTER, is used to return a table containing only those records from the **Sales** table where the value in the **Sales Quantity** column is greater than or equal to 1,000. This is then used as the table argument for the SUMX function, which iterates over the table and sums the values in the **Sales Amount** column.

Another use for table functions is in the definition of a calculated table. Unfortunately, calculated tables are not currently available with Excel Power Pivot. The following shows an example of this:

```
Product Sales =
SUMMARIZE (
    Sales,
    'Product'[ProductKey],
    "Total Sales",
    SUM ( 'Sales'[Sales Quantity] )
)
```

This will add a calculated table to your data model, called **Product Sales**, which contains the **Product Key** and the **Total Sales** amount for that product key.

Finally, table functions can be used with the EVALUATE statement to query your data model, using tools such as Excel, SQL Server Management Studio, or DAX Studio:

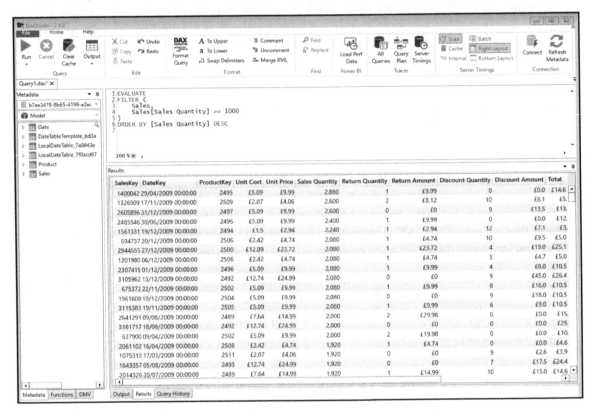

Figure 6-8: Evaluating a DAX expression in DAX Studio

Figure 6-8 is a screenshot is from DAX Studio, showing a query designed to return rows from the **Sales** table, where the **Sale Quantity** is greater than or equal to 1,000, ordered in descending order of **Sales Quantity**.

There is a special case with table functions when they return a single row with a single column - essentially a single value. In this case, DAX will attempt to automatically convert the table returned into a scalar value when needed. However, you should avoid using table functions in this way, as there is always the risk that, in the future, the function will return multiple rows, leading to an error.

Table functions cannot be used as the input to a pivot table or visual, unless the function returns a single row with a single column, as described earlier.

Function groups

DAX includes a rich set of functions that allow you to perform aggregations, look up values in related tables, and manipulate text and perform time-based business intelligence. If you have used formulas in Excel, then many will appear very similar. However, you should remember that while Excel is based around cells, DAX works with columns and tables. By default, a DAX function will reference a complete column or table, and you will need to add filters to the formula if you require a particular subset of the data held in a table.

DAX functions can be grouped depending on their functionality. The following lists each of these groups, along with a brief explanation of what functionality the functions in that group provide:

- **Aggregation functions**: These functions will aggregate the values in a column of a table, or will apply aggregation to an expression that is evaluated by iterating over a table. Functions in this group will return a scalar value.
- **Date and time functions**: These functions are very similar to the date and time functions found in Excel, except that they make use of the date and time data types used in SQL Server.
- **Filter functions**: These functions can be used to look up values in related tables, using the relationships that exist between tables in your data model. They allow you to filter tables based on specific values and manipulate filter contexts.
- **Information functions**: These functions look at the table, column, or value passed in as an argument and tell you whether the value matches the type that is expected. Most of the functions in this group will return a value of TRUE or FALSE.
- **Logical functions**: These functions will apply a logical operation against the parameters passed and return a value of TRUE or FALSE depending on the results of the logical operation performed using the parameters.
- **Mathematical and trigonometric functions**: DAX provides a large number of mathematical and trigonometric functions that are very similar to those you will find in Excel, with the exception that there are some differences in the numeric data types used.
- **Parent and child functions**: Functions in this group help to manage data presented as a parent-child hierarchy in your data model.
- **Statistical functions**: These functions carry out statistically-related aggregations, such as percentiles, standard deviations, and variances.

- **Text functions**: Functions in this group work with tables and columns and allow you to return part of a string, search for text within a string, or concatenate string values. There are also functions that allow you to format numbers and dates and times.
- **Time-intelligence functions**: These functions allow you to create time-based calculations that work with calendars and dates. When used with aggregations or calculations, it is possible to create data comparisons across different time periods. For example, using these functions, you can easily carry out year-on-year and year-to-date comparisons on data. To use these functions, you will need to include date tables in your data model.

We've gone through the function types and groups in this section. In the next section, we will learn about the aggregation functions.

Introduction to aggregation functions

As we have already seen earlier in this chapter, the DAX language consists of a large number of functions that can be grouped based on the type of functionality they provide. In this section, we are going to take our first detailed look at these groups, starting with a look at the aggregation group of functions.

Aggregation functions provide a way to summarize or group data and common examples include the AVERAGE, COUNT, MAX, MIN, and SUM functions. All of these have their equivalent X function, such as SUMX. Instead of working against a column of a table, these X functions apply the aggregation to the result of an expression that is evaluated for each row of a table.

Aggregation function reference

The following gives a list of the functions found in the aggregation function group:

- AVERAGE: Returns the average of all of the numeric values in a column
- AVERAGEA: Returns the average of all of the values in a column including non-numeric text
- AVERAGEX: Returns the average of an expression evaluated over a table
- COUNT: Counts the rows in a table where the column has a non-blank value and cannot operate on a Boolean data type

- COUNTA: Counts the rows in a table where the column has a non-blank value and can operate with Boolean data types
- COUNTBLANK: Counts the number rows where the value in the column is blank
- COUNTROWS: Counts the number of rows in a table
- COUNTX: Counts the numbers of values resulting from an expression evaluated over a table
- DISTINCTCOUNT: Counts the number of distinct values in a column
- DISTINCTCOUNTNOBLANK: Counts the number of distinct values in a column, but ignores blank values
- MAX: Returns the largest value in a column or the larger value of two scalar expressions, ignoring logical values
- MAXA: Returns the largest value in a column or the larger value of two scalar expressions, including logical values
- MAXX: Returns the largest value obtained by evaluating an expression over every row in a table
- MIN: Returns the smallest value in a column or the smaller value of two scalar expressions, ignoring logical values
- MINA: Returns the smallest value in a column or the smaller value of two scalar expressions, including logical values
- MINX: Returns the smallest value obtained by evaluating an expression over every row in a table
- PRODUCT: Returns the product of the numbers in a column
- PRODUCTX: Returns the product of an expression evaluated over every row in a table
- SUM: Returns the sum of all of the numbers in a column
- SUMX: Returns the sum of an expression evaluated over every row in a table

The MIN, MINA, and MINX functions

These functions can be used to create both calculated columns and measures. When creating a calculated column, you can create aggregations that use the current row context to sum or count values retrieved from related rows in another table. With measures, you can create aggregations that use both filters defined within the formula and filters imposed by slicers, along with those coming from the column headings, and row headings of a pivot table or matrix visual.

Let's finish off this section by looking at three related functions from this group, starting with the MIN function.

The syntax of the MIN function is as follows:

```
MIN ( <ColumnName or ScalarValue1> [, <ScalarValue2>] )
```

The MIN function gives you the choice of finding the smallest value in the given column or the smaller of two scalar values. If you want to find the smaller of two scalar values, then you will need to provide a second value as the second parameter.

The MIN function will ignore the values of the Boolean data type and will compare string values according to alphabetical order.

The syntax of the MINA function is as follows:

```
MINA ( <ColumnName> )
```

The MINA function is similar to the MIN function but does not allow for the comparison of two values—instead, working with a single specified column. Unlike the MIN function, it will handle Boolean data types and will consider TRUE as 1 and FALSE as 0.

Finally, the syntax of the MINX function is as follows:

```
MINX ( <Table>, <Expression> )
```

The MINX function works by iterating over the rows of the specified table, evaluating the given expression for every row in that table and then returning the smallest value from the result. The table given as the first parameter can be a table from your data model or a table returned by a table function.

Now, let's have a look at the next section, which covers the functions for parent-child hierarchies.

Functions for parent-child hierarchies

The last group of functions we will look at in this chapter is the one that helps to deal with a parent-child relationship in a table. A common scenario for this is an employee table, where one employee record may be related to another, for example where an employee has a manager.

Figure 6-9 shows the table we will be working with as an example. All employees other than the CEO have a parent employee ID that references their manager's employee ID:

EmployeeID	Name	Title	ParentEmployeeID
100	Peter	CEO	
200	Frank	Business Manager	100
201	Catherine	Finance Manager	100
202	Ross	IT Manager	100
300	Simon	Senior Administrator	200
301	Jane	Administrator	200
302	Richard	Finance Assistant	201
303	Julie	Finance Assistant	201
304	Saad	SharePoint Administrator	202
305	Tim	Web Developer	202
306	Kate	System Administrator	202
400	John	Junior Web Developer	305

Figure 6-9: The employees table

This can be illustrated by converting it into an organization chart. As you can see in the diagram shown in *Figure 6-10*, we have a hierarchy that consists of four levels, with the CEO at the top:

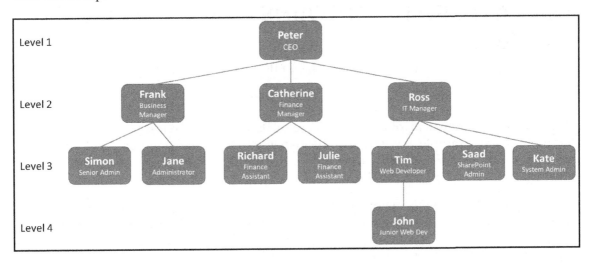

Figure 6-10: Organization chart showing employee hierarchy

In this situation, we hit a problem with the Tabular data model. It is simply not possible to create a circular relationship between a table and itself, in the way we might with a relational database. Fortunately, DAX gives us a set of functions that help to get around this problem, giving us a way to normalize the relationship as a hierarchy.

Parent and child function reference

The following gives a list of the functions found in the parent and child function group. Together, these five functions give us a way to normalize a parent-child relationship in a table and represent it as a hierarchy:

- PATH: Returns a delimited text string that contains the identifiers of all of the parents to the current identifier, starting with the root of a hierarchy
- PATHCONTAINS: Returns TRUE if the specified item exists in the given path
- PATHITEM: Returns the item in the specified position of the delimited list produced by the given path function
- PATHITEMREVERSE: Returns the item in the specified position of the delimited list produced by the given path function, but counting backward from the last item in the path
- PATHLENGTH: Returns the number of items in the delimited list produced by the given path function

The PATH, PATHCONTAINS, and PATHLENGTH functions

Let's start with the PATH function. The syntax of the PATH function is as follows:

```
PATH ( <ID_ColumnName>, <Parent_ColumnName> )
```

This function will return all of the IDs that are related to the current row, at various levels. In our employee example, it will return the manager of an employee, along with the managers of those managers and so on until it reaches the top-level manager. The list returned is delimited by a vertical bar.

The first parameter is the name of the column containing the unique identifier for the current row, while the second parameter contains the name of the column containing the unique identifier of the current row's parent. The two columns must be of the same data type, which must be either text or integer.

Any values in the <Parent_ColumnName> column must exist in the <ID_ColumnName> column. If there is no value in the <Parent_ColumnName> column, then PATH will return the value in the <ID_ColumnName> column.

With our example, we'll add a new calculated column that gives us the path for the employee and their managers using the following expression:

```
Employee Path = PATH ( Employee[EmployeeID], Employee[ParentEmployeeID] )
```

We can see the result of this in *Figure 6-11*:

EmployeeID	Name	Title	ParentEmployeeID	Employee Path
100	Peter	CEO		100
200	Frank	Business Manager	100	100|200
201	Catherine	Finance Manager	100	100|201
202	Ross	IT Manager	100	100|202
300	Simon	Senior Administrator	200	100|200|300
301	Jane	Administrator	200	100|200|301
302	Richard	Finance Assistant	201	100|201|302
303	Julie	Finance Assistant	201	100|201|303
304	Saad	SharePoint Administrator	202	100|202|304
305	Tim	Web Developer	202	100|202|305
306	Kate	System Administrator	202	100|202|306
400	John	Junior Web Developer	305	100|202|305|400

Figure 6-11: The employee table with the employee hierarchy path added

If we now look at the PATHCONTAINS function, we can see how it can be used to check for a value in the result returned by the PATH function. The syntax for the PATHCONTAINS function is as follows:

```
PATHCONTAINS ( <Path>, <Item> )
```

This checks the string created by the PATH function, given as the first parameter, to see whether it contains the value given for the second parameter.

We'll create a new calculated column to check the path for the value of **202**, which is the employee ID for the IT manager. We can do this with the following expression, which utilizes the **Employee Path** calculated column we created previously:

```
IT Employees = PATHCONTAINS ( Employee[Employee Path], "202" )
```

This will then return TRUE for all employees that are within the IT manager's group, and FALSE for all other records.

The PATHLENGTH function returns the number of items in the list returned by the PATH function. The syntax for this function is as follows:

```
PATHLENGTH ( <Path> )
```

We can create another calculated column to give the path length for a given row using the following expression. Again, we will make use of the **Employee Path** calculated column that we created earlier. The result of adding this column to our **Employee** table can be seen in *Figure 6-12*:

EmployeeID	Name	Title	ParentEmployeeID	Employee Path	IT Employees	Employee Path Length
100	Peter	CEO		100	False	1
200	Frank	Business Manager	100	100|200	False	2
201	Catherine	Finance Manager	100	100|201	False	2
202	Ross	IT Manager	100	100|202	True	2
300	Simon	Senior Administrator	200	100|200|300	False	3
301	Jane	Administrator	200	100|200|301	False	3
302	Richard	Finance Assistant	201	100|201|302	False	3
303	Julie	Finance Assistant	201	100|201|303	False	3
304	Saad	SharePoint Administrator	202	100|202|304	True	3
305	Tim	Web Developer	202	100|202|305	True	3
306	Kate	System Administrator	202	100|202|306	True	3
400	John	Junior Web Developer	305	100|202|305|400	True	4

Figure 6-12: The employee table with the employee hierarchy path length added

As we can see, this now returns the number of parents for a given row, but it also includes the row itself. So, where an employee record doesn't have a parent employee ID, it returns just one for the employee itself.

The PATHITEM and PATHITEMREVERSE functions

We can start to normalize the parent-child hierarchy in our **Employee** table by using the PATHITEM and PATHITEMREVERSE functions. These functions allow us to fetch an ID from the specified position of the delimited string returned by PATH function. The PATHITEM function uses the position going from the left of the string, while the PATHITEMREVERSE goes from the right of the string.

The syntax for the PATHITEM function is as follows:

```
PATHITEM ( <Path>, <Position> [, <Type>] )
```

The optional Type parameter allows us to specify whether we want the function to return the value as text or as an integer. If a 1 is passed, then the function returns an integer. If a 0 is passed or the parameter is left blank, then the function returns the result as text. This can be important if we want to use the returned value with the LOOKUPVALUE function, which we will in a moment. The syntax for the PATHITEMREVERSE function is the same as for the PATHITEM function.

Let's add another calculated column to our **Employee** table. This time, we'll use the PATHITEM function to get the top-level manager for each employee, using the following expression:

```
Level 1 Employee = PATHITEM ( Employee[Employee Path], 1, 1 )
```

By itself, this is not very useful. What would be more useful would be to use this as a lookup to retrieve another value from the parent employee record. For this, we can use the result of this calculated column as a parameter for the LOOKUPVALUE function. The syntax for this function is as follows:

```
LOOKUPVALUE ( <Result_ColumnName>, <Search_ColumnName>, <Search_Value>
[, <Search_ColumnName>, <Search_Value> [, ... ] ] [, <Alternate_Result>]
)
```

We can use this function to revise the expression for our previous calculated column so that it will return the name of the top-level manager:

```
Level 1 Employee =
LOOKUPVALUE (
    Employee[Name],
    Employee[EmployeeID],
    PATHITEM ( Employee[Employee Path], 1, 1 )
)
```

We can repeat the preceding expression to create additional calculated columns for employees on levels 2 to 4. This will then give us a table that looks like the one in *Figure 6-13*:

EmployeeID	Name	Title	ParentEmployeeID	Employee Path	IT Employees	Employee Path Length	Level 1 Employee	Level 2 Employee	Level 3 Employee	Level 4 Employee
100	Peter	CEO		100	False	1	Peter			
200	Frank	Business Manager	100	100|200	False	2	Peter	Frank		
201	Catherine	Finance Manager	100	100|201	False	2	Peter	Catherine		
202	Ross	IT Manager	100	100|202	True	2	Peter	Ross		
300	Simon	Senior Administrator	200	100|200|300	False	3	Peter	Frank	Simon	
301	Jane	Administrator	200	100|200|301	False	3	Peter	Frank	Jane	
302	Richard	Finance Assistant	201	100|201|302	False	3	Peter	Catherine	Richard	
303	Julie	Finance Assistant	201	100|201|303	False	3	Peter	Catherine	Julie	
304	Saad	SharePoint Administrator	202	100|202|304	True	3	Peter	Ross	Saad	
305	Tim	Web Developer	202	100|202|305	True	3	Peter	Ross	Tim	
306	Kate	System Administrator	202	100|202|306	True	3	Peter	Ross	Kate	
400	John	Junior Web Developer	305	100|202|305|400	True	4	Peter	Ross	Tim	John

Figure 6-13: The employee table showing different levels of hierarchy in separate columns

The final step in normalizing our hierarchy is to use these calculated columns to produce a hierarchy column on our **Employee** table, as shown in *Figure 6-14*:

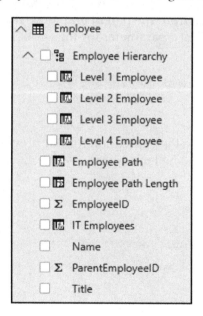

Figure 6-14: Using the separate hierarchy columns to produce a single hierarchy column

Although the Tabular data model does not support circular relationships between tables, the functions in the DAX parent and child function group go a long way toward helping you to build parent-child hierarchies into your data model, when you have the parent and child columns available in a table.

Summary

In this chapter, we took a more in-depth look at the structure of DAX syntax, including details around naming requirements. We learned more about complex relationships including how to deal with relationships, between tables that involve multiple columns and how to handle instances of tables with multiple relationships. We also learned how to use DAX functions to create virtual relationships.

We took our first look at the different groups of functions available in the DAX language, including a detailed look at the aggregation group of functions and the group of functions that help us to deal with parent and child relationships in a table. We learned how these functions can help us to use parent and child relationships to create a normalized parent-child hierarchy.

In the next chapter, we will continue our look at functions by learning more about functions that return a table as a result of their evaluation.

7
Table Functions

In this chapter, we will be looking at the table group of DAX functions. In particular, we'll focus on those functions that can be used to manipulate tables. We'll list the functions in this group, along with a description of the action that each performs.

We'll then look at a few of these functions in more detail, giving a breakdown of the syntax, along with an explanation of how the function works in practice. In addition, we'll also get hands-on with these functions, working through a practical example of each, and helping you to understand how you might use them in a real-world scenario.

The chapter is broken into the following sections:

- Introducing table functions
- Looking at table manipulation functions
- Working with table functions

Introducing table functions

In Chapter 6, *Progressive DAX Syntax and Functions*, we looked at the two types of functions found in the DAX language: scalar functions and table functions. We saw that table functions are functions that, when evaluated, return a table of data. Unlike scalar functions, which return a single value, table functions cannot directly be used to define a measure or a calculated column. Instead, they are used in conjunction with functions that accept a table expression as one of their parameters.

DAX table functions can be used for the following purposes:

- In a DAX expression that is used to define a calculated table (this excludes Excel Power Pivot, which currently does not support calculated tables).
- In the definition of a DAX function, where the function accepts a table expression as a parameter.
- To query a tabular data model using Excel or **SQL Server Management Studio (SSMS)**, or using tools such as DAX Studio, which can execute DAX queries using the EVALUATE statement.

Perhaps the most commonly used table functions in DAX are the FILTER and ALL functions. However, we will not be looking at these in this chapter. Instead, we will look at them in more detail when we come to filter functions in Chapter 9, *Filter Functions*. For this chapter, we'll focus on some other commonly used table functions, including those functions that can be used to manipulate tables.

Creating a DAX calculated table

We originally looked at calculated tables back in Chapter 3, *Building Data Models*, in the section entitled *Adding a calculated table*. In that section, we went through some practical examples of adding calculated tables to the data model we were building. When defining a calculated table, you will need to use a table function in much the same way that you need to use scalar functions when defining a measure or a calculated column.

In this example, we will create a calculated table in Power BI Desktop using the ADDCOLUMNS and SUMMARIZE functions. The table will consist of sales grouped by the **CalendarQuarter** and **CalendarYear** columns.

To create a calculated table from Power BI Desktop, proceed as follows:

1. Switch to the **Report** or **Data** view.
2. From the **Calculations** section of the **Modeling** ribbon, select **New Table,** as shown in *Figure 7-1*. This will bring up the DAX editor, where you can enter the expression that defines the new table:

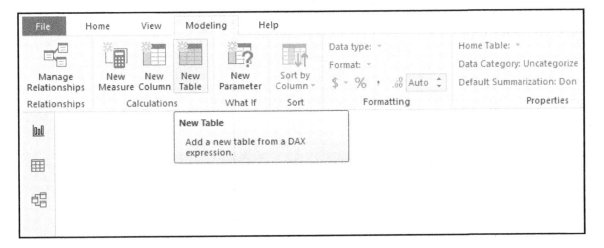

Figure 7-1: Creating a new calculated table in Power BI Desktop

3. Enter the following DAX expression into the DAX editor, and press *Return* to create a calculated table called **Sales by Quarter and Year**:

```
Sales by Quarter and Year =
SUMMARIZE (
    'Date',
    'Date'[CalendarYear],
    'Date'[CalendarQuarter]
)
```

The resulting table should look like the one shown in *Figure 7-2*:

CalendarYear	CalendarQuarter
2005	20051
2005	20052
2005	20053
2005	20054
2006	20061
2006	20062
2006	20063
2006	20064
2007	20071
2007	20072
2007	20073
2007	20074
2008	20081
2008	20082
2008	20083
2008	20084
2009	20091
2009	20092
2009	20093
2009	20094
2010	20101
2010	20102
2010	20103
2010	20104
2011	20111
2011	20112
2011	20113
2011	20114

Figure 7-2: The new table showing year and quarter

As you can see, the SUMMARIZE function takes the table given in the first parameter and groups it by the distinct combination of the columns given in the second and third parameters. In this case, it is grouping by the **CalendarYear** and **CalendarQuarter** columns.

Using a table expression as a table function parameter

As it is, our new table is not all that useful. However, we can fix this by adding another column to our table definition. To do that, we use the SUMMARIZE table expression as a parameter to the ADDCOLUMNS function.

Amend the definition for the new table using the following DAX expression:

```
Sales by Quarter and Year =
ADDCOLUMNS (
    SUMMARIZE (
        'Date',
        'Date'[CalendarYear],
        'Date'[CalendarQuarter]
    ),
    "Sales", CALCULATE ( SUM ( Sales[Sales Amount] ) )
)
```

The result of the revised table should look like what's shown shown in *Figure 7-3*. Our table now has sales summarized by quarter and year, for the quarters where sales were made:

CalendarYear	CalendarQuarter	Sales
2005	20051	
2005	20052	
2005	20053	
2005	20054	
2006	20061	
2006	20062	
2006	20063	
2006	20064	
2007	20071	£606,736,602.2517
2007	20072	£848,827,201.3114
2007	20073	£793,881,696.342
2007	20074	£894,947,792.226
2008	20081	£558,470,281.4676
2008	20082	£658,806,976.1078
2008	20083	£705,371,511.819
2008	20084	£719,764,447.638
2009	20091	£545,876,791.8135
2009	20092	£674,020,404.9164
2009	20093	£664,200,190.401
2009	20094	£670,320,468.538
2010	20101	
2010	20102	
2010	20103	
2010	20104	
2011	20111	
2011	20112	
2011	20113	
2011	20114	

Figure 7-3: The new table showing the sum of sales amount by year and quarter

The ADDCOLUMNS function is another table function. It adds a column to the result of the table passed in as the first parameter (in this case, the result of our SUMMARIZE function). The second parameter is the name of the column we are adding, and the third is the definition for creating it.

In this case, we are using the DAX expression SUM (Sales[Sales Amount]) to define the new column. However, as the ADDCOLUMNS function works with a row context and the same expression within the SUMMARIZE function works within a filter context, the SUM function must be wrapped with the CALCULATE function to force context transition.

Querying your data model using table functions

The third use for table functions is to query data in your data model. You can do this from within Excel Power Pivot, or through tools such as SSMS or DAX Studio. In this section, we'll look at examples of using all three tools.

A DAX query consists of the EVALUATE statement, followed by a table expression. This table expression can simply be a table name, or it can be a more complex example, such as the one we used in the previous section. The result of executing the EVALUATE statement is returned as a table.

Let's start by looking at how to query data in a data model using Excel. Proceed as follows:

1. Open the Excel workbook that we created in Chapter 4, *Working with DAX in Power BI, Excel, and SSAS*, as part of our look at creating data models in Excel. If you don't have that available, revisit the section in Chapter 3, *Building Data Models*, entitled *Working with DAX in Excel Power Pivot*, to see how to create a Power Pivot data model with Excel.
2. With a blank worksheet, click on the **Existing Connections** icon in the **Get External Data** section of the **Data** ribbon.
3. From the **Existing Connections** dialog, select the **Tables** tab to see a list of tables in the data model, as shown in *Figure 7-4*:

Figure 7-4: Viewing a list of available tables in Excel

4. Select the **Product** table from the list and click on the **Open** button.

5. On the **Import Data** dialog, select **Table** and click on the **OK** button to load the table onto the worksheet, as shown in *Figure 7-5*:

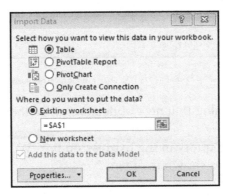

Figure 7-5: The Import Data dialog in Excel

6. With the **Product** table loaded onto the worksheet, right-click on a cell in the table and select **Table** and then **Edit DAX...** from the context menus, as shown in *Figure 7-6*:

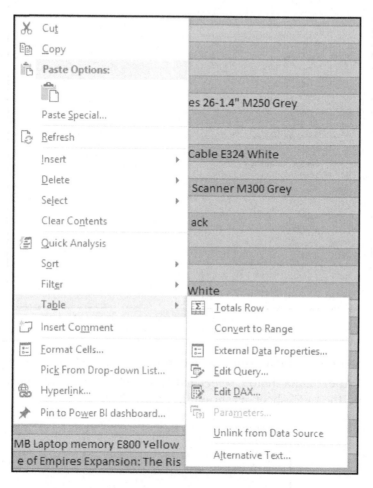

Figure 7-6: Opening the Edit DAX dialog from the table context menu

7. In the **Edit DAX** dialog that now appears, change the **Command Type** from **Table** to **DAX**.

8. We can now enter a query in the **Expression** box. We'll start with the EVALUATE Sales expression, as shown in *Figure 7-7*:

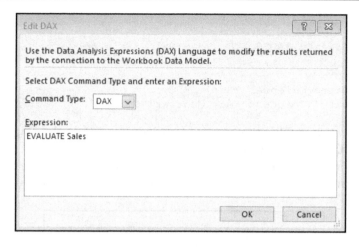

Figure 7-7: The Edit DAX dialog

9. This will result in the **Product** table, which was displayed on the worksheet, being replaced with a copy of the **Sales** table, as shown in *Figure 7-8*:

	A	B	C	D	E	F	G	H
1	ProductKey ▼	Unit Cost ▼	Unit Price ▼	StoreKey ▼	PromotionKey ▼	CurrencyKey ▼	CustomerKey ▼	OrderDateKey
2	2324	40.76	79.95	199	13	1	18901	200811
3	1553	123.24	268	199	1	1	18946	200905
4	1195	301.21	655	307	1	1	19135	200909
5	1798	21.92	43	307	14	1	19112	200901
6	2496	5.09	9.99	199	12	1	18863	200808
7	2493	12.74	24.99	306	27	1	19072	200908
8	2503	5.09	9.99	306	1	1	19052	200805
9	998	91.05	198	306	1	1	19051	200805
10	28	91.93	199.9	306	28	1	19074	200910
11	1148	215.15	422	307	16	1	19099	200805
12	1661	2.8	5.5	307	1	1	19138	200910
13	1111	150.84	328	307	14	1	19110	200811

Figure 7-8: A copy of the Sales table replaces the Product table

10. Next, repeat steps 6 to 8, but this time, we'll use a more complex query. Enter the following DAX expression into the **Expression** box on the DAX editor screen:

```
EVALUATE
ADDCOLUMNS (
    SUMMARIZE (
        'Date',
        'Date'[Calendar Year],
```

```
            'Date'[Calendar Year Quarter]
    ),
        "Sales", CALCULATE ( SUM(Sales[Sale Amount] ) ) )
    )
    ORDER BY
        'Date'[Calendar Year] DESC,
        'Date'[Calendar Year Quarter] DESC
```

11. This will return a table that is a summarized version of the **Date** table grouped by **Calendar Year** and **Calendar Year Quarter**, and then show the sum of sales made during the year and quarter. This is very similar to the example we looked at with Power BI Desktop in the previous section, as can be seen in *Figure 7-9*:

	A Calendar Year	B Calendar Year Quarter	C Sales
2	CY 2011	Q4-2011	
3	CY 2011	Q3-2011	
4	CY 2011	Q2-2011	
5	CY 2011	Q1-2011	
6	CY 2010	Q4-2010	
7	CY 2010	Q3-2010	
8	CY 2010	Q2-2010	
9	CY 2010	Q1-2010	
10	CY 2009	Q4-2009	815473.89
11	CY 2009	Q3-2009	665812.82
12	CY 2009	Q2-2009	735651.53
13	CY 2009	Q1-2009	455100.27
14	CY 2008	Q4-2008	587347.19
15	CY 2008	Q3-2008	685003.22
16	CY 2008	Q2-2008	726802.77
17	CY 2008	Q1-2008	422648.42
18	CY 2007	Q4-2007	907543.19
19	CY 2007	Q3-2007	783955.71
20	CY 2007	Q2-2007	742902.65
21	CY 2007	Q1-2007	748437.18
22	CY 2006	Q4-2006	
23	CY 2006	Q3-2006	
24	CY 2006	Q2-2006	
25	CY 2006	Q1-2006	
26	CY 2005	Q4-2005	
27	CY 2005	Q3-2005	
28	CY 2005	Q2-2005	
29	CY 2005	Q1-2005	

Figure 7-9: The sum of sales grouped by calendar year quarter and calendar year

Next, we will look at querying data using SSMS. To do this, you will need to have SQL Server 2012 (or later) installed, with a Tabular instance of **SQL Server Analysis Service (SSAS)** running. To get started, follow these steps:

1. Open SSMS and connect to the Tabular instance.
2. Right-click on the database name in **Object Explorer**, then click on **New Query**, followed by **DAX**.
3. This will open a DAX editor window, as shown in *Figure 7-10*, where you can enter a DAX table expression against the EVALUATE statement, much like we did with Excel:

Figure 7-10: The DAX editor in SQL Server Management Studio (SSMS)

Finally, we will look at querying data using a third-party tool called DAX Studio. This is a very popular third-party client tool, produced by the DAX experts at SQLBI.com. It can execute DAX queries against data models in the following packages:

- Excel Power Pivot
- Power BI Desktop
- SSAS Tabular
- Azure Analysis Services

To help connect with an Excel Power Pivot data model, it also includes an add-in for Excel that will need to be enabled first.

You can download a copy of DAX Studio by going to `https://daxstudio.org` and following the instructions from there.

If we install a copy of DAX Studio and return to our Excel spreadsheet, we can enable the Excel add-in, as follows:

1. Go to **File**, click on **Options**, and then click on **Add-Ins**.
2. In the **Manage** dialog, select **COM Add-ins** from the drop-down list, and then click on **Go**.
3. This will bring up the **COM Add-Ins** dialog, shown in *Figure 7-11*:

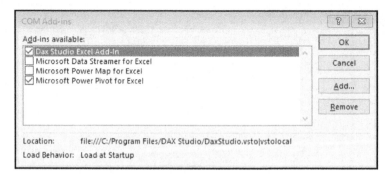

Figure 7-11: The COM Add-ins dialog in Excel

4. Check the **Dax Studio Excel Add-in** box and click on **OK**.
5. With DAX Studio enabled, you will have a new icon available on the **Add-ins** ribbon. Click on the icon to launch DAX Studio.
6. From the **Connect** dialog, accept the default option of **PowerPivot Model** and click the **Connect** button, as shown in *Figure 7-12*:

Figure 7-12: Connecting DAX Studio to Excel Power Pivot

7. We then get views of metadata, functions, and **Dynamic Management Views** (**DMVs**), along with a DAX editor pane and a results window, as can be seen in *Figure 7-13*. Here, we have run the same DAX expression as we did when we used Excel to query the data. However, using DAX Studio gives a much better user experience:

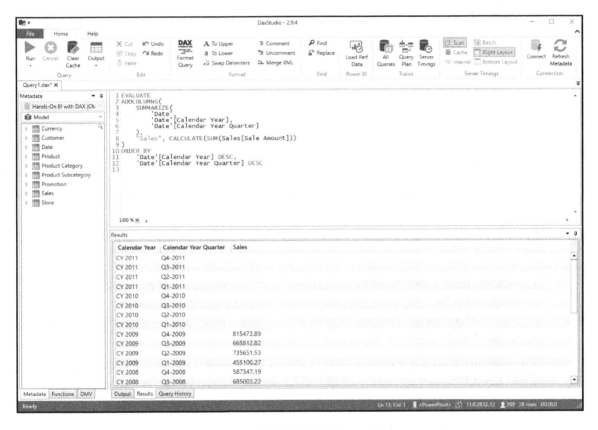

Figure 7-13: DAX Studio

In order to query data in a Power BI Desktop data model, you will need to have the Power BI file loaded in Power BI Desktop first, by doing the following:

1. Either launch DAX Studio or click on the **Connect** icon in the **Connection** section of the **Home** ribbon.
2. On the **Connect** dialog, select the option of **PBI / SSDT Model** and click the **Connect** button, as shown in *Figure 7-14*:

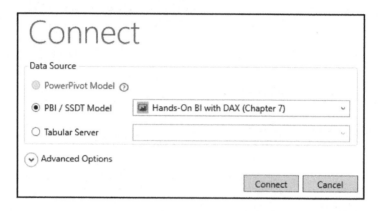

Figure 7-14: Connecting DAX Studio to Power BI Desktop

3. As with the Excel Power Pivot data model, we get views of metadata, functions, and DMVs, but this time for our Power BI data model. We also get a DAX editor pane and a results window, which we can use to query data in our data model using DAX expressions.

Finally, you can also query data in an SSAS Tabular data model using DAX Studio. To do this, you will need to know the name of the SSAS server where your data model is located, proceeding as follows:

1. If it is not already loaded, launch DAX Studio. Otherwise, click on the **Connect** icon in the **Connection** section of the **Home** ribbon.
2. From the **Connect** dialog, select the option of **PBI / SSDT Model** and click the **Connect** button, as shown in *Figure 7-15*:

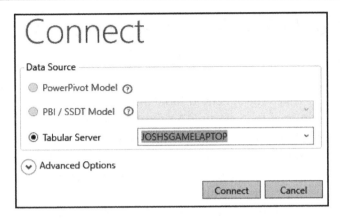

Figure 7-15: Connecting DAX Studio to SSAS Tabular

3. DAX Studio will then connect to your SSAS Tabular data model, again giving you views of the metadata, functions, and DMVs behind the data model.

Using DAX Studio to query your data brings other advantages along with ease of use. As well as outputting the results of a DAX query to the results pane, you can output the results into a text file. You can also export data from the tables in your data model to text files. Other advantages include being able to load Power BI performance data to analyze performance, and the ability to format your DAX query, following some of the rules we looked at back in Chapter 2, *Using DAX Variables and Formatting*.

Looking at table manipulation functions

In Chapter 6, *Progressive DAX Syntax and Functions*, we looked at the different groups of functions that are available in the DAX language. As we saw, individual DAX functions can be grouped depending on the functionality they provide. However, functions from across these groups can also belong to another type of group: table manipulation functions.

Table manipulation functions reference

The following is a list of the DAX functions that can be used to manipulate tables in your data model, returning the result as another table:

- ADDCOLUMNS: Takes the specified table and returns a table with additional columns, as defined by a given DAX expression and with a given name.
- CROSSJOIN: Returns a table that contains the Cartesian product of rows from all the tables given as parameters.
- DATATABLE: Returns a table that has been defined and populated by the parameters passed into the function.
- DETAILROWS: Takes the measure passed in as a parameter and returns a table that is obtained by evaluating the Detail Rows Expression of that measure.
- DISTINCT: Returns a table that contains the distinct values of a single column passed in as a parameter, or the distinct combination of columns, when a table expression is passed in as the parameter.
- EXCEPT: Takes two tables as parameters and returns the rows from the table passed in as the first parameter that are not present in the table passed in as the second parameter.
- FILTER: Takes a column name and returns a table of the filter values applied directly to that column.
- GENERATE: For each row in the table passed as the first parameter, the table expression passed in as the second parameter will be evaluated, and the cross-join of the first table with these results is returned as the result.
- GENERATEALL: For each row in the table passed as the first parameter, the table expression passed in as the second parameter will be evaluated, and the cross-join of the first table with these results is returned as the result. Includes rows where the second table expression is empty.
- GENERATESERIES: Returns a table with one column that is populated with sequential values, starting from the values passed in as the first parameter, to the values passed in as the second parameter. May also increment by the value passed in as the optional third parameter.
- GROUPBY: Returns a table summarizing the table in the first parameter, grouped by the columns specified in the parameters.

- INTERSECT: Takes two tables as parameters and returns the rows from the table that is passed in as the first parameter that are present in the table passed in as the second parameter.

- NATURALINNERJOIN: Takes two tables as parameters and joins the table passed in as the first parameter (the left table) with the table passed in as the second parameter (the right table) using an inner join. Returns a table that includes all the columns from both tables and only the rows where the values in both tables match.

- NATURALLEFTOUTERJOIN: Takes two tables as parameters and joins the table passed in as the first parameter (the left table) with the table passed in as the second parameter (the right table) using a left outer join. Returns a table that includes all the columns from both tables and all the rows from the left table with data from the right table, where the values in both tables match.

- ROW: Returns a single-row table with columns that are defined by DAX expressions, passed in as parameters.

- SELECTEDCOLUMNS: Takes the specified table and returns a table with additional columns, as defined by a given DAX expression and with a given name. Like the ADDCOLUMNS function, but starts with an empty table.

- SUBSTITUTEWITHINDEX: Returns a table that is the semi-join of the two tables passed in as parameters. The tables are joined using common columns that are replaced with a single zero-based index column. The index is a reference to rows of the right join table, sorted in the specified order.

- SUMMARIZE: Returns a table summarizing the table in the first parameter, grouped by the columns specified in the parameters.

- SUMMARIZECOLUMNS: Returns a summary table that includes combinations of values, from the columns passed in as parameters, which are given over the set of specified groups.

- TOPN: Returns a table giving the top number of rows, based on the number and table passed in as the first and second parameters, sorted by the expression given as the third parameter, and sorted in the order given as the fourth parameter.

- TOPNSKIP: Like the TOPN function, but skips the specified number of rows first, before retrieving the top number of rows.

- TREATAS: Takes the result of a table expression passed in as the first parameter and applies them as filters to columns from an unrelated table.

- UNION: Returns a table that is the union of all the tables passed in as parameters, where the columns match.

- VALUES: Returns a table that contains the distinct values of a single column passed in as a parameter, or the combination of columns (including duplicates), when a table expression is passed in as the parameter. Will include an additional blank row if the table has a one-to-many relationship where there is a violation of referential integrity.

All the functions in this group will enable you to manipulate tables in your data model in some way and return the result as another table. The resulting table can then be used as the parameter to another function, or to create a new calculated table in your data model. Like other table functions, these table manipulation functions can also be used to query data in your data model.

Let's finish off this section by looking at some of the table manipulation functions in more detail, starting with the CROSSJOIN function.

The CROSSJOIN function

The CROSSJOIN function returns a table containing the Cartesian product of all the rows from all the tables that are passed to the function as parameters. The resulting table will contain all the columns from the tables passed as parameters.

The syntax of the CROSSJOIN function is as follows:

```
CROSSJOIN ( <Table> , <Table> [, <Table> ]... )
```

You can pass two or more tables (or table expressions) to the CROSSJOIN function.

The names of the columns from the tables passed in as the parameters to the function must all be different. The function will return an error if there are two columns with the same name in the tables that are specified.

In the following example, we will apply the CROSSJOIN function to the **Product Category** and **Currency** tables. Query the data using the following DAX expression:

```
EVALUATE
CROSSJOIN ( 'Product Category', 'Currency' )
```

The screenshot in *Figure 7-16* shows an extract of the resulting table:

ProductCategoryKey	Category Code	Category	CurrencyKey	Currency Code	Currency
7	07	Games and Toys	20	GBP	British Pound
8	08	Home Appliances	20	GBP	British Pound
1	01	Audio	21	KRW	South Korean Won
2	02	TV and Video	21	KRW	South Korean Won
3	03	Computers	21	KRW	South Korean Won
4	04	Cameras and camcorders	21	KRW	South Korean Won
5	05	Cell phones	21	KRW	South Korean Won
6	06	Music, Movies and Audio Books	21	KRW	South Korean Won
7	07	Games and Toys	21	KRW	South Korean Won
8	08	Home Appliances	21	KRW	South Korean Won
1	01	Audio	22	JPY	Japanese Yen
2	02	TV and Video	22	JPY	Japanese Yen
3	03	Computers	22	JPY	Japanese Yen
4	04	Cameras and camcorders	22	JPY	Japanese Yen
5	05	Cell phones	22	JPY	Japanese Yen
6	06	Music, Movies and Audio Books	22	JPY	Japanese Yen
7	07	Games and Toys	22	JPY	Japanese Yen
8	08	Home Appliances	22	JPY	Japanese Yen
1	01	Audio	23	CNY	Renminbi Yuan
2	02	TV and Video	23	CNY	Renminbi Yuan
3	03	Computers	23	CNY	Renminbi Yuan
4	04	Cameras and camcorders	23	CNY	Renminbi Yuan
5	05	Cell phones	23	CNY	Renminbi Yuan
6	06	Music, Movies and Audio Books	23	CNY	Renminbi Yuan

Figure 7-16: Table showing the output of the CROSSJOIN function using the Product Category and Currency tables

As you can see, the table contains all the rows from the **Product Category** table, and for every row in that table, it returns all the rows from the **Currency** table. In other words, the number of rows in the resulting table will be the number of rows in the **Product Category** table, multiplied by the number of rows in the **Currency** table.

The DATATABLE function

The DATATABLE function provides a way to define an inline set of data values and can be used to create static tables in your data model.

The syntax of the `DATATABLE` function is as follows:

```
DATATABLE ( <name>, <type> [, <name>, <type> ]... ,{{ <data> } [, {
<data> }]... } )
```

- The `<name>` is the name given to the column, and must be a string and not the result of an expression.
- The `<type>` is the data type for the column, and must be one of the following values:

```
BOOLEAN
CURRENCY
DATETIME
DOUBLE
INTEGER
STRING
```

Finally, you provide the data that is being assigned to the column. Here, you provide a set of rows, embedded between a pair of curly brackets. For each row, you provide a list of values, embedded between another pair of curly brackets. You cannot use expressions for these values; only constant values are accepted.

To help make this clearer, let's look at the following example of the `DATATABLE` being used to define a calculated table, which contains different age ranges:

```
Age Ranges =
DATATABLE (
    "Age Range", STRING,
    "Min Age", INTEGER,
    "Max Age", INTEGER,
    {
        { "Under 18", 0, 17 },
        { "18 to 24", 18, 24 },
        { "25 to 34", 25, 34 },
        { "35 to 44", 35, 44 },
        { "45 to 54", 45, 54 },
        { "55 to 64", 55, 64 },
        { "65 Plus", 65, 1000 }
    }
)
```

The screenshot in *Figure 7-17* shows the result of our new calculated table after it has been created within a Power BI report:

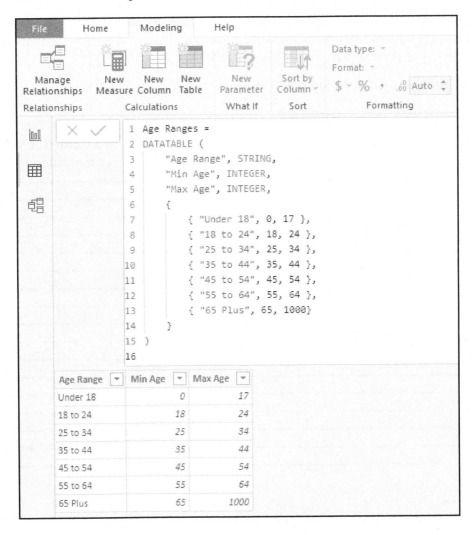

Figure 7-17: Calculated table created using the DATATABLE function

Using the DATATABLE function is a great way to create static tables as it makes it easy to see the table definition, along with the data it contains. It also makes it easier to make changes to both the definition and the contents of the table, when required.

The EXCEPT, INTERSECT, and UNION functions

Both the EXCEPT and INTERSECT functions require two tables to be passed in as parameters, and both work by carrying out a comparison of values in the two tables. The EXCEPT function returns rows from the table passed in as the first parameter that are not present in the table passed in as the second parameter.

The syntax of the EXCEPT function is as follows:

```
EXCEPT ( <Table1> , <Table2> )
```

In the following example, we have two tables for – **Color Table 1** and **Color Table 2** – each containing a list of colors. *Table 7-1* shows the colors found in each of the tables:

Color Table 1	Color Table 2
Black	Blue
Blue	Green
Brown	Gold
Green	Orange
Grey	Red
Lime	Violet
Magenta	White
Orange	Yellow
Pink	
Purple	
Red	
Teal	
Turquoise	
White	
Yellow	

Table 7-1: Colors in each of the two tables

We now query our data using these tables with the EXCEPT function using the following DAX expression:

```
EXCEPT ( 'Color Table 1', 'Color Table 2' )
```

We get the following result in return:

```
Black
Brown
Grey
Lime
Magenta
Pink
Purple
Teal
Turquoise
```

The INTERSECT function returns rows from the table passed in as the first parameter that are also present in the table passed in as the second parameter.

The syntax of the INTERSECT function is as follows:

```
INTERSECT ( <Table1> , <Table2> )
```

We now query our data using the same tables with the INTERSECT function using the following DAX expression:

```
EXCEPT ( 'Color Table 1', 'Color Table 2' )
```

We get the following result in return:

```
Blue
Green
Orange
Red
White
Yellow
```

Finally, the UNION function will join the values from the tables passed in as parameters into a single table. If the tables have duplicate values, then these will also be duplicated in the resulting table. The function requires at least two tables to be passed, but it can accept more.

The syntax of the UNION function is as follows:

```
UNION ( <Table1> , <Table2> [, <Table> ]... )
```

We now query our data using the same tables with the UNION function using the following DAX expression:

```
UNION ( 'Color Table 1', 'Color Table 2' )
```

We get the following result in return:

```
Black
Blue
Brown
Green
Grey
Lime
Magenta
Orange
Pink
Purple
Red
Teal
Turquoise
White
Yellow
Blue
Green
Gold
Orange
Red
Violet
White
Yellow
```

As you can see, this list duplicates colors that appear in both tables. We can remove duplicates by wrapping our expression using another table manipulation function.

The DISTINCT function returns a table that contains the distinct values of the table expression being passed. We can amend the expression we used previously, so that it becomes the table expression being passed, as follows:

```
DISTINCT ( UNION ( 'Color Table 1', 'Color Table 2' ) )
```

If we query our data again, using the new expression, we get the following result:

```
Black
Blue
Brown
Green
Grey
Lime
Magenta
Orange
Pink
Purple
Red
```

```
Teal
Turquoise
White
Yellow
Gold
Violet
```

This time, the duplicate values are removed from the resulting table.

The GENERATESERIES function

The final table manipulation function we're going to look at in this section is the GENERATESERIES function. The GENERATESERIES function will return a table with one column, which is populated with sequential values, starting from the value passed in as the first parameter to the value passed in as the second parameter. You can also, optionally, specify an incremental value with a third parameter.

The syntax of the GENERATESERIES function is as follows:

GENERATESERIES (<StartValue>, <EndValue> [, <IncrementValue>])

We use the following expression to create a new calculated table:

```
Generated Values = GENERATESERIES ( -5, 10 )
```

We get a table that contains the following values:

```
-5, -4, -3, -2, -1, 0, 1, 2, 3, 4, 5, 6, 7, 8, 9, 10
```

We now amend the expression to include an incremental value, as follows:

```
Generated Values = GENERATESERIES ( -5, 10, 2 )
```

We get a table that contains the following values:

```
-5, -3, -1, 1, 3, 5, 7, 9
```

You will notice that the sequence stops at the last value that is less than or equal to the end value given for the sequence.

If the specified end value is less than the start value of the sequence, then the GENERATESERIES function will return an empty table. If you are using an incremental value, then it must be a positive value.

Working with table functions

In the previous section, we focused on those table functions that can be used to manipulate tables. Many of the other table functions fall into the date, time, and time intelligence functions, which we will look at in Chapter 8, *Date, Time, and Time Intelligence Functions*. The filter functions group also contains a number of table functions, and we'll cover those in Chapter 9, *Filter Functions*.

For the remainder of this chapter, we'll look at some functions that don't fall into these groups, and where table expressions can be used as parameters. Most of these functions fall into one of the following two categories:

- Functions that will iterate over the rows returned by the table expression given as a parameter, evaluating a DAX expression for each row of the table.
- Functions that will look for a specified value, in one or more columns of the table expression given as a parameter.

The following is a list of these functions, sorted by their functions groups:

- **Aggregation Functions**:
  - AVERAGEX: Evaluates a DAX expression for each row of a table and calculates the average of the results.
  - COUNTAX: Evaluates a DAX expression for each row of a table and counts the number of values that result.
  - COUNTROWS: Counts the number of rows in a table.
  - COUNTX: Evaluates a DAX expression for each row of a table and counts the number of values that result.
  - MAXX: Evaluates a DAX expression for each row of a table and returns the largest value.
  - MINX: Evaluates a DAX expression for each row of a table and returns the smallest value.
  - PRODUCTX: Evaluates a DAX expression for each row of a table and returns the product.
  - SUMX: Evaluates a DAX expression for each row of a table and returns the sum of the values.

- **Information Functions**:
  - CONTAINS: If there exists at least one row where all columns have specified values, returns TRUE.
  - CONTAINSROW: If there exists at least one row where all columns have specified values, returns TRUE.
  - ISCROSSFILTERED: When the specified table or column is cross-filtered, returns TRUE.
  - ISEMPTY: If the specified table or table expression is empty, returns TRUE.
  - ISFILTERED: If there are direct filters on the specified table columns, returns TRUE.
- **Relationship Functions**:
  - RELATEDTABLE: Will return the related tables, filtered to include only the related rows.
- **Text Functions**:
  - CONCATENATEX: Evaluates a DAX expression for each row of a table, returning the values concatenated in a single string, separated by the specified delimiter.

The COUNTROWS function

For our first example, we'll look at one of the functions from the aggregation group. The COUNTROWS function simply counts the number of rows returned by a table expression.

The syntax of the COUNTROWS function is as follows:

```
COUNTROWS ( <Table> )
```

To demonstrate this function, we can create a new measure to count the rows of a table expression that uses the GENERATESERIES function, to create a table containing rows with the values 1 to 100.

We use the following DAX expression to create our new measure:

```
Count Rows Measure =
COUNTROWS (
    GENERATESERIES (
        1,
        100
    )
)
```

We should get the result shown in *Figure 7-18* when we place the measure on a Power BI report using a card visual:

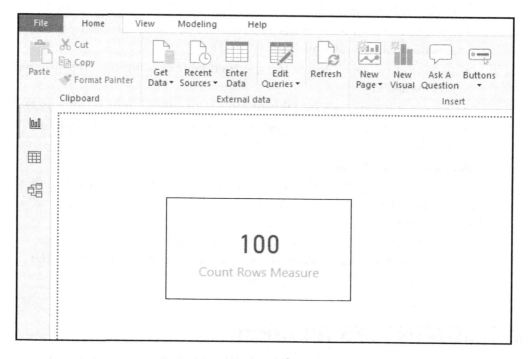

Figure 7-18: The result of the Count Rows Measure output to a card visual in Power BI Desktop

A more likely scenario for using the COUNTROWS function is to count the number of rows returned by a table expression that uses one of the filter functions we'll be looking at in Chapter 9, *Filter Functions*.

The PRODUCTX function

The PRODUCTX function is another function from the aggregation group. It returns the product of an expression that is evaluated for each row of the table expression passed as the first parameter.

The syntax of the PRODUCTX function is as follows:

```
PRODUCTX ( <Table>, <Expression> )
```

For this example, we'll use the DATATABLE function to create two new tables. One will contain the current salary of some employees, while the second will contain details of salary increases for the next 3 years. Proceed as follows:

1. To create the first table, we'll use the following DAX expression:

```
Employee Salary =
DATATABLE (
    "EmployeeID", INTEGER,
    "Salary", CURRENCY,
    {
        { "100", "150000" },
        { "200", "80000" },
        { "201", "55000" },
        { "202", "55000" },
        { "300", "45000" },
        { "301", "40000" },
        { "302", "40000" },
        { "303", "40000" },
        { "304", "50000" },
        { "305", "50000" },
        { "306", "50000" },
        { "400", "25000" }
    }
)
```

2. Next, we'll create a table detailing the annual salary increases for the next 3 years using the following DAX expression:

```
Salary Increase =
DATATABLE (
    "Year", STRING,
    "Increase", DOUBLE,
    {
        { "2019", "1.03" },
        { "2020", "1.02" },
        { "2021", "1.02" }
    }
)
```

3. Now, we can use the PRODUCTX function to create a calculated column on the **Employee Salary** table that we created with the first expression. Use the following DAX expression to create this:

```
Increased Salary =
[Salary]
    * PRODUCTX (
        'Salary Increase',
        [Increase]
    )
```

The resulting **Employee Salary** table should look like the one shown in *Figure 7-19*:

EmployeeID	Salary	Increased Salary
100	£150,000	160741.8
200	£80,000	85728.96
201	£55,000	58938.66
202	£55,000	58938.66
300	£45,000	48222.54
301	£40,000	42864.48
302	£40,000	42864.48
303	£40,000	42864.48
304	£50,000	53580.6
305	£50,000	53580.6
306	£50,000	53580.6
400	£25,000	26790.3

Figure 7-19: The result of the Employee Salary table

In this case, what the PRODUCTX function is doing is multiplying the values in the **Increase** column of the **Salary Increase** table. This is then used in the definition of the **Increased Salary** column of the **Employee Salary** table by multiplying the result of the PRODUCTX function by the value of the **Salary** column. So, for the first row, the value of the **Increased Salary** column is calculated as follows:

£150,000 * (1.03 * 1.02 * 1.02) = £160,741.80

As you can see, the PRODUCTX function is a great way of calculating future values.

The CONTAINS function

The CONTAINS function will return TRUE if there is a row where all of the specified columns contain the specified values.

The syntax of the CONTAINS function is as follows:

```
CONTAINS ( <Table>, <ColumnName>, <Value> [, <ColumnName>, <Value> [,
... ] ] )
```

In this example, we'll use the INTERSECT function to find the list of colors that appear in our two-color tables. We'll then use the result of this expression with the CONTAINS function to create a measure that checks whether this list contains the color **Red**, as follows:

```
Color Check =
CONTAINS (
    INTERSECT (
        'Color Table 1',
        'Color Table 2'
    ),
    [Color],
    "Red"
)
```

In this case, the measure would return TRUE as both tables contain the color **Red**. However, if the value was changed to **Pink**, the measure would return FALSE, as the color **Pink** only appears in **Color Table 1**.

The CONCATENATEX function

For our final example in this chapter, we're going to look at the CONCATENATEX function. This function takes a table expression for the first parameter. It then iterates over the rows in this table and evaluates the expression passed in with the second parameter. The results of the expressions are then concatenated using the delimiter specified with the third parameter.

The syntax of the CONCATENATEX function is as follows:

```
CONCATENATEX ( <Table>, <Expression> [, <Delimiter> ] )
```

In this example, we'll use the INTERSECT function to find the list of colors that appear in our two color tables. We'll then use the result of this expression with the CONCATENATEX function to create a new measure that we can use to display these colors as a comma-separated list.

We can create the new measure using the following DAX expression:

```
Colors =
CONCATENATEX (
    INTERSECT (
        'Color Table 1',
        'Color Table 2'
    ),
    [Color],
    ","
)
```

We can then use that measure with a card visual in Power BI Desktop to display the result, which should look like the one shown in *Figure 7-20*:

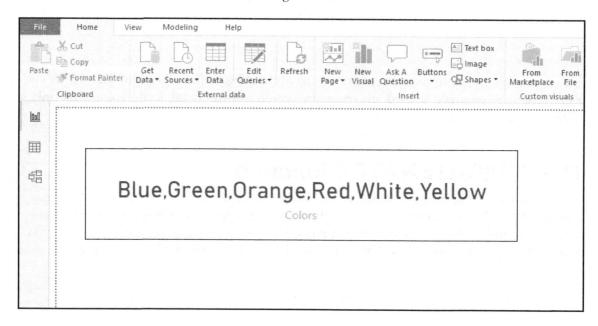

Figure 7-20: The result of the colors measure output to a card visual in Power BI Desktop

The CONCATENATEX function is a great way of displaying the result of a table expression. For example, you could use it in conjunction with the VALUES table function to display the current values of a filter or slicer as a dynamic title on a report.

Summary

In this chapter, we looked at the DAX table functions. We looked at how they can be used to create calculated tables and how they can be used as parameters to functions that require a table expression for a parameter. We learned how to use table functions with Excel, SSMS, and DAX Studio to query data in our data model.

We then moved on to look at those table functions that are classed as table manipulation functions, and how they can be used to manipulate data in our data model. We looked in detail at the CROSSJOIN, DATATABLE, EXCEPT, INTERSECT, UNION, and GENERATESERIES functions.

Finally, we looked at some examples of working with table functions. In particular, we looked at using table functions as parameters to other functions and we worked through some examples of using the COUNTROWS, PRODUCTX, CONTAINS, and CONCATENATEX functions.

In the next chapter, we will continue our look at functions by learning about the date, time, and time intelligence functions that are available in the DAX language.

8
Date, Time, and Time Intelligence Functions

We'll start this chapter by looking at the group of DAX functions that deal with date and time. Starting with a brief description of each of the functions currently available in this group, we'll then turn our attention to some hands-on examples.

In the second half of this chapter, we'll be working with the time intelligence group of functions. Again, we'll start with a list of the functions in this group, before moving on to look at how these functions work with a date table in your data model to bring you new insights. We'll also work through some examples of using these functions to aggregate and compare data over different time periods.

This chapter will cover the following topics:

- Introduction to date and time functions
- Working with date and time functions
- Looking at time intelligence functions
- Making your data more intelligent over time

Introduction to date and time functions

The DAX language contains a number of functions relating to date and time, including a couple of functions that allow you to automatically create simple date tables. Many of the remaining date and time functions give you the ability to expand these automatically generated tables with additional columns of date-related information. If you've worked with date and time functions in Excel, then these are very similar, with the exception that DAX date and time functions work with the datetime data type.

Almost all the data models you'll work with will involve some form of calculation relating to date and time, and they'll usually contain at least one date table. In fact, if you are working with a data model in Power BI Desktop and you don't have your own date table, then, by default, it will automatically create a hidden date table for every date field in the data model.

> Time tables are less commonly found in data models. Where they are, they will have a similar structure, with one row for every unit of time. That unit of time will depend on the granularity of your time table, be it hour, minute, second, or lower. Generally, you will have rows covering the time between midnight and 23:59:59.

Whenever you have dates in a data model that you want use for analysis, you will need to have a related date table. Where you have multiple dates that you want to analyze, you have the following choices:

- Use a single date table where you have a single active relationship and multiple inactive relationships. You will then need to use the USERELATIONSHIP function to indicate which relationship to use.
- Use multiple date tables, each related to its own date column.

In Chapter 3, *Building Data Models*, in the section titled *It's a date*, we looked at building a custom date table using some of these date and time functions. In that example, we started by building a simple table with the CALENDAR function, and then expanded it by adding numerous calculated columns. In this chapter, we're going to build a similar date table. However, this time, we'll do it using a single DAX expression and use the ADDCOLUMNS function to add the additional date-related columns.

Date and time function reference

The following list of DAX functions are found in the date and time function group, along with a brief description of the functionality provided by each:

- CALENDAR: Returns a table that contains a single column called 'Date', which holds a set of contiguous dates. These dates range from a specified start date to a specified end date, inclusively.
- CALENDARAUTO: Returns a table that contains a single column called 'Date', which holds a set of contiguous dates. The range for these dates is calculated automatically based on the earliest date found in your data model through to the latest.
- DATE: Returns the specified date in datetime format.

- DATEDIFF : Returns the number of units specified as the interval between two specified dates.
- DATEVALUE: Converts a date specified in text format into a date in datetime format.
- DAY: Returns an integer number between 1 and 31, representing the day of the month of the specified date.
- EDATE: Returns a date in datetime format, which is the date that is the specified number of months before or after the given start date.
- EOMONTH: Returns a date in datetime format, which is the last day of the month for the specified number of months, before or after the given start date.
- HOUR: Returns an integer number between 0 and 23, representing the hour of the specified date/time.
- MINUTE: Returns an integer number between 0 and 59, representing the minute of the specified date/time.
- MONTH: Returns an integer number between 1 and 12, representing the month of the specified date.
- NOW: Returns the current date and time in datetime format.
- SECOND: Returns an integer number between 0 and 59, representing the second of the specified date/time.
- TIME: Converts the specified hours, minutes, and seconds, given as numbers, to a time in datetime format.
- TIMEVALUE: Converts a specified time given in text format into a time in datetime format.
- TODAY: Returns the current date in datetime format.
- UTCNOW: Returns the current **Coordinated Universal Time (UTC)** date and time in datetime format.
- UTCTODAY: Returns the current UTC date in datetime format.
- WEEKDAY: Returns an integer number between 1 and 7, representing the day of the week of the specified date. Gives you the option to specify whether to use Sunday or Monday as the first day of the week.
- WEEKNUM: Returns an integer number representing the week number of the year for the specified date. Gives you the option to specify whether to use Sunday or Monday as the first day of the week.
- YEAR: Returns a four-digit integer number between 1900 and 9999 representing the year for the specified date.
- YEARFRAC: Returns the fraction of a year based on whole days between a specified start and end date.

Now, let's have a look at the date and time functions in the next section.

Working with date and time functions

In this section, we're going to look at some of the date and time functions in more detail by using them with some hands-on examples. We'll start by looking at a DAX expression to build a date table.

 As we'll see in the *Looking at time intelligence functions* section of this chapter on time intelligence functions, we need at least one table in our data model that contains all the days for the years being analyzed for those functions to work correctly.

Unlike the date table we built in `Chapter 3`, *Building Data Models* where we built the table in sections using calculated columns, we'll build this date table with a single DAX expression.

Building a date table

For this example, we will be building a date table using Power BI Desktop. We'll start by creating a calculated table. From Power BI Desktop, do the following:

1. Switch to the **Report** or **Data** view.
2. From the **Calculations** section of the **Modeling** ribbon, select **Create New Table**. This will bring up the DAX editor where we can name the table and add the DAX expression to define it. In the DAX editor, enter the following expression to create the new date table:

```
Date Table =
VAR StartYear = 2005
VAR EndYear = 2020
VAR CalendarDates =
    CALENDAR ( DATE ( StartYear, 1, 1 ), DATE ( EndYear, 12, 31 ) )
RETURN
    ADDCOLUMNS (
        CalendarDates,
        "Year", YEAR ( [Date] ),
        "Quarter Name", "Q" & TRUNC ( ( MONTH ( [Date] ) - 1 ) /
            3 ) + 1,
        "Quarter Number", TRUNC ( ( MONTH ( [Date] ) - 1 ) / 3 ) +
            1,
        "Month Name", FORMAT ( [Date], "mmmm" ),
        "Month Number", MONTH ( [Date] ),
```

```
        "Week Name", "Week " & FORMAT ( WEEKNUM ( [Date] ), "00"
            ),
        "Week Number", WEEKNUM ( [Date] ),
        "Day Name", FORMAT ( [Date], "dddd" ),
        "Day Number", WEEKDAY ( [Date] )
    )
```

3. This will create a new date table with a date column called **Date**. Check that this column is correctly formatted as a date.

4. Finally, mark the new table as a date table. To do this, right-click on the new date table in the **Fields** pane and select **Mark as date table**. This will bring up the **Make as date table** dialog. In the drop-down **Date** column, select **Date** and click **OK**.

In this example, we have used the CALENDAR function with a start and end date. We could have just as easily used the CALENDARAUTO function to automatically detect the earliest and latest dates in our data model. However, the CALENDAR function gives us greater control over the date range of the table. Let's look at these two functions in more detail.

The CALENDAR and CALENDARAUTO functions

The CALENDAR function will return a table that contains a single column called **Date**, which holds a set of contiguous dates. These dates range from a specified start date to a specified end date, inclusively.

The syntax of the CALENDAR function is as follows:

```
CALENDAR ( <StartDate> , <EndDate> )
```

To ensure that the DAX time intelligence functions work correctly, you should always include an entire year in a date table.

In the expression we used to create our date table in the previous example, we effectively used the following DAX to return a table with dates between January 1, 2005 and December 31, 2020:

```
CALENDAR (
    DATE ( 2005, 1, 1 ),
    DATE ( 2020, 12, 31 )
)
```

- The CALENDARAUTO function also returns a table with a set of contiguous dates and a single column called **Date**. However, the start and end dates for the date range are calculated automatically based on the data in your data model.
- The syntax of the CALENDARAUTO function is CALENDARAUTO ([<FiscalYearEndMonth>]).
- The function takes an optional parameter, which is an integer between 1 to 12 that represents the end month of the fiscal year. By default, the fiscal year ends in month 12 (December).
- While the CALENDARAUTO function can be useful for populating a date table, it has a major drawback. If your data model contains dates that you are not using for analysis, such as date of birth, then it will also pick these up. This will potentially give a much wider date range than you want.

The DATEDIFF function

The DATEDIFF function returns the amount of time between the specified start and end dates, with a specified time interval of seconds, minutes, hours, days, weeks, months, quarters, or years.

The syntax of the DATEDIFF function is as follows:

DATEDIFF (<Date1>, <Date2>, <Interval>)

The <Date1> and <Date2> parameters are dates in datetime format that represent the two dates that we want to measure the interval between. The interval is specified with the third parameter.

Let's create two measures to illustrate the function being used with day and week as the intervals by using the following DAX expressions:

```
DATEDIFF Day Example =
DATEDIFF (
    DATE ( 2019, 1, 1 ),
    DATE ( 2020, 12, 31 ),
    DAY
)

DATEDIFF Week Example =
DATEDIFF (
    DATE ( 2019, 1, 1 ),
    DATE ( 2020, 12, 31 ),
    WEEK
)
```

If we now display these measures using a couple of card visuals with Power BI, we get the results shown in *Figure 8-1*:

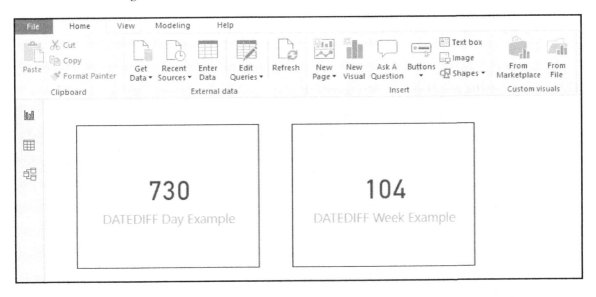

Figure 8-1: Using the $\mathrm{DATEDIFF}$ function with day and week intervals

In this example, for each of the measures, the end date is after the start date, so the difference is returned as a positive figure. However, in instances where the start date is after the end date, then the difference would be returned as a negative number.

The EDATE function

The EDATE function returns the date that is the specified number of months before or after the given start date.

The syntax of the EDATE function is as follows:

```
EDATE ( <StartDate>, <Months> )
```

The first parameter is a date in datetime or text format that represents the start date. The second parameter represents the number of months before or after the start date to return.

To illustrate this, create a new measure using the following DAX expression:

```
EDATE Example =
EDATE (
    DATE ( 2019, 1, 31 ),
    1
)
```

This then gives the result shown in *Figure 8-2*:

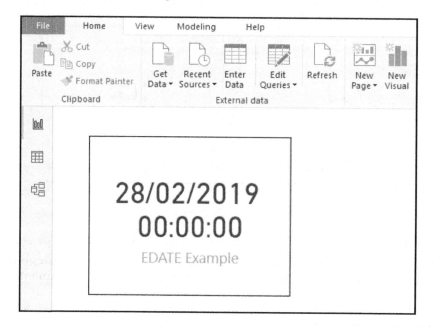

Figure 8-2: Using the EDATE function

In cases like our example, where the day of the month of the specified start date is past the last day of the corresponding month, then the last day of the corresponding month is returned.

The EOMONTH function

The EOMONTH function is like the EDATE function except that it will return the last date of the month where the specified number of months is before or after the given start date.

The syntax of the EOMONTH function is as follows:

```
EOMONTH ( <StartDate>, <Months> )
```

The first parameter is a date in datetime or text format that represents the start date. The second parameter represents the number of months before or after the start date to return.

Again, let's illustrate this by creating a new measure using the following DAX expression:

```
EOMONTH Example =
EOMONTH (
    DATE ( 2019, 12, 15 ),
    -2
)
```

This will then give the result shown in *Figure 8-3*:

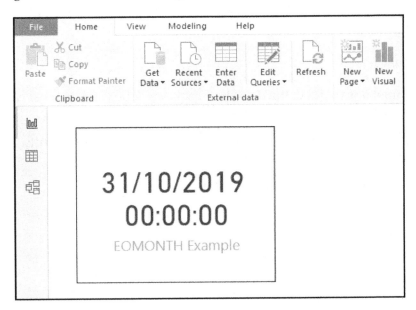

Figure 8-3: Using the EOMONTH function

Even though both the EDATE and EOMONTH functions return a date, they return it in datetime format. If you only want the date, without the time, then you should wrap the EDATE or EOMONTH function with the FORMAT function, and format the date as required.

The YEARFRAC function

The last function in the date and time group that we're going look at is the YEARFRAC function. This function returns the number of days between the specified start and end dates as a year fraction.

The syntax of the YEARFRAC function is as follows:

```
YEARFRAC ( <StartDate>, <EndDate> [, <Basis>] )
```

The third optional parameter is an integer number between 0 and 4 and it allows you to specify the type of day count basis to be used. The following gives the meaning for each value:

0 – US (NASD) 30/360
1 – Actual/actual
2 – Actual/360
3 – Actual/365
4 – European 30/360

If the third parameter is omitted, the default of basis 0 will be used. In most cases, if you are not sure which basis to use, you should use basis 1.

Where possible, you should use four-digit years to avoid unexpected results. If the year is omitted, then the current year will be used.

Let's create an example measure using the following DAX expression:

```
YEARFRAC Example =
YEARFRAC (
    DATE ( 1968, 4, 1 ),
    DATE ( 2019, 10, 1 ),
    1
)
```

This will then give the result shown in *Figure 8-4*:

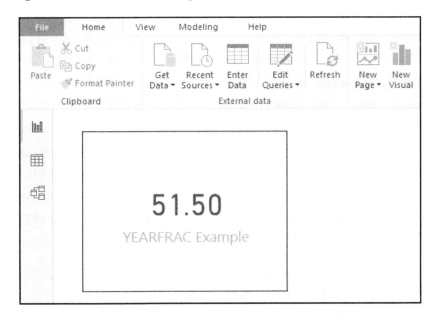

Figure 8-4: Using the YEARFRAC function

The YEARFRAC function is useful for financial and HR-related calculations, where the calculation requires the portion of a whole year. In the previous example, we created the measure using set dates, but these could just as easily be dates coming from tables in our data model.

We worked with the date and time functions in this section. In the next section, we'll move on toward the time intelligence functions.

Looking at time intelligence functions

Now that we've spent some time working with date and time functions in more detail, it's time to move on to looking at the time intelligence group of DAX functions.

The DAX language contains a number of functions related to time intelligence. This set of functions will enable you to get insight into your data by making it easy to perform analysis over different time periods. For example, you can get figures such as months, quarters, and year to date, or the same period last year. Each of these functions belongs to one of three categories:

- Functions that return a single date
- Functions that return a table of dates
- Functions that evaluate expressions over a period of time

In order to be able to use any of these time intelligence functions, your data model must contain at least one date table. This date table will also need to conform to the following rules:

- It must start on January 1 of the year of the earliest date being analyzed.
- It must end on December 31 of the year of the latest date being analyzed.
- It will need one record, and only one record, for each date.
- The dates must be contiguous. There can be no missing dates between the start and end dates for the range of dates covered by the date table.

As we have already seen, if you are using Power BI Desktop, then you have two options available. You can either work with the hidden data tables that are automatically created by default when you have dates in your data model, or you can create your own custom date table. If you create a custom table, then any hidden date tables will be removed from your data model.

 It is recommended that you always create your own custom date table when working with time intelligence functions as you will have greater control over it.

As you will see when we come to the examples of using these functions, we will use some of them with the CALCULATE function. As such, you will need a good understanding of how the CALCULATE function works to be able to understand how a particular time intelligence function works. If you need a reminder of how the CALCULATE function works, check out the section entitled *The CALCULATE function* in Chapter 1, *What is DAX?*.

Time intelligence function reference

The following is a list of the DAX functions found in the time intelligence group of functions, along with a brief description of the functionality provided by each:

- CLOSINGBALANCEMONTH, CLOSINGBALANCEQUARTER, and CLOSINGBALANCEYEAR evaluate a given expression at the last date of the month/quarter/year for the specified dates in the current context. They also take an optional argument for a filter expression to apply to the current context. The CLOSINGBALANCEYEAR function also allows you to specify a literal string with a date that defines the year-end date.

- DATEADD: Returns a table containing a column of dates, shifted either forward or backward in time by the specified number of intervals from the dates in the current context. Intervals can be specified as day, month, quarter, or year.

- DATESBETWEEN: Returns a table containing a column of dates that begin with the specified start date and end with the specified end date.

- DATESINPERIOD: Returns a table containing a column of dates that begin with the specified start date and continues for the specified number of intervals. Intervals can be specified as day, month, quarter, or year.

- DATESMTD, DATESQTD, and DATESYTD: Returns a table containing a column of the dates for the month/quarter/year to date in the current context.

- ENDOFMONTH, ENDOFQUARTER, and ENDOFYEAR: Returns the last date of the month/quarter/year in the current context for the specified column of dates.

- FIRSTDATE: Returns the first date in the current context for the specified column of dates.

- FIRSTNONBLANK: Returns the first value in the column, filtered by the current context, where the expression is not blank.

- LASTDATE: Returns the last date in the current context for the specified column of dates.

- LASTNONBLANK: Returns the last value in the column, filtered by the current context, where the expression is not blank.

- NEXTDAY, NEXTMONTH, NEXTQUARTER, and NEXTYEAR: Returns a table containing a column of all dates from the next day/month/quarter/year, based on the first date specified in the date column in the current context.

- OPENINGBALANCEMONTH, OPENINGBALANCEQUARTER, and OPENINGBALANCEYEAR: Evaluates the expression at the first date of the month/quarter/year in the current context.

- PARALLELPERIOD: Returns a table that contains a column of dates that represents a period parallel to the dates in the specified date column, in the current context, with the dates shifted by a specified number of intervals either forward in time or back in time. Intervals can be specified as month, quarter, or year.
- PREVIOUSDAY, PREVIOUSMONTH, PREVIOUSQUARTER, and PREVIOUSYEAR: Returns a table that contains a column of all dates from the previous day/month/quarter/year, based on the first date in the date column in the current context.
- SAMEPERIODLASTYEAR: Returns a table that contains a column of dates shifted one year back in time from the dates in the specified date column in the current context.
- STARTOFMONTH, STARTOFQUARTER, and STARTOFYEAR: Returns the first date of the month/quarter/year in the current context for the specified column of dates.
- TOTALMTD, TOTALQTD, and TOTALYTD: Evaluates the value of the expression for the dates in the month/quarter/year to date in the current context.

All the functions in this group take dates as one of their parameters. The dates passed to these functions can be any of the following:

- A reference to a date/time column
- A table expression that returns a single column of date/time values
- A Boolean expression that defines a single-column table of date/time values

Making your data more intelligent over time

In this section, we're going to look at some of the time intelligence functions in more detail by using them with some hands-on examples. As we mentioned in the previous section, you must have at least one date table in your data model for the functions in this group to work. If you don't have a date table in your data model already, make sure you add one, as outlined in the previous section on the date and time functions. This date table will also need to have a relationship with the **SalesDateKey** column in the **Sales** table.

DAX functions that return a single date

The first category of time intelligence functions that we are going to look at are those that return a single value. In reality, they return a single row of a single column table, so they can be used with any function that requires a table as a parameter.

The functions in this category are as follows:

- FIRSTDATE and LASTDATE
- FIRSTNONBLANK and LASTNONBLANK
- STARTOFMONTH and ENDOFMONTH
- STARTOFQUARTER and ENDOFQUARTER
- STARTOFYEAR and ENDOFYEAR

Let's look at the first of these functions to help us understand how the functions in this category work.

The syntax of the FIRSTDATE function is as follows:

```
FIRSTDATE ( <Dates> )
```

The syntax of the LASTDATE functions is as follows:

```
LASTDATE ( <Dates> )
```

These functions have only one parameter, which is either the name of a column containing dates or a one-column table containing dates. From these dates, it will then return the first date in the current context.

The FIRSTNONBLANK and LASTNONBLANK functions work slightly differently to the others in this group, in that they don't just work with date columns, but also work with columns of any data type.

The syntax of the FIRSTNONBLANK function is as follows:

```
FIRSTNONBLANK ( <ColumnName>, <Expression> )
```

The syntax of the LASTNONBLANK function is as follows:

```
LASTNONBLANK ( <ColumnName>, <Expression> )
```

For the first parameter, we give it the name of the column that we want to return the value from. For the second parameter, we need to supply an expression that is to be evaluated for each value of the column passed in the first parameter for non-blank values. Let's illustrate this with an example:

1. Create a new measure using the following DAX expression:

```
First Sales Date =
FIRSTNONBLANK (
    'Date Table'[Date],
```

```
CALCULATE (
    SUM ( Sales[Sales Amount] )
)
)
```

This will give the first date where the sales amount was not blank. On its own, this is not very useful. However, if we add this to a table visual, along with the product name, we get the date that each product achieved its first sale. We can see this in *Figure 8-5*:

Product Name	First Sales Date
A. Datum Advanced Digital Camera M300 Azure	31/03/2007
A. Datum Advanced Digital Camera M300 Black	01/01/2007
A. Datum Advanced Digital Camera M300 Green	01/01/2007
A. Datum Advanced Digital Camera M300 Grey	01/01/2007
A. Datum Advanced Digital Camera M300 Orange	01/01/2007
A. Datum Advanced Digital Camera M300 Pink	01/01/2007
A. Datum Advanced Digital Camera M300 Silver	01/01/2007
A. Datum All in One Digital Camera M200 Azure	04/01/2009
A. Datum All in One Digital Camera M200 Black	01/01/2007
A. Datum All in One Digital Camera M200 Green	01/01/2007
A. Datum All in One Digital Camera M200 Grey	01/01/2007
A. Datum All in One Digital Camera M200 Orange	31/03/2007
A. Datum All in One Digital Camera M200 Pink	01/01/2007
A. Datum All in One Digital Camera M200 Silver	01/01/2007
A. Datum Bridge Digital Camera M300 Azure	01/01/2007
A. Datum Bridge Digital Camera M300 Black	28/02/2007
A. Datum Bridge Digital Camera M300 Green	01/01/2007
A. Datum Bridge Digital Camera M300 Grey	01/01/2007
A. Datum Bridge Digital Camera M300 Orange	01/01/2007
A. Datum Bridge Digital Camera M300 Pink	01/01/2007
A. Datum Bridge Digital Camera M300 Silver	30/09/2008
A. Datum Compact Digital Camera M200 Azure	01/01/2007
A. Datum Compact Digital Camera M200 Green	01/01/2007
A. Datum Compact Digital Camera M200 Grey	01/01/2007

Figure 8-5: Showing the first date of sale for each product

2. We can expand on this to find the total sales amount for that first day's sales by using the same expression as a filter with the CALCULATE function. Create a new measure using the following expression:

```
First Sales Date Sales Amount =
CALCULATE (
    SUM ( sales[sales amount] ),
    FIRSTNONBLANK (
        'Date Table'[Date],
        CALCULATE (
            SUM ( Sales[Sales Amount] )
        )
    )
)
```

Here, we are using the fact that FIRSTNONBLANK returns a table, which can then be used as a filter for the CALCULATE function.

The last functions we're going to look at in this category are the STARTOFYEAR and ENDOFYEAR functions. These functions return the date of the start of the year and the date of the end of the year, respectively.

The syntax of the STARTOFYEAR function is as follows:

```
STARTOFYEAR ( <Dates> [, <YearEndDate>] )
```

For the first parameter, you need to supply either the name of a column containing dates or a one-column table containing dates. The second, optional, parameter allows you to specify the end date of the year, which may be different to the calendar year if you're working with financial years, for example.

The YearEndDate parameter is a string literal of a date. This will be in the locale of the client where a workbook was created, and the year part of the date will be ignored. It is advisable to use the format day/month to ensure the correct interpretation.

3. For this example, create a measure using the following expression:

```
Financial Year Start Date =
STARTOFYEAR (
    Sales[SalesDateKey],
    "03/31"
)
```

In this example, we have included the optional parameter to specify an alternative year-end date of March 31 for our financial year. When combined with the date column of our date table in a table visual, we get the start date of the financial year for each quarter, as can be seen in *Figure 8-6*:

Year	Quarter	Financial Year Start Date
2007	Qtr 1	01/01/2007
2007	Qtr 2	01/04/2007
2007	Qtr 3	01/04/2007
2007	Qtr 4	01/04/2007
2008	Qtr 1	01/04/2007
2008	Qtr 2	01/04/2008
2008	Qtr 3	01/04/2008
2008	Qtr 4	01/04/2008
2009	Qtr 1	01/04/2008
2009	Qtr 2	01/04/2009
2009	Qtr 3	01/04/2009
2009	Qtr 4	01/04/2009

Figure 8-6: Getting the start date of the financial year

The financial year start date for Q1 2007 is January 1, 2007 as this is the first date that has sales in the **Sales** table.

The STARTOFMONTH, ENDOFMONTH, STARTOFQUARTER, and ENDOFQUARTER functions are very similar to the STARTOFYEAR and ENDOFYEAR functions, with the exception that they don't have an optional parameter for an alternative end date.

Comparing values over different periods of time

Another category within the time intelligence group of functions are those that return a table of dates. These functions are largely used as the filter parameter, for the CALCULATE function and are used to create comparisons of values over different time periods.

The functions in this category are as follows:

- DATEADD, DATESBETWEEN, and DATESINPERIOD
- DATESMTD, DATESQTD, and DATESYTD
- NEXTDAY, NEXTMONTH, NEXTQUARTER, and NEXTYEAR
- PARALLELPERIOD and SAMEPERIODLASTYEAR
- PREVIOUSDAY, PREVIOUSMONTH, PREVIOUSQUARTER, and PREVIOUSYEAR

We'll begin our look at this category of time intelligence functions with the DATEADD function. This function will take a set of dates and then move them by the given number of the specified time interval.

The syntax of the DATEADD function is as follows:

```
DATEADD ( <Dates>, <NumberOfIntervals>, <Interval> )
```

The first parameter is either the name of a column containing dates or a one-column table containing dates. The second parameter is the number of the specified intervals that you want to move the dates by, and the third parameter is the interval type. The interval type can be day, month, quarter, or year. To demonstrate this, do the following:

1. Create a new measure using the following expression:

```
Sales Amount Last Month =
CALCULATE (
    SUM ( Sales[Sales Amount] ),
    DATEADD (
        'Date Table'[Date],
        -1,
        MONTH
    )
)
```

This takes our table of dates and returns a table with the date shifted back by one month. The result from this is then used as the filter parameter of the CALCULATE function, which evaluates the expression that sums the **Sales Amount** column of the **Sales** table.

With this measure, we can compare the sales amount for a month with the sales amount of the previous month, as can be seen in *Figure 8-7*:

Year	Month	Sales Amount	Sales Amount Last Month
2007	January	£193,305,554.64	
2007	February	£209,439,067.93	£193,305,554.6355
2007	March	£203,991,979.69	£209,439,067.9252
2007	April	£276,891,048.16	£203,991,979.691
2007	May	£288,749,508.61	£276,891,048.1564
2007	June	£283,186,644.54	£288,749,508.611
2007	July	£272,818,635.11	£283,186,644.544
2007	August	£263,780,279.28	£272,818,635.112
2007	September	£257,282,781.95	£263,780,279.28
2007	October	£288,853,903.92	£257,282,781.95
2007	November	£308,752,784.65	£288,853,903.918
2007	December	£297,341,103.65	£308,752,784.654
2008	January	£183,970,020.28	£297,341,103.654
2008	February	£191,106,948.30	£183,970,020.2795
2008	March	£183,393,312.89	£191,106,948.2956
2008	April	£223,849,292.33	£183,393,312.8925
2008	May	£220,502,302.24	£223,849,292.3268
2008	June	£214,455,381.54	£220,502,302.237
2008	July	£246,239,251.91	£214,455,381.544
2008	August	£231,189,642.07	£246,239,251.905
2008	September	£227,942,617.84	£231,189,642.073
2008	October	£211,203,579.42	£227,942,617.841

Figure 8-7: Comparing the sales amount for a month with the sales amount of the previous month

This same result could also be obtained by using the PARALLELPERIOD function. This function is very similar to the DATEADD function and the syntax for it is as follows:

PARALLELPERIOD (<Dates>, <NumberOfIntervals>, <Interval>)

2. To use this function instead, amend the previous measure by using the following expression:

```
Sales Amount Last Month =
CALCULATE (
    SUM ( Sales[Sales Amount] ),
    PARALLELPERIOD (
        'Date Table'[Date],
        -1,
        MONTH
    )
)
```

There is a third way this result could be obtained, this time using the PREVIOUSMONTH function. Unlike DATEADD, this function only has one parameter, and the syntax for it is as follows:

```
PREVIOUSMONTH ( <Dates> )
```

3. To use this function instead, amend the previous measure using the following expression:

```
Sales Amount Last Month =
CALCULATE (
    SUM ( Sales[Sales Amount] ),
    PREVIOUSMONTH ( 'Date Table'[Date] )
)
```

All the NEXT and PREVIOUS functions work in the same way as the PREVIOUSMONTH function – they just move the date by different intervals.

The DATESMTD, DATESQTD, and DATESYTD functions all return a table containing a column of the dates for the month, quarter, or year to date in the current context. They all take one parameter, which is the name of the column containing dates or a one-column table containing dates.

In the next part of this chapter, we'll look at the DATESYTD function being used as a filter with the CALCULATE function to create a measure that returns the year-to-date sales amount.

The opening and closing balance functions

The last intelligence function that we're going to focus on is the CLOSINGBALANCEMONTH function. This function belongs to the third category of time intelligence functions that evaluate expressions over a period of time.

The CLOSINGBALANCEMONTH function evaluates an expression for the last date of the month in the current context. The CLOSINGBALANCEQUARTER and CLOSINGBALANCEYEAR functions work in the same way, except they evaluate an expression for the last date of the quarter and year, respectively. The CLOSINGBALANCEYEAR function also has an additional optional parameter that allows you to specify a different year-end date (the default being December 31).

The syntax of the CLOSINGBALANCEMONTH function is as follows:

```
CLOSINGBALANCEMONTH ( <Expression>, <Dates> [, <Filter>] )
```

The first parameter is the expression that is to be evaluated. This can be a DAX expression or an existing measure. In our example, we are going to use a measure called **YTD Sales**. This measure calculates a cumulative total of sales to date for each year:

1. There are a couple of ways we can calculate this measure using other functions from the time intelligence group. Firstly, we could use the DATESYTD function with the CALCULATE function, as in the following example:

```
YTD Sales =
CALCULATE (
    SUM ( Sales[Sales Amount] ),
    DATESYTD ( 'Date Table'[Date] )
)
```

Alternatively, we could use a function from the category of functions that evaluate expressions over a time period; the TOTALYTD function:

```
YTD Sales 2 =
TOTALYTD (
    SUM ( Sales[Sales Amount] ),
    'Date Table'[Date]
)
```

We can see the results of both measures in *Figure 8-8*, which shows daily sales amounts, along with the results of both versions of our year-to-date total sales measures:

Year	Quarter	Month	Day	Sales Amount	YTD Sales	YTD Sales 2
2007	Qtr 1	January	1	£6,085,839.18	£6,085,839.1825	£6,085,839.1825
2007	Qtr 1	January	2	£6,270,657.17	£12,356,496.352	£12,356,496.352
2007	Qtr 1	January	3	£6,096,024.11	£18,452,520.464	£18,452,520.464
2007	Qtr 1	January	4	£5,979,164.13	£24,431,684.5935	£24,431,684.5935
2007	Qtr 1	January	5	£5,926,584.02	£30,358,268.609	£30,358,268.609
2007	Qtr 1	January	6	£6,150,610.75	£36,508,879.3615	£36,508,879.3615
2007	Qtr 1	January	7	£6,517,040.34	£43,025,919.697	£43,025,919.697
2007	Qtr 1	January	8	£5,856,724.52	£48,882,644.2165	£48,882,644.2165
2007	Qtr 1	January	9	£6,184,820.44	£55,067,464.6555	£55,067,464.6555
2007	Qtr 1	January	10	£6,612,222.96	£61,679,687.613	£61,679,687.613
2007	Qtr 1	January	11	£6,524,046.81	£68,203,734.4195	£68,203,734.4195
2007	Qtr 1	January	12	£5,889,201.15	£74,092,935.5675	£74,092,935.5675
2007	Qtr 1	January	13	£6,330,346.71	£80,423,282.282	£80,423,282.282
2007	Qtr 1	January	14	£5,945,346.59	£86,368,628.8765	£86,368,628.8765
2007	Qtr 1	January	15	£6,385,077.45	£92,753,706.323	£92,753,706.323
2007	Qtr 1	January	16	£6,173,139.29	£98,926,845.6095	£98,926,845.6095
2007	Qtr 1	January	17	£6,709,543.94	£105,636,389.549	£105,636,389.549
2007	Qtr 1	January	18	£6,143,140.45	£111,779,529.9975	£111,779,529.9975
2007	Qtr 1	January	19	£6,034,566.93	£117,814,096.929	£117,814,096.929
2007	Qtr 1	January	20	£6,354,141.60	£124,168,238.5275	£124,168,238.5275
2007	Qtr 1	January	21	£6,617,879.81	£130,786,118.334	£130,786,118.334
2007	Qtr 1	January	22	£6,800,149.52	£137,586,267.858	£137,586,267.858
2007	Qtr 1	January	23	£6,226,790.07	£143,813,057.927	£143,813,057.927
2007	Qtr 1	January	24	£5,884,406.49	£149,697,464.416	£149,697,464.416
2007	Qtr 1	January	25	£5,702,550.69	£155,400,015.1105	£155,400,015.1105
2007	Qtr 1	January	26	£6,108,977.86	£161,508,992.9685	£161,508,992.9685
2007	Qtr 1	January	27	£6,301,865.73	£167,810,858.6935	£167,810,858.6935
2007	Qtr 1	January	28	£6,273,568.46	£174,084,427.1525	£174,084,427.1525
2007	Qtr 1	January	29	£6,359,243.46	£180,443,670.6085	£180,443,670.6085
2007	Qtr 1	January	30	£6,360,062.75	£186,803,733.3535	£186,803,733.3535
2007	Qtr 1	January	31	£6,501,821.28	£193,305,554.6355	£193,305,554.6355
2007	Qtr 1	February	1	£6,824,039.74	£200,129,594.3759	£200,129,594.3759
2007	Qtr 1	February	2	£7,050,235.15	£207,179,829.5274	£207,179,829.5274

Figure 8-8: Displaying both versions of the YTD sales measures

For the second parameter of the CLOSINGBALANCEMONTH function, we need to give either the name of a column containing dates or a one-column table containing dates. In our example, it will be the **date** field from our date table.

Finally, we can specify an optional filter for the third parameter. In this example, we're going to restrict the year-to-date sales figures to just those for products in the **Economy** class.

2. We'll now create our example measure using the following DAX expression:

```
EOM Sales Balance =
CLOSINGBALANCEMONTH (
    [YTD Sales],
    'Date Table'[Date],
    'Product'[Class] = "Economy"
)
```

Figure 8-9 shows the result of using this measure, splitting our year-to-date sales amount by month, quarter, and then by year:

Year	Quarter	Month	EOM Sales Balance
2007	Qtr 1	January	£21,190,753.942
2007	Qtr 1	February	£41,812,972.5876
2007	Qtr 1	March	£62,556,439.5748
2007	Qtr 2	April	£90,673,680.3726
2007	Qtr 2	May	£119,784,981.9186
2007	Qtr 2	June	£148,389,108.8536
2007	Qtr 3	July	£174,865,281.5046
2007	Qtr 3	August	£198,848,035.8156
2007	Qtr 3	September	£222,232,643.5096
2007	Qtr 4	October	£249,172,463.7976
2007	Qtr 4	November	£275,036,272.3541
2007	Qtr 4	December	£299,544,303.4121
2008	Qtr 1	January	£27,618,611.5265
2008	Qtr 1	February	£55,242,289.4096
2008	Qtr 1	March	£81,699,342.8523
2008	Qtr 2	April	£113,271,988.9115
2008	Qtr 2	May	£144,388,945.5115
2008	Qtr 2	June	£173,989,360.6865
2008	Qtr 3	July	£207,444,915.5575
2008	Qtr 3	August	£238,453,047.0435
2008	Qtr 3	September	£268,804,523.5495
2008	Qtr 4	October	£296,231,594.7475
2008	Qtr 4	November	£329,210,907.3535
2008	Qtr 4	December	£362,693,099.241
Total			

Year	Quarter	EOM Sales Balance
2007	Qtr 1	£62,556,439.5748
2007	Qtr 2	£148,389,108.8536
2007	Qtr 3	£222,232,643.5096
2007	Qtr 4	£299,544,303.4121
2008	Qtr 1	£81,699,342.8523
2008	Qtr 2	£173,989,360.6865
2008	Qtr 3	£268,804,523.5495
2008	Qtr 4	£362,693,099.241
2009	Qtr 1	£119,587,598.3756
2009	Qtr 2	£257,815,265.4974
2009	Qtr 3	£401,866,568.3004
2009	Qtr 4	£545,996,947.1699
Total		

Year	EOM Sales Balance
2007	£299,544,303.4121
2008	£362,693,099.241
2009	£545,996,947.1699
Total	

Figure 8-9: Using the CLOSINGBALANCEMONTH function

In this example, we used a running sales total over the course of a year. A more typical example of using the CLOSINGBALANCE function would be where you have a different total for each day; for example, stock levels or the balance of a bank account.

The OPENINGBALANCE function is very similar to the CLOSINGBALANCE function except that it evaluates the expression at the first date of the month, quarter, or year in the current context instead of the last date.

Summary

In this chapter, we started off by looking at the DAX date and time group of functions. We looked at how these functions can be used to create a custom date table in our data model, and how they can be used to find out date-related information, such as the number of days between two dates.

We then moved on to look at the time intelligence group of functions. We looked at the three different categories of function available in this group and how they can be used to help us gain further insight into the data held in our data model. We worked through a number of hands-on examples of these functions, using them to return single dates, tables of dates, and learning how to compare values over different time periods.

In the next chapter, we will continue our look at DAX functions by learning about the filter group of functions.

9

Filter Functions

In this chapter, we are going to be looking at the DAX group of functions that are used to filter data. We'll start off with a brief description of each of the functions in this group before turning our attention to some hands-on examples.

This chapter is broken down into the following sections:

- Introduction to filter functions
- Filtering your data with filter functions

Introduction to filter functions

We've already looked at some of the filter functions in previous chapters when we were looking at the evaluation contexts. In Chapter 1, *What is DAX?* and Chapter 5, *Getting it into Context*, we looked in some detail at the CALCULATE function. We also touched on the ALL, FILTER, and KEEPFILTERS functions. In this chapter, we'll revisit these and take a more detailed look at some of the other functions in this group.

Filter function reference

The following gives a list of the DAX functions found in the filter function group, along with a brief description of the functionality provided by each:

- ALL: This returns a table that includes all of the rows of a specified table or all of the values of the specified column or combination of columns. It ignores any filters that have been applied to the table. The ALL function can be used with the CALCULATE and CALCULATETABLE functions to remove filters from the filter context.

- ALLEXCEPT: This is similar to the ALL function in that it returns a table that includes all of the values for the combination of columns from the specified table, excluding the specified columns. Like the ALL function, it can be used with the CALCULATE and CALCULATETABLE functions to remove filters from all but the specified columns.

- ALLNOBLANKROW: This works much like the ALL function, but unlike that function, it does not include the blank row that is generated when there is a missing record on one side of a table relationship.

- ALLSELECTED: This returns a table that includes all of the rows of a specified table or all of the values in a column or combination of columns. It ignores filters applied inside the query, whilst retaining any external filters. The ALLSELECTED function can be used with the CALCULATE and CALCULATETABLE functions to restore explicit filters and contexts.

- CALCULATE: This evaluates an expression with a context that is modified by filters. Filter parameters can either remove or restore filters.

- CALCULATETABLE: This evaluates a table expression in a context modified by filters. Filter parameters can either remove or restore filters.

- FILTER: This returns a filtered table or table expression using a Boolean expression that is used to evaluate each row of the table.

- KEEPFILTERS: This changes the way filters are applied when evaluating a CALCULATE or CALCULATETABLE function by overriding the standard behavior of both functions. Where the filter parameters of the CALCULATE and CALCULATETABLE functions replace the current context, the KEEPFILTERS function adds filters to the current context.

- LOOKUPVALUE: This returns a single value that is retrieved by searching for a value in a table. If no match satisfies all of the search values, BLANK is returned.
- REMOVEFILTERS: This removes filters from the specified tables or columns. The REMOVEFILTERS function is equivalent to the ALL function when used as a modifier with the CALCULATE and CALCULATETABLE functions.
- SELECTEDVALUE: This returns the value of the specified column when there's only one value to return; otherwise, it returns the alternate specified result.

Filtering your data with filter functions

From the brief descriptions given in the previous section, it's not always clear exactly what each filter function does. The easiest way to understand these functions is by going through some of them using hands-on examples. In this section, we're going to do just that, starting with a look at the ALL and ALLEXCEPT functions.

The ALL and ALLEXCEPT functions

When used as a table function, and depending on the parameters used, the ALL function returns a table that contains all of the values of a column, all of the values of a combination of columns, or all of the rows of a specified table. More importantly, the ALL function ignores any filters or slicers that may be set, effectively removing them from the current filter context.

However, when the ALL function is used as a parameter with the CALCULATE and CALCULATETABLE functions, its functionality is different. Instead of returning a table that contains all of the values of a specified column or combination of columns, it removes the specified columns from the current filter context.

The syntax for the ALL function is as follows:

```
ALL ( [<TableNameOrColumnName>] [, <ColumnName> [, <ColumnName> [, ... ]
] ] )
```

Let's start by demonstrating how the ALL function works as a table function. In *Figure 9-1*, we have the following simple report that shows records from the **Product** table, filtered using a couple of slicers. It currently shows products that have a value in the **Color column** of **Red** and a value in the **Class** column of **Regular**. Also, there is a count of the selected rows:

Class				
☐ Deluxe				
☐ Economy				
▣ Regular				

ProductKey	Product Name	Color	Class
17	Contoso 8GB Super-Slim MP3/Video Player M800 Red	Red	Regular
28	Contoso 16GB Mp5 Player M1600 Red	Red	Regular
30	Contoso 32GB Video MP3 Player M3200 Red	Red	Regular
84	NT Wireless Bluetooth Stereo Headphones M402 Red	Red	Regular
92	NT Wireless Transmitter and Bluetooth Headphones M150 Red	Red	Regular
356	Fabrikam Laptop14.1W M4180 Red	Red	Regular
359	Fabrikam Laptop12 M2002 Red	Red	Regular
360	Fabrikam Laptop13.3 M3000 Red	Red	Regular
361	Fabrikam Laptop13.3W M3080 Red	Red	Regular
381	Adventure Works Laptop15 M1501 Red	Red	Regular
382	Adventure Works Laptop12 M1201 Red	Red	Regular
383	Adventure Works Laptop16 M1601 Red	Red	Regular
384	Adventure Works Laptop15.4W M1548 Red	Red	Regular
1592	SV DVD 48 DVD Storage Binder M50 Red	Red	Regular
1593	SV DVD 58 DVD Storage Binder M55 Red	Red	Regular
1596	SV DVD 55DVD Storage Binder M56 Red	Red	Regular
1637	Contoso DVD 48 DVD Storage Binder M50 Red	Red	Regular
1638	Contoso DVD 58 DVD Storage Binder M55 Red	Red	Regular
1641	Contoso DVD 55DVD Storage Binder M56 Red	Red	Regular

Color: ☐ Azure, ☐ Black, ☐ Blue, ☐ Brown, ☐ Gold, ☐ Green, ☐ Grey, ☐ Orange, ☐ Pink, ☐ Purple, ▣ Red, ☐ Silver, ☐ Silver Grey, ☐ White, ☐ Yellow

19
Count of Selected Products

Figure 9-1: Filtering a table with slicers in a Power BI Desktop report

The measure to show the count of selected products was created using the following expression:

```
Count of Selected Products = COUNTROWS ( 'Product' )
```

Now, let's create another new measure, this time using a DAX expression that uses the **Product** table as the parameter to the ALL function, as shown:

```
Count of ALL Products = COUNTROWS ( ALL ( 'Product' ) )
```

This measure is similar to the first but makes use of the ALL function to ignore the filters coming from our two slicers. This produces the result shown in *Figure 9-2*, which equals the total number of records in the **Product** table:

Figure 9-2: Ignoring slicers with the ALL function

When the column of a table is used as a parameter, the ALL function returns a table containing a distinct list of values from that column. We will demonstrate this by creating a new table using the following expression:

```
Product Color = ALL ( 'Product'[Color] )
```

If we look at the new table, we see the result shown in *Figure 9-3*, which is the distinct list of values found in the **Color** column of the **Product** table:

Figure 9-3: Creating a calculated table with a distinct list of values from a single column of another table

If we supply several columns from the same table as parameters, the ALL function will return a table that contains a distinct list of values from the combination of those columns. Again, we will demonstrate this by creating another new table, this time using the following expression:

```
Product Color Class and Brand =
ALL (
    'Product'[Color],
    'Product'[Class],
    'Product'[Brand]
)
```

If we look at the new table, we see the following result as shown in *Figure 9-4*, which is the distinct list of values coming from the combination of the **Color**, **Class**, and **Brand** columns of the **Product** table:

Color	Class	Brand
Silver	Regular	Contoso
Silver	Regular	Wide World Importers
Silver	Regular	Northwind Traders
Silver	Regular	Adventure Works
Silver	Regular	Southridge Video
Silver	Regular	Litware
Silver	Regular	The Phone Company
Silver	Regular	Fabrikam
Silver	Regular	Proseware
Silver	Regular	A. Datum
Blue	Regular	Contoso
Blue	Regular	Wide World Importers
Blue	Regular	Northwind Traders
Blue	Regular	Adventure Works
Blue	Regular	Southridge Video
Blue	Regular	Fabrikam
Blue	Regular	A. Datum

Figure 9-4: Creating a calculated table with a distinct list of values from a combination of columns of another table

When specifying multiple columns for the parameters of the ALL function, they must all be from the same table.

Now, let's turn our attention to using the ALL function as a filter parameter of the CALCULATE and CALCULATETABLE functions. As already mentioned, when used in this manner, the ALL function removes the specified table or columns from the current filter context.

In the latest versions of DAX, there is a new function called REMOVEFILTERS. This function is equivalent to the ALL function when used as a modifier with the CALCULATE and CALCULATETABLE functions.

We can demonstrate this action by creating two new measures using the following expressions:

```
Count of Products with Class =
  CALCULATE (
      COUNTROWS ( 'Product' ),
      ALL ( 'Product'[Color] )
  )

Count of Products with Color =
  CALCULATE (
      COUNTROWS ( 'Product' ),
      ALL ( 'Product'[Class] )
  )
```

The first measure will remove the filter created by selecting a value in the **Color** slicer, whilst the second will remove the filter created by selecting a value in the **Class** slicer. This has the effect of giving us a row count for the total number of products from the selected class and a row count for the total number of products with the selected color. This can be seen in *Figure 9-5*:

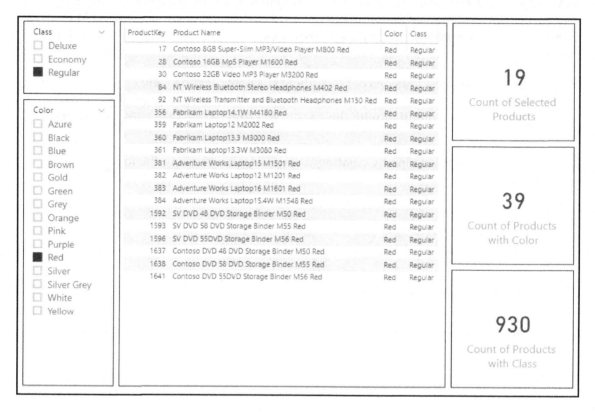

Figure 9-5: Using the ALL function to remove individual slicers from a measure

Here, we have 19 products in the **Product** table that are both **Red** in color and are from the **Regular** class. The first of our measures tells us that there is a total of 39 products in the **Product** table that are **Red** in color irrespective of their class. The second measure tells us that the **Regular** class of products contains a total of 930 products, this time irrespective of their color.

On its own, this may not be particularly useful information, but it does enable us to work out percentages. So, for example, to work out the selected products as a percentage of products for a particular class, you could create a measure using the following expression:

```
% Selected of Product Class =
DIVIDE (
    COUNTROWS ( 'Product' ),
    'Product'[Count of Products with Class]
)
```

And to do the same for color, you would create the following measure:

```
% Selected of Product Color =
DIVIDE (
    COUNTROWS ( 'Product' ),
    'Product'[Count of Products with Color]
)
```

We will now add these products, correctly formatted as percentages, to our final report, as shown in the *Figure 9-6*:

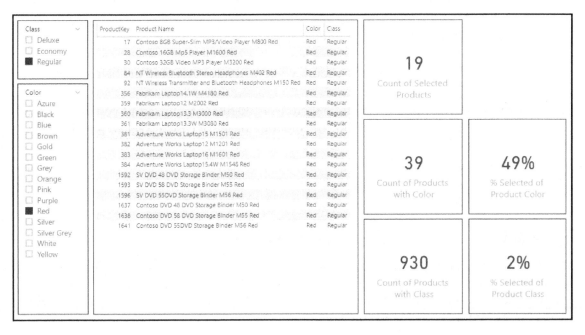

Figure 9-6: Power BI Desktop report showing all of our new measures

As we can see from *Figure 9-6*, the 19 selected products represent 49% of the total number of red-colored products. However, they only represent 2% of products from the **Regular** class of products.

 For more information on using the ALL function, check out the section in Chapter 5, *Getting it into Context*, titled *Using the ALL function*.

Now, let's look at the ALLEXCEPT function. The syntax for the ALLEXCEPT function is as follows:

```
ALLEXCEPT ( <TableName>, <ColumnName> [, <ColumnName> [, ... ] ] )
```

- As mentioned in the description in the preceding reference list, this function is very similar to the ALL function.
- However, instead of specifying the columns to be removed from the filter context, you specify the columns that should remain.
- It will remove all of the columns in the specified table, except those given as the column parameters.
- Unlike the ALL function, you must specify both the table name and one or more column names.
- The ALLEXCEPT function is useful where you have lots of filters being applied to the filter context.
- Suppose you had a case where there were 30 filters applied and you only wanted to retain one of them for your calculation. In such a case, if you were using the ALL function, you would need to pass 29 columns as parameters.
- With the ALLEXCEPT function, you would only need to pass the table name and the name of the column that you wanted to retain the filter for.

The ALLSELECTED function

Much like the ALL and ALLEXCEPT functions, the ALLSELECTED function removes filters from the current filter context. It ignores filters applied inside a query, but will retain any external filters. When used with the CALCULATE and CALCULATETABLE functions, it enables you to restore explicit filters and contexts.

The syntax for the `ALLSELECTED` function is as follows:

```
ALLSELECTED ( [<TableNameOrColumnName>] [, <ColumnName> [, <ColumnName>
[, ... ] ] ] )
```

To demonstrate the `ALLSELECTED` function, let's create two new measures using the following expressions:

```
Total ALL Sales =
 CALCULATE (
     SUM ( Sales[Sales Amount] ),
     ALL ( 'Product' )
 )

Total SELECTED Sales =
 CALCULATE (
     SUM ( Sales[Sales Amount] ),
     ALLSELECTED ( 'Product' )
 )
```

The first of these measures creates a total value that removes all filters applied to any of the columns in the **Product** table. The second only removes filters from inside a query, leaving those applied by any external filters intact. This means, for example, that any filters being applied by slicers will still be included in the filter context.

We will now use these measures in the following code to create another two measures to calculate the percentage of the overall sales total and the percentage of the sales total for the products selected using an external filter, such as a slicer:

```
% ALL Sales =
 DIVIDE (
     SUM ( Sales[Sales Amount] ),
     [Total ALL Sales]
 )

% SELECTED Sales =
 DIVIDE (
     SUM ( Sales[Sales Amount] ),
     [Total SELECTED Sales]
 )
```

We can now see these measures applied to a new version of our report, as shown in *Figure 9-7*:

Class											

Class		ProductKey	Product Name	Color	Class	Sales Amount	Total ALL Sales	% ALL Sales	Total SELECTED Sales	% SELECTED Sales
☐ Deluxe		17	Contoso 8GB Super-Slim MP3/Video Player M800 Red	Red	Regular	£1,061,417.72	£8,341,224,364.8324	0.01%	£93,399,791.1945	1.14%
☐ Economy		28	Contoso 16GB Mp5 Player M1600 Red	Red	Regular	£672,255.70	£8,341,224,364.8324	0.01%	£93,399,791.1945	0.72%
■ Regular		30	Contoso 32GB Video MP3 Player M3200 Red	Red	Regular	£1,961,753.25	£8,341,224,364.8324	0.02%	£93,399,791.1945	2.10%
		84	NT Wireless Bluetooth Stereo Headphones M402 Red	Red	Regular	£747,894.20	£8,341,224,364.8324	0.01%	£93,399,791.1945	0.80%
Color		92	NT Wireless Transmitter and Bluetooth Headphones M150 Red	Red	Regular	£921,684.05	£8,341,224,364.8324	0.01%	£93,399,791.1945	0.99%
☐ Azure		356	Fabrikam Laptop14.1W M4180 Red	Red	Regular	£9,678,096.92	£8,341,224,364.8324	0.12%	£93,399,791.1945	10.36%
☐ Black		359	Fabrikam Laptop12 M2002 Red	Red	Regular	£7,612,065.28	£8,341,224,364.8324	0.09%	£93,399,791.1945	8.15%
☐ Blue		360	Fabrikam Laptop13.3 M3000 Red	Red	Regular	£7,968,527.80	£8,341,224,364.8324	0.10%	£93,399,791.1945	8.53%
☐ Brown		361	Fabrikam Laptop13.3W M3080 Red	Red	Regular	£8,301,260.00	£8,341,224,364.8324	0.10%	£93,399,791.1945	8.89%
☐ Gold		381	Adventure Works Laptop15 M1501 Red	Red	Regular	£15,140,542.71	£8,341,224,364.8324	0.18%	£93,399,791.1945	16.21%
☐ Green		382	Adventure Works Laptop12 M1201 Red	Red	Regular	£8,117,134.57	£8,341,224,364.8324	0.10%	£93,399,791.1945	8.69%
☐ Grey		383	Adventure Works Laptop16 M1601 Red	Red	Regular	£13,170,254.93	£8,341,224,364.8324	0.16%	£93,399,791.1945	14.10%
☐ Orange		384	Adventure Works Laptop15.4W M1548 Red	Red	Regular	£16,138,722.02	£8,341,224,364.8324	0.19%	£93,399,791.1945	17.28%
☐ Pink		1592	SV DVD 48 DVD Storage Binder M50 Red	Red	Regular	£375,476.67	£8,341,224,364.8324	0.00%	£93,399,791.1945	0.40%
☐ Purple		1593	SV DVD 58 DVD Storage Binder M55 Red	Red	Regular	£295,645.18	£8,341,224,364.8324	0.00%	£93,399,791.1945	0.32%
■ Red		1596	SV DVD 55DVD Storage Binder M56 Red	Red	Regular	£274,034.94	£8,341,224,364.8324	0.00%	£93,399,791.1945	0.29%
☐ Silver		1637	Contoso DVD 48 DVD Storage Binder M50 Red	Red	Regular	£388,018.03	£8,341,224,364.8324	0.00%	£93,399,791.1945	0.42%
☐ Silver Grey		1638	Contoso DVD 58 DVD Storage Binder M55 Red	Red	Regular	£299,315.33	£8,341,224,364.8324	0.00%	£93,399,791.1945	0.32%
☐ White		1641	Contoso DVD 55DVD Storage Binder M56 Red	Red	Regular	£275,691.88	£8,341,224,364.8324	0.00%	£93,399,791.1945	0.30%
☐ Yellow		Total				£93,399,791.19	£8,341,224,364.8324	1.12%	£93,399,791.1945	100.00%

Figure 9-7: Power BI Desktop report with measures added to a table

As can be seen, the **Total ALL Sales** measure removes all filters coming from columns in the **Product** table, whilst the **Total SELECTED Sales** measure only removes filters from within the query being created by the table visual. It does not remove the external filters coming from the two slicers. This gives us the overall total for sales of the products selected using the slicers.

The FILTER function

Next, we are going to look at the FILTER function. This function returns a filtered table, using a Boolean expression that is used to evaluate each row of a specified table.

The syntax for the FILTER function is as follows:

```
FILTER ( <Table>, <FilterExpression> )
```

- The first parameter is the name of the table that is to be filtered.
- The second parameter is the DAX expression that is to be applied to each row of the table specified with the first parameter.
- The expression must evaluate to TRUE or FALSE.

Let's look at a practical example of this function in operation. Consider the following measure:

```
Count of Regular Products =
    COUNTROWS (
        FILTER (
            'Product',
            'Product'[Class] = "Regular"
        )
    )
```

The result of this measure can be seen in *Figure 9-8*:

Brand	Count of ProductKey	Count of Regular Products
A. Datum	132	89
Adventure Works	128	71
Contoso	560	269
Fabrikam	163	107
Litware	48	36
Northwind Traders	27	10
Proseware	177	105
Southridge Video	170	71
The Phone Company	152	104
Wide World Importers	133	68
Total	**1690**	**930**

Figure 9-8: Using the FILTER function in a measure

Here, we can see that the FILTER function has iterated through the **Product** table, looking for products with a value in the **Class** column equal to **Regular**. The rows that evaluated to TRUE were then returned, as a table, to the COUNTROWS function, giving the values we see in the **Count of Regular Products** column in the preceding screenshot.

You can add additional constraints to the DAX expression being used as a filter, including the use of the AND and OR operators. You can also use the RELATED function to check for conditions in tables related to the table specified as the table parameter of the FILTER function.

You should also remember that any explicit filters you create using the FILTER function are on top of any implicit filters that may be coming from external sources such as slicers.

The KEEPFILTERS function

As a function, the KEEPFILTERS function does not return a value as such. Instead, it is a filter modifier that overrides the standard behavior of the CALCULATE and CALCULATETABLE functions.

The syntax for the KEEPFILTERS function is as follows:

```
KEEPFILTERS ( <Expression> )
```

The KEEPFILTERS function changes the way filters are applied when evaluating a function. Where the filter parameters of the CALCULATE and CALCULATETABLE functions would normally remove columns from the filter context, the KEEPFILTERS function will prevent them being removed if they conflict with the expression being given as the parameter of the KEEPFILTER function.

Let's demonstrate this with an example. Suppose we have the following measure:

```
Sales Amount for Red Products =
 CALCULATE (
     SUM ( Sales[Sales Amount] ),
     'Product'[Color] = "Red"
 )
```

This measure may give us undesired results. By default, it will remove the **Color** column of the **Product** table from the filter context. We can see the results of this in *Figure 9-9*, where the measure has been used in a table visual:

Brand	Color	Sales Amount for Red Products
A. Datum	Azure	
A. Datum	Black	
A. Datum	Blue	
A. Datum	Gold	
A. Datum	Green	
A. Datum	Grey	
A. Datum	Orange	
A. Datum	Pink	
A. Datum	Silver	
A. Datum	Silver Grey	
Adventure Works	Black	86135967
Adventure Works	Blue	86135967
Adventure Works	Brown	86135967
Adventure Works	Red	86135967
Adventure Works	Silver	86135967
Adventure Works	White	86135967
Contoso	Black	27650572
Contoso	Blue	27650572
Contoso	Brown	27650572
Contoso	Gold	27650572
Contoso	Green	27650572
Contoso	Grey	27650572
Contoso	Orange	27650572
Contoso	Pink	27650572
Contoso	Purple	27650572
Total		**188643986**

Figure 9-9: Displaying a measure that doesn't use the KEEPFILTERS function

As it is, the filter parameter of the CALCULATE function overrides the **Color** filter that is being passed from the **Color** column of the visual. Where a **Brand** does not have a red-colored product, the measure returns a null; otherwise, it returns the total value for the **Brand**.

If we now modify the measure to use the KEEPFILTERS function with the filter parameter of the CALCULATE function, then the filters being applied by the visual to the **Color** column will be preserved.

Suppose we modify our original measure to the following:

```
Sales Amount for Red Products =
 CALCULATE (
     SUM ( Sales[Sales Amount] ),
     KEEPFILTERS ( 'Product'[Color] = "Red" )
 )
```

Then we get the desired result, as can be seen in *Figure 9-10*:

Brand	Color	Sales Amount for Red Products
A. Datum	Silver Grey	
Adventure Works	Black	
Adventure Works	Blue	
Adventure Works	Brown	
Adventure Works	Red	86135967
Adventure Works	Silver	
Adventure Works	White	
Contoso	Black	
Contoso	Blue	
Contoso	Brown	
Contoso	Gold	
Contoso	Green	
Contoso	Grey	
Contoso	Orange	
Contoso	Pink	
Contoso	Purple	
Contoso	Red	27650572
Contoso	Silver	
Contoso	Silver Grey	
Contoso	Transparent	
Contoso	White	
Contoso	Yellow	
Fabrikam	Black	
Fabrikam	Blue	
Total		**188643986**

Figure 9-10: Using the KEEPFILTERS function

Now, the **Color** filter being generated by the table visual is preserved in the filter context, despite the column being used as a filter parameter of the CALCULATE function. As expected, we only get a figure against the brand when the color is equal to **Red**.

The LOOKUPVALUE function

The LOOKUP function returns a single value, which is retrieved by searching for a value in a lookup table. If a match that satisfies all of the search values cannot be found, either an alternative result can be specified or, if not, BLANK will be returned.

This function is useful when you have a situation where you need to obtain a value from a lookup table that is not related to the table that contains the source value.

The syntax for the LOOKUPVALUE function is as follows:

```
LOOKUPVALUE ( <Result_ColumnName>, <Search_ColumnName>, <Search_Value>
[, <Search_ColumnName>, <Search_Value> [, ... ] ] [, <Alternate_Result>]
)
```

- For the first parameter, we need to specify the name of the column containing the values you want returned as the end result. This is usually a fully qualified name that includes both the table name and the column name. We cannot use an expression for this parameter.
- For the second parameter, we need to specify the name of a column that will be used as the lookup value. This column must be in the same table used for the first parameter or a table that is related to it. Again, it cannot be an expression.
- The third parameter is a scalar expression, which must not refer to a column in the table that is being searched.
- Finally, we can also supply an alternate result, which will be used if a lookup value is not found, or multiple results are returned by the search criteria.

If an alternate result is not specified, then no value being returned will result in BLANK, and multiple values being returned will result in an error.

You can have multiple search columns and values, and the result that is returned will be the value of the column specified in the first parameter, where all of the search columns and values match.

Now, let's show this function in action. We'll start with a very simple data model containing two tables, as shown in *Figure 9-11*, which are not connected by a relationship:

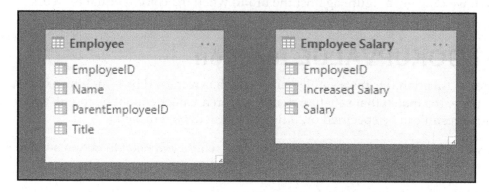

Figure 9-11: Simple data model with two unrelated tables

The **Employee** table contains the data shown in *Figure 9-12*:

EmployeeID	Name	Title	ParentEmployeeID
100	Peter	CEO	
200	Frank	Business Manager	100
201	Catherine	Finance Manager	100
202	Ross	IT Manager	100
300	Simon	Senior Administrator	200
301	Jane	Administrator	200
302	Richard	Finance Assistant	201
303	Julie	Finance Assistant	201
304	Saad	SharePoint Administrator	202
305	Tim	Web Developer	202
306	Kate	System Administrator	202
400	John	Junior Web Developer	305

Figure 9-12: The Employee table

On the other hand, the **Employee Salary** table contains the values shown in *Figure 9-13*:

EmployeeID	Salary	Increased Salary
100	£150,000	160741.8
200	£80,000	85728.96
201	£55,000	58938.66
202	£55,000	58938.66
300	£45,000	48222.54
301	£40,000	42864.48
302	£40,000	42864.48
303	£40,000	42864.48
304	£50,000	53580.6
305	£50,000	53580.6
306	£50,000	53580.6

Figure 9-13: The Employee Salary table

Now, let's create a new calculated column in the **Employee** table that takes the value of the **Salary** column in the **Employee Salary** table, where the **Employee ID** values match. We will do this with the following DAX expression:

```
Salary Lookup =
LOOKUPVALUE(
    'Employee Salary'[Salary],
    'Employee Salary'[EmployeeID],
    Employee[EmployeeID],
    0
)
```

Figure 9-14 shows the **Employee** table with the new **Salary Lookup** column added:

EmployeeID	Name	Title	ParentEmployeeID	Salary Lookup
100	Peter	CEO		£150,000
200	Frank	Business Manager	100	£80,000
201	Catherine	Finance Manager	100	£55,000
202	Ross	IT Manager	100	£55,000
300	Simon	Senior Administrator	200	£45,000
301	Jane	Administrator	200	£40,000
302	Richard	Finance Assistant	201	£40,000
303	Julie	Finance Assistant	201	£40,000
304	Saad	SharePoint Administrator	202	£50,000
305	Tim	Web Developer	202	£50,000
306	Kate	System Administrator	202	£50,000
400	John	Junior Web Developer	305	£0

Figure 9-14: Adding the Salary Lookup column to the Employee table

You can see that John's salary has a value of zero, which is the alternate result value, as he does not have a corresponding record in the **Salary** table.

The SELECTEDVALUE function

The final filter function that we're going to look at in this chapter is the SELECTEDVALUE function. This function returns the value of the specified column when there's only one value in the current filter context to return. If no value is selected, or more than one value is selected, it can return an optionally specified alternate result.

The syntax for the SELECTEDVALUE function is as follows:

```
SELECTEDVALUE ( <ColumnName> [, <AlternateResult>] )
```

We will demonstrate a potential use of this function by creating a new measure using the following DAX expression:

```
Selected Class =
 SELECTEDVALUE (
     'Product'[Class],
     "N/A"
 )
```

Internally, the SELECTEDVALUE function is just simplified syntax for the combined use of the HASONEVALUE and VALUES functions. The measure can be written using the following expression:

```
Selected Class =
 IF (
     HASONEVALUE ( 'Product'[Class] ),
     VALUES ( 'Product'[Class] ),
     "N/A"
 )
```

We can now use the first measure to display a dynamic title, as shown in *Figure 9-15*:

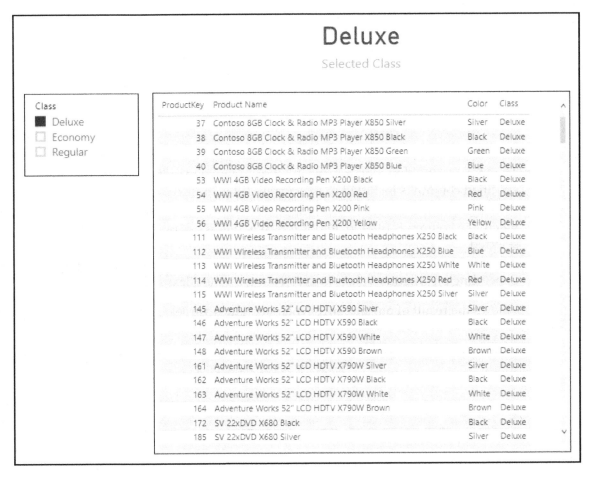

Figure 9-15: Displaying a dynamic title

As we can see, the **Class** slicer is adding one value in the **Class** column of the **Product** table to the filter context. As such, the title displays the selected value coming from the **Class** slicer. However, there is an issue with this. If no values are selected with the slicer, or more than one value is selected, the SELECTEDVALUE function will return the alternate result, which, in our example, is N/A.

If an alternate result is not specified in the parameters, then when no value is selected, or more than one value is selected, the SELECTEDVALUE function will return BLANK.

To overcome this problem, we can amend our measure to use the IF and ISFILTERED functions, as follows:

```
Selected Class =
SELECTEDVALUE (
    'Product'[Class],
    IF (
        ISFILTERED ( 'Product'[Class] ),
        "Multiple Selected Values",
        "No Selected Values"
    )
)
```

- The ISFILTERED function returns TRUE or FALSE depending on whether the specified column is included in the current filter context.
- By using this in conjunction with the SELECTEDVALUE function, we can tell whether a column is filtered, and if it is, whether it has one or more values selected.
- Based on this, our revised measure will return one of two alternate results, depending on whether values are selected with the **Class** slicer.

Figure 9-16 shows the result of our measure when no values are selected with the **Class** slicer:

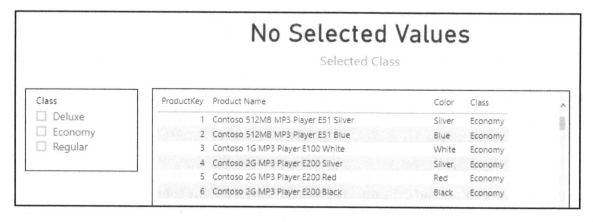

Figure 9-16: Dynamic title when no values are selected with the slicer

Figure 9-17 shows the result of our measure when multiple values are selected with the **Class** slicer:

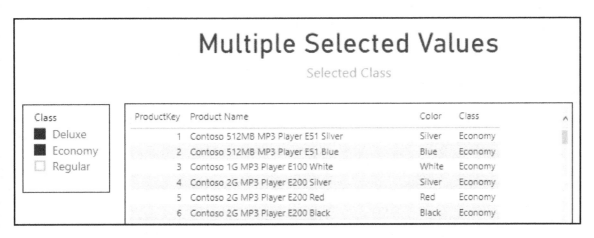

Figure 9-17: Dynamic title when multiple values are selected with the slicer

In addition to being a great way of creating dynamic titles, the SELECTEDVALUE function can be used anytime you need to retrieve a single value from the filter context. However, you should remember that the SELECTEDVALUE function only works with the filter context, not the row context.

Summary

In this chapter, we looked at the group of DAX functions used to filter data. We revisited the ALL and ALLEXCEPT functions, looking at how they can be used as standalone table functions and how they behave differently when used with the CALCULATE function. We looked at the ALLSELECTED function and how it can be used to remove filters inside a query, whilst retaining those filers coming from outside the query.

We also took a more detailed look at some of the other functions in this group, exploring their use through a number of hands-on examples.

In the next chapter, we will take our final look at DAX functions, this time looking at the statistical group of functions.

10
Statistical Functions

This is the last chapter in which we will be looking at the different groups of DAX functions. In this chapter, we will be looking at the group of functions that help us to perform statistical aggregations.

As in previous chapters, we will start this chapter with a complete list of the functions found in this group, along with a brief description of each. We'll then move on and look in more detail at some of the more commonly used functions in this group, all while using hands-on examples to explain how they work.

The chapter is broken into the following sections:

- Introducing statistical functions
- Calculating averages
- Working with percentiles
- Ranking your data
- Calculating standard deviation and variance

Introducing statistical functions

The statistical group of DAX functions is one of the largest, with over 40 different functions currently available. Recently, several new functions were added to this group that replicate some of the advanced statistical functions found in Excel.

As well as some of the more specialist functions found in this group, it also contains functions that will help you compute more frequently needed statistical values, such as averages, percentiles, ranking, and standard deviation.

In this section of this chapter, we will look at the list of functions that are currently available in this group.

Statistical function reference

The following list details the DAX functions currently found in the statistical function group, along with a brief description of what each function does:

- AVERAGE: Calculates the average value of all the numbers in a column. This function only works with numeric values and cannot handle text or non-numeric values.
- AVERAGEA: Calculates the average value of all the values in a column. In addition to numeric values, this function will attempt to handle text and non-numeric values.
- AVERAGEX: Calculates the average value of a set of expressions evaluated over a table.
- BETA.DIST: Calculates the value of the beta distribution.
- BETA.INV: Calculates the value of the inverse of the beta cumulative probability density function (BETA.DIST).
- CHISQ.DIST: Calculates the value of the chi-squared distribution.
- CHISQ.DIST.RT: Calculates the value of the right-tailed probability of the chi-squared distribution.
- CHISQ.INV: Calculates the value of the inverse of the left-tailed probability of the chi-squared distribution.
- CHISQ.INV.RT: Calculates the value of the inverse of the right-tailed probability of the chi-squared distribution.
- COMBIN: Calculates the value of the number of combinations, excluding repetitions, for a specified number of items.
- COMBINA: Calculates the value of the number of combinations, including repetitions, for a specified number of items.
- CONFIDENCE.NORM: Using a normal distribution, calculates a value for the confidence interval for a population mean.

- CONFIDENCE.T: Using a Student's t-distribution, calculates a value for the confidence interval for a population mean.
- EXPON.DIST: Calculates the value of the exponential distribution.
- GEOMEAN: Calculates the value of the geometric mean of a specified column.
- GEOMEANX: Calculates the value of the geometric mean of a set of expressions evaluated over a table.
- MEDIAN: Calculates the value of the 50th percentile of values in a column.
- MEDIANX: Calculates the 50th percentile of a set of expressions evaluated over a table.
- NORM.DIST: Calculates the value of the normal distribution for the specified mean and standard deviation.
- NORM.INV: Calculates the value of the inverse of the normal cumulative distribution for the specified mean and standard deviation.
- NORM.S.DIST: Calculates the value of the standard normal distribution.
- NORM.S.INV: Returns the inverse of the standard normal cumulative distribution.
- PERCENTILE.EXC: Calculates the value of the *k*th percentile of values in a column, with *k* in the range *0..1* exclusive.
- PERCENTILE.INC: Calculates the value of the *k*th percentile of values in a column, with *k* in the range *0..1* inclusive.
- PERCENTILEX.EXC: Calculates the value of the *k*th percentile of a set of expressions evaluated over a table, with *k* in the range *0..1* exclusive.
- PERCENTILEX.INC: Calculates the value of the *k*th percentile of a set of expressions evaluated over a table, with *k* in the range *0..1* inclusive.
- PERMUT: Calculates the number of permutations for the specified number of objects that can be selected from number objects.
- POISSON.DIST: Calculates the value of the Poisson distribution.
- RANK.EQ: Calculates a value for the rank of a number in a column of numbers.
- RANKX: Calculates a value for the rank of a set of expressions evaluated over a table.
- SAMPLE: Returns a table containing a sample subset, consisting of a specified number of rows from a specified table expression.
- STDEV.P: Calculates the value of the standard deviation for the entire population of the specified column. Ignores logical values and text.

- `STDEV.S`: Calculates the value of the standard deviation for a sample population from the specified column. Ignores logical values and text in the sample.
- `STDEVX.P`: Calculates the value of the standard deviation for the entire population, which results from a set of expressions evaluated over a table.
- `STDEVX.S`: Calculates the value of the standard deviation for a sample population, which results from a set of expressions evaluated over a table.
- `T.DIST`: Calculates the value of the Student's left-tailed t-distribution.
- `T.DIST.2T`: Calculates the value of the two-tailed Student's t-distribution.
- `T.DIST.RT`: Calculates the value of the right-tailed Student's t-distribution.
- `T.INV`: Calculates the value of the left-tailed inverse of the Student's t-distribution.
- `T.INV.2T`: Calculates the value of the two-tailed inverse of the Student's t-distribution.
- `VAR.P`: Calculates the value of the variance for the entire population of the specified column.
- `VAR.S`: Calculates the value of the variance for a sample population of the specified column.
- `VARX.P`: Calculates the value of the variance for the entire population, which results from a set of expressions evaluated over a table.
- `VARX.S`: Calculates the value of the variance for a sample population, which results from a set of expressions evaluated over a table.
- `XIRR`: Calculates the value of the **internal rate of return (IRR)** for a schedule of cash flows, which is not necessarily periodic.
- `XNPV`: Calculates the value of the **net present value (NPV)** for a schedule of cash flows.

Many of the statistical functions in this group are used for advanced calculations, and a full understanding of how they are applied is beyond the scope of this book. However, as these functions can also be found in Excel, they are well documented, and you should have no problem finding detailed articles about them online.

We will only be looking at a selection of the statistical functions in this chapter. If you want details about all the statistical functions, then the official Microsoft documentation can be found at `https://docs.microsoft.com/en-us/dax/statistical-functions-dax`.

In the following section, we will look at some of the more frequently used functions that, as a business intelligence professional, you are more likely to come across or need to use to gain further insight into your data. Specifically, we are going to look at some examples of calculating averages, percentiles, rankings, standard deviations, and variances.

Calculating averages

In this section, we're going to focus on two of the DAX functions designed specifically for calculating averages: the AVERAGE and AVERAGEX functions.

The AVERAGE function

The syntax for the AVERAGE function is as follows:

```
AVERAGE ( <ColumnName> )
```

This is a very simple function that is used to calculate the average value (or the arithmetic mean) of all the numbers in a specified column. It's important to remember that this function only works with numeric values, and it cannot handle text or non-numeric values. If you want to include non-numeric values in your calculation, you will need to use the AVERAGEA function instead, which uses the same syntax as the AVERAGE function.

> The AVERAGEA function deals with Boolean values as if they are integers, with TRUE returning a 1 and FALSE returning a 0. Any string values, including empty strings, will result in a 0, even if the string contains a number. This limits the usefulness of the AVERAGEA function. It is better to use the AVERAGEX function, where you can convert string values that contain a number using the VALUE function.

To demonstrate the AVERAGE function, create a new measure by using the following expression:

```
Avg Sales Amount = AVERAGE ( Sales[Sales Amount] )
```

This gives us a very simple measure, which is the average amount of all sales made to date, or the average of all the values in the **Sales Amount** column of the **Sales** table. We can use this measure to slice and dice the sales data. For example, we can create a chart to show the average sales amount for each year, as shown in *Figure 10-1*:

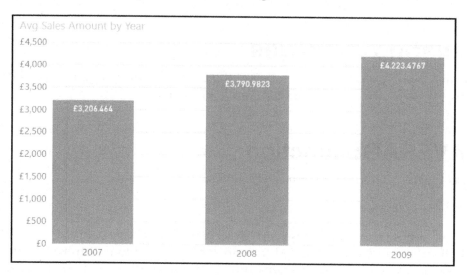

Figure 10-1: Average sales for each year

We can create a slightly more sophisticated measure by using the following expression:

```
Avg Sales Amount for Red Products =
  CALCULATE (
      AVERAGE ( Sales[Sales Amount] ),
      KEEPFILTERS ( 'Product'[Color] = "Red" )
  )
```

This measure will give us the average sales amount, but only for those products with a color of **Red**. We could use this measure to show a comparison of the average sales for red-colored products against the average of all sales, as can be seen in *Figure 10-2*:

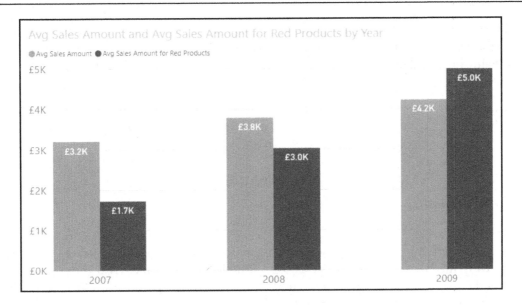

Figure 10-2: Average sales per year compared to average sales for red products

Here, we can easily see that the average sales amount for red products compared to the overall average sales amount is increasing year by year.

Calculating rolling averages with the AVERAGEX function

Like the other iterator functions, the AVERAGEX function will iterate over the table passed in as the first parameter, and will then give the average of values returned by the expression given as the second parameter. As such, this gives us a very flexible way to calculate averages, including being able to calculate a rolling average.

The syntax for the AVERAGEX function is as follows:

```
AVERAGEX ( <Table>, <Expression> )
```

For the first parameter, we need to specify a table or table expression over which we want to iterate. For the second parameter, we need to give a measure. For our rolling average, we need to create a measure for the total sales amount. We can do this by using the following simple expression:

```
Total Sales = SUM ( Sales[Sales Amount] )
```

Next, we need to create a measure using the AVERAGEX function, which will go through the dates in the **Date** table and calculate the average based on the daily total sales amounts, up to and including the date of the current row. This can be done by using the following expression:

```
Rolling Avg Total Sales =
AVERAGEX (
    FILTER (
        ALL ( 'Date Table' ),
        'Date Table'[Date]
            <= MAX ( 'Date Table'[Date] )
    ),
    [Total Sales]
)
```

The FILTER function in this expression returns all the dates prior to the current date, up to and including the current date. The AVERAGEX function then iterates over these dates and calculates the average of the values returned by the **Total Sales** measure. We can see the result of this more clearly by looking at the table shown in *Figure 10-3*:

Date	Total Sales	Rolling Avg Total Sales
01/01/2007 00:00:00	£6,085,839.1825	6,085,839.18
02/01/2007 00:00:00	£6,270,657.1695	6,178,248.18
03/01/2007 00:00:00	£6,096,024.112	6,150,840.15
04/01/2007 00:00:00	£5,979,164.1295	6,107,921.15
05/01/2007 00:00:00	£5,926,584.0155	6,071,653.72
06/01/2007 00:00:00	£6,150,610.7525	6,084,813.23
07/01/2007 00:00:00	£6,517,040.3355	6,146,559.96
08/01/2007 00:00:00	£5,856,724.5195	6,110,330.53
09/01/2007 00:00:00	£6,184,820.439	6,118,607.18
10/01/2007 00:00:00	£6,612,222.9575	6,167,968.76
11/01/2007 00:00:00	£6,524,046.8065	6,200,339.49
12/01/2007 00:00:00	£5,889,201.148	6,174,411.30
13/01/2007 00:00:00	£6,330,346.7145	6,186,406.33
14/01/2007 00:00:00	£5,945,346.5945	6,169,187.78
15/01/2007 00:00:00	£6,385,077.4465	6,183,580.42
Total	£8,341,224,364.8324	7,610,606.17

Figure 10-3: Rolling average of sales

So, for the first date, the measure calculates the average for this date only. For the second date, it calculates the average based on the totals for the first two dates, while for the third date, it's based on the totals for the first three dates. It will continue through all the dates in the **Date** table, calculating the rolling average for the total sales amount.

Working with percentiles

There are six DAX functions in this function group that will help you calculate percentile values for a given set of data. They are PERCENTILE.EXC, PERCENTILE.INC, PERCENTILEX.EXC, PERCENTILEX.INC, MEDIAN, and MEDIANX.

 A percentile is a statistical measure that gives the value where a certain percentage of values in a dataset fall below it. For example, the 30th percentile will be the value in a dataset where 30% of the values fall below it, and the remaining 70% are above it.

Before we start to look at these functions, let's use the following expression to create a new table, which will contain the numbers 1 through to 20:

```
Numbers = GENERATESERIES ( 1, 20 )
```

Now, we can use this table as our dataset to help us understand how these functions work. We'll start by looking at the first of these functions.

The PERCENTILE.EXC and PERCENTILE.INC functions

The syntax for the PERCENTILE.EXC function is as follows:

```
PERCENTILE.EXC ( <Column>, <K> )
```

The syntax for the PERCENTILE.INC function is as follows:

```
PERCENTILE.INC ( <Column>, <K> )
```

For the first parameter, we need to give the column that contains the values for the dataset that we want to work with. For the second parameter, we need to give the percentile value (the *k*th) that we want to calculate, with the value being between 0 and 1—in other words, the point at which a certain percentage of values in the dataset are below.

We can demonstrate this function by creating a measure that will calculate the 25th percentile for the values in the **Numbers** table that we've just created. We can do this with the following expression:

```
Numbers 25th Percentile = PERCENTILE.EXC ( 'Numbers'[Value], 0.25 )
```

This will return the value shown in *Figure 10-4*:

Figure 10-4: The 25th percentile figure

So, any numbers in our **Numbers** table that are below this value are said to be in the 25th percentile. This is also equivalent to the first quartile.

If we want to find the remaining quartiles, then we need to find the values for the 50th percentile and the 75th percentile. We can do this by creating two more measures using the following expressions:

```
Numbers 50th Percentile = PERCENTILE.EXC ( 'Numbers'[Value], 0.50 )
Numbers 75th Percentile = PERCENTILE.EXC ( 'Numbers'[Value], 0.75 )
```

This will give us the results shown in *Figure 10-5*:

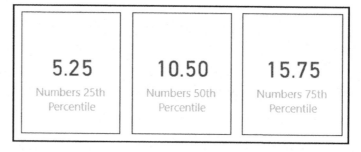

Figure 10-5: The 25th, 50th and 75th percentile figures

One thing to note about the PERCENTILE.EXC function is that the values for the second parameter must be in the range *1/(N+1)* to *N/(N+1)*, where *N* is the number of values in the dataset. So, for example, if the value of the second parameter for our **Numbers** table was 0.047, it would generate the error shown in *Figure 10-6*:

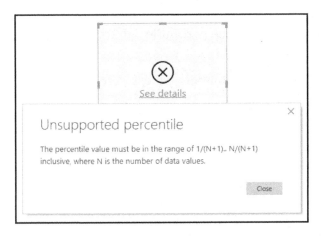

Figure 10-6: Error generated when using an invalid value with the PERCENTILE.EXE function

However, if you use the PERCENTILE.INC function, the value for the second parameter can be any value between 0 and 1.

Essentially, what the PERCENTILE.EXC function is saying is that there are no values in the dataset that are below the 4.7th percentile, while the PERCENTILE.INC function uses a different formula to calculate a number. If accuracy is more important, then it is recommended that you use the PERCENTILE.EXC function over the PERCENTILE.INC function.

The PERCENTILEX.EXC and PERCENTILEX.INC functions

The syntax for the PERCENTILEX.EXC function is as follows:

```
PERCENTILEX.EXC ( <Table>, <Expression>, <K> )
```

The syntax for the PERCENTILEX.INC function is as follows:

```
PERCENTILEX.INC ( <Table>, <Expression>, <K> )
```

These functions work much like their standard counterparts, except that, like all the x functions, these will calculate the value of the percentile by iterating over the rows of a specified table, evaluating a set of expressions.

For the first parameter, we need to specify the table over which to iterate. For the second parameter, we need to give the expression that will be evaluated. For the third—and final—parameter, we need to give the percentile value (the *k*th) that we want to calculate, with the value being between 0 and 1.

Let's demonstrate this, using our **Numbers** table, by creating a new measure by using the following expression:

```
Numbersx10 25th Percentile =
PERCENTILEX.EXC (
    Numbers,
    [Value] * 10,
    0.25
)
```

What this is doing is calculating the value for the 25th percentile, for the values in the **Numbers** table multiplied by 10. In other words, for numbers between 10 to 200, find the value below which you would find the bottom 25% of the numbers.

This will return the value shown in *Figure 10-7*:

52.50

Numbersx10 25th Percentile

Figure 10-7: The 25th percentile figure

Again, with the PERCENTILEX.EXC function, the value for the third parameter must be in the range *1/(N+1)* to *N/(N+1)*, where *N* is the number of values in the dataset. If you use the PERCENTILEX.INC function, the value for the third parameter can be any value between 0 and 1.

The MEDIAN and MEDIANX functions

The syntax for the MEDIAN function is as follows:

```
MEDIAN ( <Column> )
```

The syntax for the MEDIANX function is as follows:

```
MEDIANX ( <Table>, <Expression> )
```

The MEDIAN and MEDIANX functions will calculate the value of the 50th percentile of the values in a column or a set of expressions evaluated over a table. They are equivalent to the percentile functions being used to calculate the 50th percentile. In fact, we can demonstrate this by creating a new measure, using the following expression:

```
Numbers Median = MEDIAN ( 'Numbers'[Value] )
```

This will return the median value for the numbers in our **Numbers** table, which—as we can see from *Figure 10-8*—matches the value we got for the 50th percentile in our previous example:

Figure 10-8: The median figure

The MEDIANX function, like the other iterator functions, requires a table for its first parameter, which it will use to iterate over. For its second parameter, it requires an expression, which it will evaluate for each row in the table over which it is iterating. From the dataset it computes, it will then calculate the value of the median.

Ranking your data

DAX has a couple of functions that enable us to sort and rank data in a table. The first of these—the RANK.EQ function—will calculate a value for the rank of a number in a specified column of numbers.

The RANK.EQ function

The syntax for the RANK.EQ function is as follows:

```
RANK.EQ ( <Value>, <ColumnName> [, <Order>] )
```

For the first parameter, we need to specify the value that is to be ranked. For the second parameter, we need to give the column against which the value will be ranked. Finally, we can specify an optional order over which the ranking is to be applied. This can be either ascending (ASC) or descending (DESC). If it is not specified, then the default order will be descending.

> It is quite common to use the same column for both the value and the column name parameters.

We can demonstrate the use of the RANK.EQ function by adding a new calculated column to the **Numbers** table we created in the previous section on working with percentiles. Create a new column using the following expression:

```
Rank of value = RANK.EQ ( Numbers[Value], Numbers[Value], ASC )
```

This will produce the result shown in *Figure 10-9*:

Value	Rank of value
1	1
2	2
3	3
4	4
5	5
6	6
7	7
8	8
9	9
10	10
11	11
12	12
13	13
14	14
15	15
16	16
17	17
18	18
19	19
20	20

Figure 10-9: Ranking values in a table with the RANK.EQ function

The RANK.EQ is mostly used for compatibility with Excel and is usually only used when migrating a formula. The RANKX function provides more flexibility and is the function that is more often used for ranking data.

The RANKX function

Unlike many of the other iterator X functions, RANKX is not just an iterator version of the RANK.EQ function. It offers us much more flexibility in how we can rank our data.

The syntax for the RANKX function is as follows:

```
RANKX ( <Table>, <Expression> [, <Value>] [, <Order>] [, <Ties>] )
```

For the first parameter, we need to give a table name or an expression that returns a table. The second parameter is an expression that will evaluate to a scalar value. The function will iterate through the table, ordering the values returned by the expression with a ranking number.

The remaining parameters are all optional. The third parameter is a scalar DAX expression, whose value will be used to find the ranking. If this parameter is omitted, then the value of the expression given for the second parameter will be evaluated for the current row and used instead. In practice, the third parameter is usually omitted, unless there is a special reason to use it.

The fourth parameter defines the order over which the ranking is to be applied. This can either be ascending (ASC) or descending (DESC). If it is not specified, then the default order will be descending.

Finally, the fifth optional parameter defines how the ranking for tied values will be treated. Specifying Dense for this parameter will mean that the next rank value, after a tie, will be the next rank value in the sequence. For example, you may have a ranking sequence that looks like this: *1,2,3,3,4,5*. Specifying Skip for this parameter means that the next rank value, after a tie, will skip over the count of tied values. For example, you may have a ranking sequence that looks like this: *1,2,3,3,3,6,7*.

Slightly confusingly, the RANKX function can be used in expressions that create both calculated columns and measures. We'll start our practical examples by creating a new calculated column for the **Product** table that ranks values for the **Total Sales** measure for a row against all the other rows in the **Product** table. The following expression can be used to create the new column:

```
RANKX Total Sales by Product =
RANKX (
    'Product',
    [Total Sales]
)
```

We can see the result of adding this new column in *Figure 10-10*:

Product Name	Total Sales	RANKX Total Sales by Product
Proseware Projector 1080p DLP86 White	£51,901,056.27	1
Proseware Projector 1080p DLP86 Silver	£51,484,223.07	2
Proseware Projector 1080p DLP86 Black	£49,266,460.53	3
Proseware Projector 1080p LCD86 White	£47,504,870.55	4
Contoso Projector 1080p X980 White	£47,499,546.15	5
Proseware Projector 1080p LCD86 Black	£46,883,476.35	6
Contoso Projector 1080p X980 Silver	£46,779,948.90	7
Contoso Projector 1080p X980 Black	£45,935,343.00	8
Proseware Projector 1080p LCD86 Silver	£45,886,757.85	9
Fabrikam Independent Filmmaker 1" 25mm X400 Blue	£31,744,337.40	10
Fabrikam Independent Filmmaker 1/2" 3mm X300 Black	£28,884,788.40	11
Adventure Works Desktop PC1.80 ED182 Brown	£25,815,220.92	12
Adventure Works Laptop19W X1980 White	£25,499,421.96	13
Adventure Works Laptop19W X1980 Blue	£25,354,960.17	14
Adventure Works Desktop PC1.80 ED182 White	£25,298,914.21	15
Fabrikam Independent Filmmaker 2/3" 17mm X100 Black	£25,212,825.00	16
Adventure Works Desktop PC1.80 ED182 Silver	£25,047,404.52	17
Fabrikam Laptop19W M9800 Black	£25,022,218.76	18
Adventure Works Desktop PC1.80 ED182 Black	£24,550,173.98	19
Fabrikam Laptop19 M9000 Black	£24,280,404.82	20
Adventure Works Laptop19W X1980 Silver	£24,083,654.85	21
Adventure Works Laptop19W X1980 Red	£23,689,681.14	22

Figure 10-10: Ranking values in a table with the RANKX function

The new column ranks each of the products based on the value in the **Total Sales** column, with the product with the highest value in the **Total Sales** column ranked as 1. This is because, by default, the RANKX function will order those products with a higher total sales amount with a lower ranking.

We can change this order by specifying the order parameter. Let's amend the definition of the expression we used to create our calculated column by adding ASC as the fourth parameter, like this:

```
RANKX Total Sales by Product =
RANKX (
    'Product',
    [Total Sales],,
    ASC
)
```

This will give us a new result, which can be seen in *Figure 10-11*:

Product Name	Total Sales	RANKX Total Sales by Product
Proseware Projector 1080p DLP86 White	£51,901,056.27	1690
Proseware Projector 1080p DLP86 Silver	£51,484,223.07	1689
Proseware Projector 1080p DLP86 Black	£49,266,460.53	1688
Proseware Projector 1080p LCD86 White	£47,504,870.55	1687
Contoso Projector 1080p X980 White	£47,499,546.15	1686
Proseware Projector 1080p LCD86 Black	£46,883,476.35	1685
Contoso Projector 1080p X980 Silver	£46,779,948.90	1684
Contoso Projector 1080p X980 Black	£45,935,343.00	1683
Proseware Projector 1080p LCD86 Silver	£45,886,757.85	1682
Fabrikam Independent Filmmaker 1" 25mm X400 Blue	£31,744,337.40	1681
Fabrikam Independent Filmmaker 1/2" 3mm X300 Black	£28,884,788.40	1680
Adventure Works Desktop PC1.80 ED182 Brown	£25,815,220.92	1679
Adventure Works Laptop19W X1980 White	£25,499,421.96	1678
Adventure Works Laptop19W X1980 Blue	£25,354,960.17	1677
Adventure Works Desktop PC1.80 ED182 White	£25,298,914.21	1676
Fabrikam Independent Filmmaker 2/3" 17mm X100 Black	£25,212,825.00	1675
Adventure Works Desktop PC1.80 ED182 Silver	£25,047,404.52	1674
Fabrikam Laptop19W M9800 Black	£25,022,218.76	1673
Adventure Works Desktop PC1.80 ED182 Black	£24,550,173.98	1672
Fabrikam Laptop19 M9000 Black	£24,280,404.82	1671
Adventure Works Laptop19W X1980 Silver	£24,083,654.85	1670
Adventure Works Laptop19W X1980 Red	£23,689,681.14	1669

Figure 10-11: Ranking values in a table with the RANKX function in ascending order

Now, the products with higher values in the **Total Sales** column are ranked with a higher ranking.

Although we don't have any tied rankings in the preceding screenshot, if we did, by default, they would skip rankings. If we didn't want any gaps in the rankings, then we could override the default behavior by specifying Dense for the fifth optional parameter.

Next, we are going to look at how you we create a calculated column that enables us to apply rankings within a subgroup. To do this, we need to make use of the FILTER function.

Let's create a new calculated column in the **Product** table by using the following expression:

```
RANKX Total Sales by Product (by Subgroup) =
RANKX (
    FILTER (
        'Product',
        'Product'[Manufacturer] = EARLIER( 'Product'[Manufacturer] )
    ),
    [Total Sales]
)
```

The use of the FILTER function adds an additional row context to the calculation, based on the value in the **Manufacturer** column. The RANKX function is now only evaluating rows in the **Product** table where the value of the **Manufacturer** is equal to the value of the **Manufacturer** of the current row.

We can see the result of this new column in *Figure 10-12*:

Manufacturer	Total Sales	RANKX Total Sales by Product (by Subgroup)
Fabrikam SLR Camera 35" M358 Pink	£2,928,902.24	155
Fabrikam Social Videographer 2/3" 17mm E100 Black	£2,922,328.00	156
Fabrikam Social Videographer 2/3" 17mm E100 Orange	£2,803,043.20	157
Fabrikam Laptop8.9W E0880 Silver	£2,556,136.80	158
Fabrikam Social Videographer 2/3" 17mm E100 White	£2,534,280.50	159
Fabrikam Social Videographer 2/3" 17mm E100 Blue	£2,338,087.16	160
Fabrikam Laptop8.9 M0801 Silver	£1,356,403.89	161
Fabrikam SLR Camera M148 Gold	£1,077,389.80	162
Fabrikam Laptop8.9 E0800 Silver	£538,713.60	163
Contoso, Ltd		
Contoso Projector 1080p X980 White	£47,499,546.15	1
Contoso Projector 1080p X980 Silver	£46,779,948.90	2
Contoso Projector 1080p X980 Black	£45,935,343.00	3
Contoso Projector 720p M621 White	£20,212,497.27	4
Contoso Projector 720p M621 Silver	£20,068,391.52	5
Contoso Home Theater System 7.1 Channel M1700 Black	£19,903,696.54	6
Contoso Projector 720p M621 Black	£19,480,799.70	7
Contoso Home Theater System 7.1 Channel M1700 Brown	£19,413,759.75	8
Contoso Home Theater System 7.1 Channel M1700 White	£19,086,278.82	9
Contoso Home Theater System 7.1 Channel M1700 Silver	£18,633,911.17	10
Contoso Projector 720p M620 White	£14,527,275.06	11
Contoso Projector 720p M620 Black	£14,499,042.45	12
Contoso SLR Camera X143 Grey	£13,933,838.86	13
Contoso SLR Camera X144 Silver Grey	£13,790,961.21	14

Figure 10-12: Applying rankings using subgroups

As we can see, the new column now gives a ranking that is reset when the value of the **Manufacturer** column changes.

Now, we are going to move on to looking at using the RANKX function with a measure. We'll start by creating a simple measure that ranks products by the value of total sales, by the manufacturer. We can do this by creating a new measure with the following expression:

```
RANKX Products by Manufacturer =
RANKX (
    ALL ( 'Product'[Manufacturer] ),
    [Total Sales],,
    ASC,
    Dense
)
```

With this measure, we have also specified that the order should be ascending and that tied values should use a Dense ranking. This means that manufacturers with a higher value for total sales will be ranked with a higher-ranking number. It also means that where there are tied values, the next rank number, after a tie, will be the next rank number in the sequence.

The result of this expression can be seen in *Figure 10-13*:

Manufacturer	Total Sales	RANKX Products by Manufacturer
Fabrikam, Inc.	£1,874,455,854.35	10
Contoso, Ltd	£1,497,920,768.36	9
Adventure Works	£1,089,734,248.74	8
Proseware, Inc.	£954,540,220.53	7
Wide World Importers	£811,532,851.91	6
The Phone Company	£673,525,407.96	5
A. Datum Corporation	£619,803,753.56	4
Southridge Video	£471,653,445.03	3
Litware, Inc.	£327,894,810.44	2
Northwind Traders	£20,163,003.97	1

Figure 10-13: Using the RANKX function with a measure

For this measure, we are making use of the ALL function. In this case, instead of being used to remove filters from the filter context, as it would when used with the CALCULATE function, it is being used to return a table that contains a distinct list of manufacturers from the **Product** table. The RANKX function will then use this to iterate over, using the **Total Sales** measure to calculate the order of ranking.

If we now add another column from the **Product** table to act as a subgroup, we will find that the RANKX measure automatically ranks the value of the **Total Sales** measure, by **Manufacturer**, within that subgroup.

This can be seen in *Figure 10-14*, and is when we add the **Class** column from the **Product** table to our visual:

Class	Total Sales	RANKX Products by Manufacturer ▼
Deluxe		
Fabrikam, Inc.	£420,114,104.80	10
Contoso, Ltd	£379,160,840.05	9
Proseware, Inc.	£375,496,320.92	8
Adventure Works	£227,126,317.70	7
Wide World Importers	£201,039,835.86	6
The Phone Company	£197,094,815.33	5
Southridge Video	£79,416,013.42	4
A. Datum Corporation	£71,882,480.30	3
Litware, Inc.	£6,606,812.05	2
Economy		
Contoso, Ltd	£277,868,875.39	10
Wide World Importers	£191,553,277.11	9
Fabrikam, Inc.	£150,969,141.35	8
Adventure Works	£148,905,083.74	7
Southridge Video	£129,786,863.57	6
Proseware, Inc.	£101,011,593.31	5
A. Datum Corporation	£97,045,726.08	4
Litware, Inc.	£51,517,141.64	3
The Phone Company	£48,025,341.10	2

Figure 10-14: Using the ranking measure with subgroups

However, if we want to look at ranking based on the combination of values from the **Manufacturer** and **Class** columns, we will need to change the definition of our measure. We will need to add the **Class** column from the **Product** table to the parameters of the ALL function. The following code shows the expression that's used for our revised measure:

```
RANKX Products by Class and Manufacturer =
RANKX (
    ALL (
        'Product'[Class],
        'Product'[Manufacturer]
```

```
    ),
    [Total Sales],
    ,
    ASC,
    Dense
)
```

The result of this revised measure can be seen in *Figure 10-15*, where we now have the ranking for the value of the **Total Sales** measure applied over the combination of the **Class** and **Manufacturer** columns:

Class	Manufacturer	Total Sales	RANKX Products by Class and Manufacturer
Regular	Fabrikam, Inc.	£1,303,372,608.20	29
Regular	Contoso, Ltd	£840,891,052.92	28
Regular	Adventure Works	£713,702,847.29	27
Regular	Proseware, Inc.	£478,032,306.30	26
Regular	A. Datum Corporation	£450,875,547.18	25
Regular	The Phone Company	£428,405,251.53	24
Deluxe	Fabrikam, Inc.	£420,114,104.80	23
Regular	Wide World Importers	£418,939,738.94	22
Deluxe	Contoso, Ltd	£379,160,840.05	21
Deluxe	Proseware, Inc.	£375,496,320.92	20
Economy	Contoso, Ltd	£277,868,875.39	19
Regular	Litware, Inc.	£269,770,856.75	18
Regular	Southridge Video	£262,450,568.03	17
Deluxe	Adventure Works	£227,126,317.70	16
Deluxe	Wide World Importers	£201,039,835.86	15
Deluxe	The Phone Company	£197,094,815.33	14
Economy	Wide World Importers	£191,553,277.11	13
Economy	Fabrikam, Inc.	£150,969,141.35	12

Figure 10-15: Using the revised ranking measure

We could calculate the ranking over additional columns from the **Product** table simply by adding them to the parameters of the ALL function and then adding them to our table visual.

Calculating standard deviation and variance

This group of DAX functions contains several aggregation functions that will help you to calculate the standard deviation and variance of a population. There are two variations of each function: one with a suffix of .P and the other with a suffix of .S. The functions that end with .P calculate the result using a formula that is based on the assumption that the data represents the entire population. Those ending with .S use a slightly different formula that is based on the assumption that the data represents a sample of the entire population.

As with the other functions in this group, there are also versions of the functions that work with a single column and versions that iterate over a table, evaluating an expression. Let's start by looking at the four functions that will help you to calculate standard deviation.

 A detailed explanation of standard deviation is beyond the scope of this book. However, if you would like to find out more about it, check out the Wikipedia page on standard deviation at `https://en.wikipedia.org/wiki/standard_deviation`.

The syntax for the STDEV.P function is as follows:

```
STDEV.P ( <ColumnName> )
```

The syntax for the STDEV.S function is as follows:

```
STDEV.S ( <ColumnName> )
```

The syntax for the STDEVX.P function is as follows:

```
STDEVX.P ( <Table>, <Expression> )
```

The syntax for the STDEVX.S function is as follows:

```
STDEVX.S ( <Table>, <Expression> )
```

To demonstrate the use of these standard deviation functions, we are going to create some new measures, based around the sales quantity. Create these by using the following expressions:

```
Avg Sales Quantity = AVERAGE ( Sales[Sales Quantity] )
Min Sale Quantity = MIN ( Sales[Sales Quantity] )
Max Sales Quantity = MAX ( Sales[Sales Quantity] )
StdDevP Sales Quantity = STDEV.P ( Sales[Sales Quantity] )
StdDevS Sales Quantity = STDEV.S ( Sales[Sales Quantity] )
```

Now, we can add these to a table visual, along with the **Product Name** column from the **Product** table. This gives us the result shown in *Figure 10-16*:

Product Name	Avg Sales Quantity	Min Sale Quantity	Max Sales Quantity	StdDevP Sales Quantity	StdDevS Sales Quantity
A. Datum Advanced Digital Camera M300 Azure	12.18	8	52	5.10	5.10
A. Datum Advanced Digital Camera M300 Black	12.10	8	78	5.26	5.26
A. Datum Advanced Digital Camera M300 Green	12.44	8	60	5.91	5.91
A. Datum Advanced Digital Camera M300 Grey	12.26	8	72	5.67	5.67
A. Datum Advanced Digital Camera M300 Orange	12.35	8	72	5.89	5.89
A. Datum Advanced Digital Camera M300 Pink	12.16	8	108	5.66	5.66
A. Datum Advanced Digital Camera M300 Silver	12.02	8	54	5.04	5.05
A. Datum All in One Digital Camera M200 Azure	12.47	8	40	5.14	5.15
A. Datum All in One Digital Camera M200 Black	12.25	8	72	5.76	5.76
A. Datum All in One Digital Camera M200 Green	12.31	8	78	5.86	5.86
A. Datum All in One Digital Camera M200 Grey	12.49	8	182	7.31	7.31
A. Datum All in One Digital Camera M200 Orange	12.28	8	52	5.18	5.18
A. Datum All in One Digital Camera M200 Pink	12.11	8	72	5.48	5.48
A. Datum All in One Digital Camera M200 Silver	12.11	8	60	5.13	5.13
A. Datum Bridge Digital Camera M300 Azure	12.10	8	52	5.08	5.09
A. Datum Bridge Digital Camera M300 Black	12.27	8	65	5.40	5.40
A. Datum Bridge Digital Camera M300 Green	12.26	8	72	5.74	5.75
A. Datum Bridge Digital Camera M300 Grey	12.28	8	104	6.02	6.02
A. Datum Bridge Digital Camera M300 Orange	12.11	8	78	5.42	5.42
A. Datum Bridge Digital Camera M300 Pink	12.31	8	104	6.03	6.03
A. Datum Bridge Digital Camera M300 Silver	12.21	8	39	4.82	4.82
A. Datum Compact Digital Camera M200 Azure	11.35	4	78	9.11	9.11
A. Datum Compact Digital Camera M200 Green	11.48	4	72	9.27	9.27
A. Datum Compact Digital Camera M200 Grey	11.03	4	78	8.74	8.74
A. Datum Compact Digital Camera M200 Orange	11.53	4	80	9.21	9.22
A. Datum Compact Digital Camera M200 Pink	11.30	4	96	9.21	9.21
A. Datum Compact Digital Camera M200 Silver	11.19	4	78	8.49	8.49
A. Datum Consumer Digital Camera E100 Azure	11.54	6	104	5.53	5.54
A. Datum Consumer Digital Camera E100 Black	11.56	6	78	5.74	5.75
Total	16.17	4	2880	39.35	39.35

Figure 10-16: Table using standard deviation functions

You will see that, in some cases, there is a slight variation in the results calculated by the STDEV.P and STDEV.S functions. The STDEV.S function may calculate a higher standard deviation than the STDEV.P function.

Now, let's turn our attention to the functions that will calculate variance.

The syntax for the VAR.S function is as follows:

```
VAR.S ( <columnName> )
```

The syntax for the VAR.P function is as follows:

```
VAR.P ( <columnName> )
```

The syntax for the VARX.S function is as follows:

```
VARX.S ( <table>, <expression> )
```

The syntax for the VARX.P function is as follows:

```
VARX.P ( <table>, <expression> )
```

We can demonstrate the use of these variance functions by creating a couple more measures, based on sales quantity. Create these new measures by using the following expressions:

```
VarP Sales Quantity = VAR.P ( Sales[Sales Quantity] )
VarS Sales Quantity = VAR.S ( Sales[Sales Quantity] )
```

We can then add these to the table we created in this example, which will give us the result shown in *Figure 10-17*:

Product Name	Avg Sales Quantity	Min Sale Quantity	Max Sales Quantity	StdDevP Sales Quantity	StdDevS Sales Quantity	VarP Sales Quantity	VarS Sales Quantity
A. Datum Advanced Digital Camera M300 Azure	12.18	8	52	5.10	5.10	26.02	26.03
A. Datum Advanced Digital Camera M300 Black	12.10	8	78	5.26	5.26	27.64	27.66
A. Datum Advanced Digital Camera M300 Green	12.44	8	60	5.91	5.91	34.88	34.90
A. Datum Advanced Digital Camera M300 Grey	12.26	8	72	5.67	5.67	32.11	32.13
A. Datum Advanced Digital Camera M300 Orange	12.35	8	72	5.89	5.89	34.72	34.74
A. Datum Advanced Digital Camera M300 Pink	12.16	8	108	5.66	5.66	32.03	32.05
A. Datum Advanced Digital Camera M300 Silver	12.02	8	54	5.04	5.05	25.44	25.45
A. Datum All in One Digital Camera M200 Azure	12.47	8	40	5.14	5.15	26.42	26.49
A. Datum All in One Digital Camera M200 Black	12.25	8	72	5.76	5.76	33.21	33.23
A. Datum All in One Digital Camera M200 Green	12.31	8	78	5.86	5.86	34.32	34.34
A. Datum All in One Digital Camera M200 Grey	12.49	8	182	7.31	7.31	53.46	53.49
A. Datum All in One Digital Camera M200 Orange	12.28	8	52	5.18	5.18	26.81	26.83
A. Datum All in One Digital Camera M200 Pink	12.11	8	72	5.48	5.48	30.06	30.08
A. Datum All in One Digital Camera M200 Silver	12.11	8	60	5.13	5.13	26.28	26.30
A. Datum Bridge Digital Camera M300 Azure	12.10	8	52	5.08	5.09	25.85	25.87
A. Datum Bridge Digital Camera M300 Black	12.27	8	65	5.40	5.40	29.19	29.21
A. Datum Bridge Digital Camera M300 Green	12.26	8	72	5.74	5.75	33.00	33.02
A. Datum Bridge Digital Camera M300 Grey	12.28	8	104	6.02	6.02	36.21	36.23
A. Datum Bridge Digital Camera M300 Orange	12.11	8	78	5.42	5.42	29.36	29.38
A. Datum Bridge Digital Camera M300 Pink	12.31	8	104	6.03	6.03	36.33	36.35
A. Datum Bridge Digital Camera M300 Silver	12.21	8	39	4.82	4.82	23.19	23.24
A. Datum Compact Digital Camera M200 Azure	11.35	4	78	9.11	9.11	82.90	82.95
A. Datum Compact Digital Camera M200 Green	11.48	4	72	9.27	9.27	85.91	85.96
A. Datum Compact Digital Camera M200 Grey	11.03	4	78	8.74	8.74	76.32	76.36
A. Datum Compact Digital Camera M200 Orange	11.53	4	80	9.21	9.22	84.91	84.96
A. Datum Compact Digital Camera M200 Pink	11.30	4	96	9.21	9.21	84.75	84.80
A. Datum Compact Digital Camera M200 Silver	11.19	4	78	8.49	8.49	72.09	72.13
A. Datum Consumer Digital Camera E100 Azure	11.54	6	104	5.53	5.54	30.63	30.65
A. Datum Consumer Digital Camera E100 Black	11.56	6	76	5.74	5.75	32.99	33.01
Total	16.17	4	2880	39.35	39.35	1,548.45	1,548.45

Figure 10-17: Table with variance functions added

As with the standard deviation functions, the variance functions will calculate the variance slightly differently. The VAR.S function may calculate a higher variance than the VAR.P function.

Summary

In this chapter, we looked at the group of DAX functions used to help us calculate statistical data. We started with a look at the complete list of the functions in this group, along with a brief description of each. We then moved on to look in more detail at some of the more commonly used functions in this group.

We looked at those functions that can be used to calculate averages, percentiles, and to rank our data, all while working through some examples of each function being used. We rounded off this chapter by taking a brief look at those functions that can be used to calculate standard deviation and variance.

In the next chapter, we will move beyond the different groups of DAX functions and take a look at some examples of DAX patterns.

11
Working with DAX Patterns

In this chapter, we're going to look at the concept of DAX patterns. As with other software design patterns, a DAX pattern consists of a template that forms the basis of a reusable solution to a commonly encountered problem.

We'll start with an introduction to the Quick Measures feature in Power BI Desktop. As the name suggests, this is a quick and easy way to create a DAX measure, without needing to know any DAX code. Behind the scenes, it uses predefined DAX patterns that are completed using the responses you provide through the Quick Measures dialog.

Having explored how the Quick Measures feature works, we'll look at some examples of the measures that are available by using them with hands-on examples.

The chapter is broken into the following sections:

- Introducing Power BI Quick Measures
- Calculating cumulative totals
- Binning data using segmentation
- Comparing equivalent periods
- Working with mathematical patterns

Introducing Power BI Quick Measures

In software engineering, a coding pattern refers to a coding solution in the form of a template or partially completed code that can be used repeatedly in different scenarios. It provides a way to develop software using a tried-and-tested approach.

The idea of DAX patterns also centers around the concept of reusable templates that contain a set of DAX expressions. There are plenty of examples of DAX patterns available on the internet, but the easiest way to get started is through the Quick Measures feature in Power BI Desktop.

> If you want a great example of a site that provides a wide range of DAX patterns, check out the following site: `https://www.daxpatterns.com/`.

The Quick Measures feature in Power BI Desktop provides a great way to quickly create commonly used and powerful measures in your Power BI report. Better still, like all measures, they are built using a set of DAX expressions that you can access and modify to meet your exact requirements. They are also created using proven DAX code, which means they are a reliable way to start creating DAX measures.

> Although the idea behind Quick Measures is that you can start creating measures without needing to know any DAX, understanding how the code they generate works does require a good level of DAX knowledge.

At the time of writing this book, the Quick Measures feature contains patterns that fall within the following categories:

- Aggregations per category
- Filters
- Time intelligence
- Totals
- Mathematical operations
- Text

Another great thing about the DAX patterns that are created by Quick Measures is that the DAX code they generate can be reused in Excel Power Pivot, **SQL Server Analysis Services (SSAS)** Tabular, and anywhere else that DAX is used.

Creating your first quick measure

There are a couple of ways you can get started with creating a quick measure in Power BI Desktop, as follows:

1. Right-click on any item in the **Fields** pane and select **New quick measure** from the context menu that appears, as shown in *Figure 11-1*:

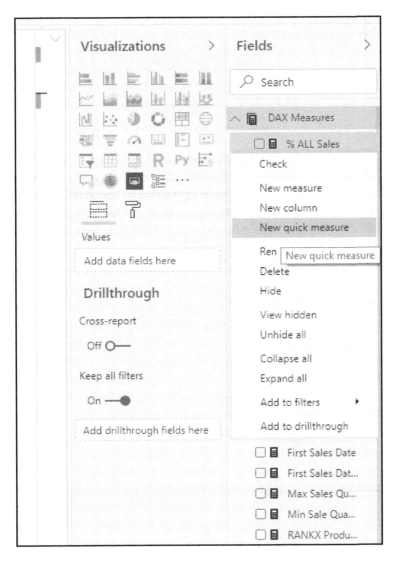

Figure 11-1: Create a new quick measure from the field context menu in Power BI Desktop

2. Alternatively, click on the **New Quick Measure** button on the **Calculations** section of the **Home** ribbon, as shown in *Figure 11-2*:

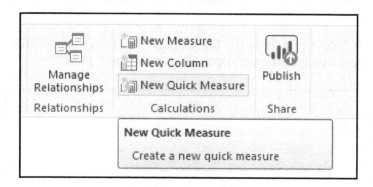

Figure 11-2: Create a new quick measure from the Calculations section of the Home ribbon in Power BI Desktop

3. This will bring up the **Quick Measures** dialog, where you will be able to select, from a drop-down menu, the type of calculation you want to use to create your new measure, along with the fields you want to use with the calculation.

4. *Figure 11-3* shows the **Quick Measures** dialog. On the left-hand side is the list of available calculations, while on the right-hand side is the list of the tables and fields available from your data model:

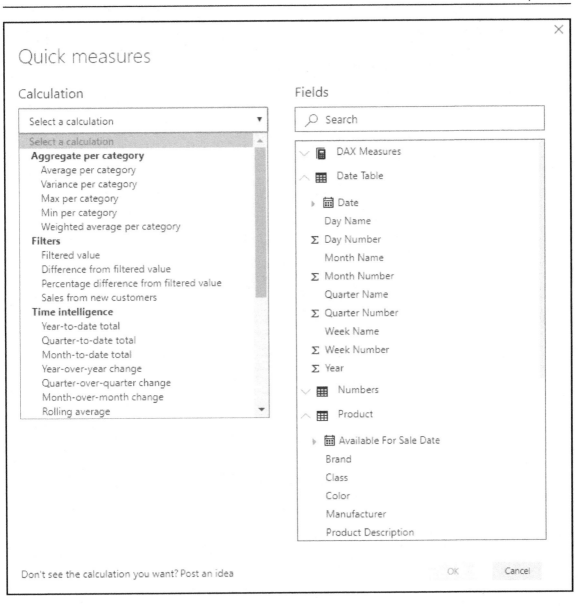

Figure 11-3: The Quick measures dialog

5. To create a quick measure, select a calculation from the list on the left-hand side. In the example shown in *Figure 11-4*, we have picked the **Year-to-date total** measure from the **Time intelligence** group:

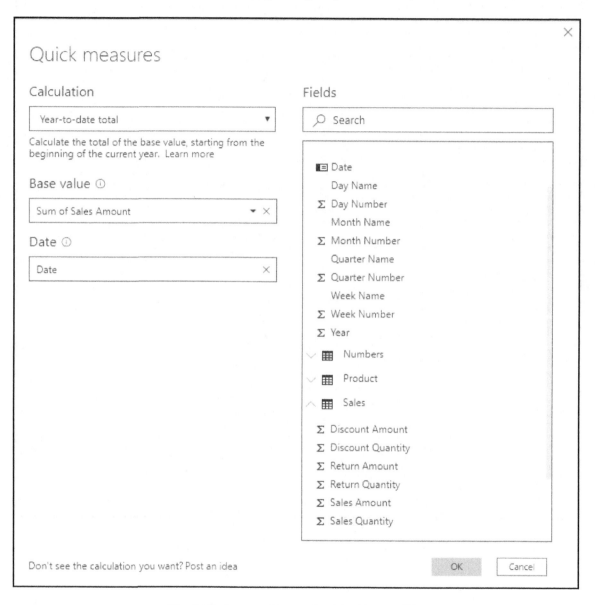

Figure 11-4: Creating a year-to-date measure through the quick measures dialog

6. For this measure, we'll populate the **Date** parameter with the **Date** field from the table called **Date table.**
7. For the **Base value** parameter, we'll use the **Sales Amount** from the **Sales** table. The **Sales Amount** will be aggregated using the SUM function by default, but you can select other aggregations.
8. Click on the **OK** button to create the new quick measure.

Once the measure is created, you will have an example of an expression that follows a defined code pattern:

Date	Sales Amount	Sales Amount running total in Date
01/01/2007 00:00:00	£6,085,839.18	£6,085,839.18
02/01/2007 00:00:00	£6,270,657.17	£12,356,496.35
03/01/2007 00:00:00	£6,096,024.11	£18,452,520.46
04/01/2007 00:00:00	£5,979,164.13	£24,431,684.59
05/01/2007 00:00:00	£5,926,584.02	£30,358,268.61
06/01/2007 00:00:00	£6,150,610.75	£36,508,879.36
07/01/2007 00:00:00	£6,517,040.34	£43,025,919.70
08/01/2007 00:00:00	£5,856,724.52	£48,882,644.22
09/01/2007 00:00:00	£6,184,820.44	£55,067,464.66
10/01/2007 00:00:00	£6,612,222.96	£61,679,687.61
11/01/2007 00:00:00	£6,524,046.81	£68,203,734.42
12/01/2007 00:00:00	£5,889,201.15	£74,092,935.57
13/01/2007 00:00:00	£6,330,346.71	£80,423,282.28
14/01/2007 00:00:00	£5,945,346.59	£86,368,628.88
15/01/2007 00:00:00	£6,385,077.45	£92,753,706.32
16/01/2007 00:00:00	£6,173,139.29	£98,926,845.61
17/01/2007 00:00:00	£6,709,543.94	£105,636,389.55
18/01/2007 00:00:00	£6,143,140.45	£111,779,530.00
19/01/2007 00:00:00	£6,034,566.93	£117,814,096.93
20/01/2007 00:00:00	£6,354,141.60	£124,168,238.53
Total	**£8,341,224,364.83**	**£8,341,224,364.83**

Figure 11-5: Adding the year-to-date quick measure to a table

Figure 11-5 shows this measure added to a table that also shows the total **Sales Amount** for each day. As you can see, our new measure gives us a way of calculating a running total. In the next section, we'll be looking at the code behind this measure, along with some other examples of code that have been created following a DAX pattern.

Calculating cumulative totals

In the previous section of this chapter, we looked at creating a quick measure for year-to-date totals. The DAX expression that is created for this measure is an example of the Cumulative Total pattern. In this case, the pattern is used to create a running total of the **Sales Amount** field by the **Date** field.

The following code is the DAX expression that was created for this example:

```
Sales Amount running total in Date =
CALCULATE (
    SUM ( 'Sales'[Sales Amount] ),
    FILTER (
        ALLSELECTED ( 'Date Table'[Date] ),
        ISONORAFTER ( 'Date Table'[Date], MAX ( 'Date Table'[Date] ), DESC
)
    )
)
```

- The expression works by using the FILTER and ISONORAFTER functions to return a table of dates that are less than or equal to the date of the current row.
- The measure then calculates the SUM of **Sales Amount** for all sales made on dates that are equal to those returned by this table.

The following code block shows a very similar pattern that could be used to calculate the same result, but is slightly easier to understand:

```
Sales Amount running total in Date 2 =
CALCULATE (
    SUM ( 'Sales'[Sales Amount] ),
    FILTER (
        ALLSELECTED ( 'Date Table'[Date] ),
        'Date Table'[Date] <= MAX ( 'Date Table'[Date] )
    )
)
```

The Cumulative Total pattern we are following here requires that your data model contains a **Date Table** that is correctly marked as a date table. The date referred to in the pattern must be the date column from that **Date Table**.

Although not strictly necessary, we can enhance the pattern to include a check that will prevent totals being displayed for any dates that are greater than any of the dates in the **Sales** table, as follows:

```
Sales Amount running total in Date 3 =
IF (
    MIN ( 'Date Table'[Date] )
        <= CALCULATE ( MAX ( Sales[SalesDateKey] ), ALL ( Sales ) ),
    CALCULATE (
        SUM ( 'Sales'[Sales Amount] ),
        FILTER (
            ALLSELECTED ( 'Date Table'[Date] ),
            'Date Table'[Date] <= MAX ( 'Date Table'[Date] )
        )
    )
)
```

Figure 11-6 shows the table of sales by date extended to include our two additional measures:

Date	Sales Amount	Sales Amount running total in Date	Sales Amount running total in Date 2	Sales Amount running total in Date 3
21/12/2009 00:00:00	£7,192,199.87	£8,268,672,851.09	£8,268,672,851.0889	£8,268,672,851.0889
22/12/2009 00:00:00	£7,297,809.94	£8,275,970,661.03	£8,275,970,661.0259	£8,275,970,661.0259
23/12/2009 00:00:00	£7,166,257.40	£8,283,136,918.43	£8,283,136,918.4294	£8,283,136,918.4294
24/12/2009 00:00:00	£7,291,113.96	£8,290,428,032.39	£8,290,428,032.3909	£8,290,428,032.3909
25/12/2009 00:00:00	£7,131,232.46	£8,297,559,264.85	£8,297,559,264.8509	£8,297,559,264.8509
26/12/2009 00:00:00	£7,263,444.05	£8,304,822,708.90	£8,304,822,708.8999	£8,304,822,708.8999
27/12/2009 00:00:00	£7,244,858.75	£8,312,067,567.65	£8,312,067,567.6499	£8,312,067,567.6499
28/12/2009 00:00:00	£6,958,378.37	£8,319,025,946.02	£8,319,025,946.0199	£8,319,025,946.0199
29/12/2009 00:00:00	£7,514,756.49	£8,326,540,702.51	£8,326,540,702.5054	£8,326,540,702.5054
30/12/2009 00:00:00	£7,175,234.68	£8,333,715,937.19	£8,333,715,937.1854	£8,333,715,937.1854
31/12/2009 00:00:00	£7,508,427.65	£8,341,224,364.83	£8,341,224,364.8324	£8,341,224,364.8324
01/01/2010 00:00:00		£8,341,224,364.83	£8,341,224,364.8324	
02/01/2010 00:00:00		£8,341,224,364.83	£8,341,224,364.8324	
03/01/2010 00:00:00		£8,341,224,364.83	£8,341,224,364.8324	
04/01/2010 00:00:00		£8,341,224,364.83	£8,341,224,364.8324	
05/01/2010 00:00:00		£8,341,224,364.83	£8,341,224,364.8324	
06/01/2010 00:00:00		£8,341,224,364.83	£8,341,224,364.8324	
07/01/2010 00:00:00		£8,341,224,364.83	£8,341,224,364.8324	
08/01/2010 00:00:00		£8,341,224,364.83	£8,341,224,364.8324	
09/01/2010 00:00:00		£8,341,224,364.83	£8,341,224,364.8324	
Total	£8,341,224,364.83	£8,341,224,364.83	£8,341,224,364.8324	£8,341,224,364.8324

Figure 11-6: Table showing additional versions of year-to-date measures

As you can see, unlike the measures we created using the first two versions of the pattern, our third measure does not repeat the cumulative total when the dates go beyond the last date for which we have sales data in the **Sales** table.

Binning data using segmentation

Next, we are going to look at a DAX pattern that can be used to create a calculated column to segment data into different groups. Typical examples include age groups, product groups, and price banding. This process is also known as value binning, and it is particularly useful when you want to visualize data using histograms.

In this example, we are going to create a new column in the **Products** table that will group products based on the value of the **Unit Price** field.

The following code is the DAX expression for the new calculated column:

```
Unit Price Segment =
SWITCH (
    TRUE (),
    'Product'[Unit Price] < 100, "0-99",
    'Product'[Unit Price] < 200, "100-199",
    'Product'[Unit Price] < 300, "200-299",
    'Product'[Unit Price] < 400, "300-399",
    'Product'[Unit Price] < 500, "400-499",
    'Product'[Unit Price] < 600, "500-599",
    'Product'[Unit Price] < 700, "600-699",
    'Product'[Unit Price] < 800, "700-799",
    'Product'[Unit Price] < 900, "800-899",
    "900+"
)
```

This pattern uses the SWITCH function to create the groupings. *Figure 11-7* shows the number of products in each group as a histogram:

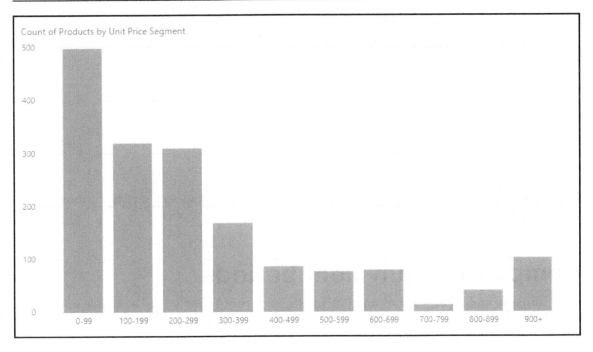

Figure 11-7: Binning products by price groups

In this example, the segments display in the correct order. However, depending on the names of your segment groups, you may also need to create an additional column to sort the segments by. So, for example, we might create a unit price band that consists of three segments: Low, Medium, and High.

The following DAX expression would create the segment column:

```
Unit Price Segment =
SWITCH (
    TRUE (),
    'Product'[Unit Price] < 200,  "Low",
    'Product'[Unit Price] < 600,  "Medium",
    "High"
)
```

When used in a visual, these groups would not display in the correct order. To correct this, we need to create a segment sorting column. The following DAX expression can be used to create this column:

```
Unit Price Segment Sort =
SWITCH (
    TRUE (),
    'Product'[Unit Price] < 200, 1,
    'Product'[Unit Price] < 600, 2,
    3
)
```

The segment column could then be configured to sort by the segment sorting column so that it displays in the correct order when used with visuals in reports.

Comparing equivalent periods

We've already looked at some of the time intelligence functions that are available in the DAX language. However, in this section, we are going look at how these—and other—functions can be applied to create a range of date and time patterns.

Comparing previous periods

For the first set of date patterns, we are going to look at some DAX expressions to create measures that will compare values over equivalent periods. The first of these will give the total sales quantity for the same period of the previous year.

The following expression will create a measure called **Sales Quantity PY** that will give the total sales quantity for the equivalent date in the previous year:

```
Sales Quantity PY =
CALCULATE (
    SUM ( Sales[Sales Quantity] ),
    SAMEPERIODLASTYEAR ( 'Date Table'[Date] )
)
```

Figure 11-8 shows this measure being used to create a graph showing a comparison of sales quantity with the same period for the previous year:

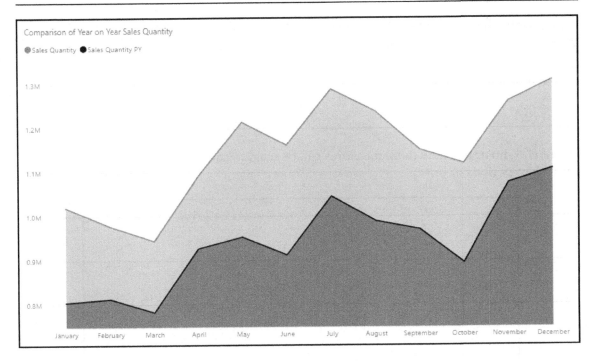

Figure 11-8: Comparison of sales quantity with the same period for the previous year

- The **Sales Quantity PY** measure makes use of the SAMEPERIODLASTYEAR time intelligence function to obtain the date from the previous year.
- However, this does restrict our comparison capability to the previous year only.
- If we want to go back beyond the previous year with our comparisons, then we need to use a pattern that utilizes the DATEADD function instead.

The following expression will create a measure called **Sales Quantity PY + 1** that will give the total sales quantity for the equivalent date 2 years previously:

```
Sales Quantity PY + 1 =
CALCULATE (
    SUM ( Sales[Sales Quantity] ),
    DATEADD ( 'Date Table'[Date], -2, YEAR )
)
```

As we will see with the next two examples, by simply changing the interval type and the number of intervals through the parameters of the DATEADD function, we can use this as a pattern to create measures that will calculate the values for previous quarters and previous months.

For example, the following expression will create a measure called **Sales Quantity PQ** that gives the total sales quantity for the equivalent date in the previous quarter:

```
Sales Quantity PQ =
CALCULATE (
    SUM ( Sales[Sales Quantity] ),
    DATEADD( 'Date Table'[Date], -1, QUARTER )
)
```

Figure 11-9 illustrates how these measures can be used to compare values against equivalent periods of time:

Year	Quarter Name	Sales Quantity	Sales Quantity PQ	Sales Quantity PY
2007	Q1	2,373,754		
2007	Q2	3,222,875	2,373,754	
2007	Q3	2,943,359	3,222,875	
2007	Q4	3,311,940	2,943,359	
2008	Q1	2,397,546	3,311,940	2,373,754
2008	Q2	2,791,503	2,397,546	3,222,875
2008	Q3	3,004,083	2,791,503	2,943,359
2008	Q4	3,077,267	3,004,083	3,311,940
2009	Q1	2,941,906	3,077,267	2,397,546
2009	Q2	3,467,389	2,941,906	2,791,503
2009	Q3	3,678,532	3,467,389	3,004,083
2009	Q4	3,690,256	3,678,532	3,077,267
Total		**36,900,410**	**33,210,154**	**23,122,327**

Figure 11-9: Using measures to compare sales quantity over different periods of time

Let's complete our set of equivalent period measures using this pattern by creating a measure to calculate the total sales quantity for the equivalent date in the previous month, as follows:

```
Sales Quantity PM =
CALCULATE (
    SUM ( Sales[Sales Quantity] ),
    DATEADD ( 'Date Table'[Date], -1, MONTH )
)
```

- Unfortunately, when it comes to comparing values for weekly periods, this pattern will not work since the available interval parameter options are days, months, quarters, and years.
- There is no interval option for weeks. Therefore, if we want to compare values against weeks, then the pattern we need to use will be more complex.

The following expression uses a pattern for comparing the value of sales quantity with the previous week:

```
Sales Quantity PW =
VAR CurrentWeek =
    SELECTEDVALUE ( 'Date Table'[Week Number] )
VAR CurrentYear =
    SELECTEDVALUE ( 'Date Table'[Year] )
VAR MaxWeekNumber =
    CALCULATE (
        MAX ( 'Date Table'[Week Number] ),
        FILTER ( ALL ( 'Date Table' ), 'Date Table'[Year] = CurrentYear )
    )
RETURN
    SUMX (
        FILTER (
            ALL ( 'Date Table' ),
            IF (
                CurrentWeek = 1,
                'Date Table'[Week Number] = MaxWeekNumber
                    && 'Date Table'[Year] = CurrentYear - 1,
                'Date Table'[Week Number] = CurrentWeek - 1
                    && 'Date Table'[Year] = CurrentYear
            )
        ),
        CALCULATE ( SUM ( Sales[Sales Quantity] ) )
    )
```

This pattern starts by setting variables for the current week, the current year, and the number of weeks in the current year, based on the row context. It then calculates the sales quantity for the previous week in the same year, unless it is week 1. If it is week **1**, it calculates the sales quantity for the last week (MaxWeekNumber) of the previous year.

This completes the set of previous period comparison patterns. Next, we will look at how we can calculate the period-on-period percentages.

Comparing the period-on-period percentages

Now that we have some measures to compare values over equivalent periods, we need a pattern to allow us to calculate the percentage difference between periods. To help us with this, there are a set of quick measures in the time intelligence group that will allow us to calculate the following:

- Year-over-year change
- Quarter-over-quarter change
- Month-over-month change

Let's start with the first option, to calculate the year-over-year percentage change. If we provide the **Sales Quantity** from the **Sales** table as the base value and **Date** from **Date Table** and specify 1 for the period, it will generate DAX code that we can use for our pattern.

The following expression will create a measure called **Sales Quantity YoY%**. This will give the percentage change between the total sales quantity for a given date and the equivalent date in the previous year, as follows:

```
Sales Quantity YoY% =
VAR __PREV_YEAR =
    CALCULATE (
        SUM ( 'Sales'[Sales Quantity] ),
        DATEADD ( 'Date Table'[Date], -1, YEAR )
    )
RETURN
    DIVIDE ( SUM ( 'Sales'[Sales Quantity] ) - __PREV_YEAR, __PREV_YEAR )
```

Figure 11-10 shows this measure being used to compare sales quantities year-over-year:

Year	Sales Quantity	Sales Quantity PY	Sales Quantity YoY%
2007	11,851,928		
2008	11,270,399	11,851,928	-4.91%
2009	13,778,083	11,270,399	22.25%
Total	**36,900,410**	**23,122,327**	**59.59%**

Figure 11-10: Comparing sales quantity year-over-year

We can use the same pattern to create measures that give the quarter-over-quarter percentage change and the month-over-month percentage change.

The following expression will create a measure to calculate the quarter-over-quarter percentage change:

```
Sales Quantity QoQ% =
VAR __PREV_QUARTER =
    CALCULATE (
        SUM ( 'Sales'[Sales Quantity] ),
        DATEADD ( 'Date Table'[Date], -1, QUARTER )
    )
RETURN
    DIVIDE ( SUM ( 'Sales'[Sales Quantity] ) - __PREV_QUARTER,
__PREV_QUARTER )
```

The following expression will create a measure to calculate the month-over-month percentage change:

```
Sales Quantity MoM% =
VAR __PREV_MONTH =
    CALCULATE (
        SUM ( 'Sales'[Sales Quantity] ),
        DATEADD ( 'Date Table'[Date], -1, MONTH )
    )
RETURN
    DIVIDE ( SUM ( 'Sales'[Sales Quantity] ) - __PREV_MONTH, __PREV_MONTH )
```

The only difference between the three measures in this group is the interval given as the third parameter of the DATEADD function.

This completes the set of patterns for calculating the period-on-period percentage changes. Next, we will look at a set of patterns for calculating period-to-date totals.

Calculating period-to-date totals

The patterns in this section make use of the time intelligence functions TOTALMTD, TOTALQTD, and TOTALYTD. We'll also look at a pattern for creating a DAX measure to calculate a week-to-date total. Let's start with a measure that will give us a running total of sales quantity for the month to date.

The following expression uses the TOTALMTD function to create a measure that calculates a running total of sales quantity for the month to date:

```
Sales Quantity MTD =
TOTALMTD (
    SUM ( 'Sales'[Sales Quantity] ),
    'Date Table'[Date]
)
```

The following expression uses a very similar pattern to create equivalent measures for the sales quantity totals for the quarter to date and year to date. This expression uses the TOTALQTD function to create a measure that calculates a running total of sales quantity for the quarter to date, as follows:

```
Sales Quantity QTD =
TOTALQTD (
    SUM ( 'Sales'[Sales Quantity] ),
    'Date Table'[Date]
)
```

The following expression uses the TOTALYTD function to create a measure that calculates a running total of sales quantity for the year to date:

```
Sales Quantity YTD =
TOTALYTD (
    SUM ( 'Sales'[Sales Quantity] ),
    'Date Table'[Date]
)
```

- The only difference between these three measures is the time intelligence function used.
- However, as with the previous period patterns, there is no time intelligence function to calculate week to date.
- When it comes to calculating the total for the week to date, then the pattern is more complicated.

The following expression follows a pattern for calculating a running total of sales quantity for the week to date:

```
Sales Quantity WTD =
VAR CurrentDate =
    LASTDATE ( 'Date Table'[Date] )
VAR DayNumberOfWeek =
    WEEKDAY (
        CurrentDate,
        3
```

```
    )
RETURN
    CALCULATE (
        SUM ( Sales[Sales Quantity] ),
        DATESBETWEEN (
            'Date Table'[Date],
            DATEADD (
                CurrentDate,
                -1 * DayNumberOfWeek,
                DAY
            ),
            CurrentDate
        )
    )
```

- The pattern starts by setting a variable for the current date.
- It then sets a variable for the day number of the week. For this, it uses the WEEKDAY function, with a value of 3 being passed as the return type parameter, to specify that the week starts on a Monday, with a day number of 0.
- Finally, in the return part of the expression, it calculates the sales quantity for the days between the start of the current week and the current date.

This completes the set of patterns for calculating period-to-date totals and our overall look at patterns for comparing values of equivalent periods. In the next section, we are going to finish off our look at DAX patterns with some examples of mathematical patterns.

Working with mathematical patterns

We are going to round off this chapter with a look at some examples of mathematical patterns, both simple and complex.

The following examples are based on the measures included in the *Mathematical operations* section of the Quick Measures feature found in Power BI Desktop:

1. First, we have some examples of basic mathematical operation patterns, starting with an expression that will create a measure using the addition pattern:

```
Sales Amount plus Sales Tax =
SUM ( 'Sales'[Sales Amount] ) + SUM ( 'Sales'[Sales Tax] )
```

2. The following expression will create a measure that uses the subtraction pattern:

```
Sales Amount minus Discount Amount =
SUM ( 'Sales'[Sales Amount] ) - SUM ( 'Sales'[Discount Amount] )
```

3. The following expression will create a measure that uses the multiplication pattern:

```
Unit Price x Sales Quantity =
SUM ( 'Sales'[Unit Price] ) * SUM ( 'Sales'[Sales Quantity] )
```

4. Finally, we have an expression that will create a measure that uses the division pattern:

```
Sales Amount divided by Sales Quantity =
DIVIDE ( SUM ( 'Sales'[Sales Amount] ), SUM ( 'Sales'[Sales
Quantity] ) )
```

5. Next, we have a couple of patterns that will calculate the percentage difference between two values. We'll start with an expression that will create a measure to calculate the percentage difference between the total sales amount and the total return amount, as follows:

```
Return Amount % difference from Sales Amount =
VAR __BASELINE_VALUE = SUM ( 'Sales'[Sales Amount] )
VAR __VALUE_TO_COMPARE = SUM ( 'Sales'[Return Amount] )
RETURN
    DIVIDE ( __VALUE_TO_COMPARE - __BASELINE_VALUE,
__BASELINE_VALUE )
```

6. With this measure, blanks are treated as zeros in the calculation. However, in the following example, the pattern is amended so that blanks will produce blanks in the output:

```
Return Amount % difference from Sales Amount 2 =
VAR __BASELINE_VALUE = SUM ( 'Sales'[Sales Amount] )
VAR __VALUE_TO_COMPARE = SUM ( 'Sales'[Return Amount] )
RETURN
    IF (
        NOT ISBLANK ( __VALUE_TO_COMPARE ),
        DIVIDE ( __VALUE_TO_COMPARE - __BASELINE_VALUE,
__BASELINE_VALUE )
    )
```

7. For the final mathematical pattern, we are going to look at a more complex operation. The following expression will create a measure that will calculate the **Pearson Correlation Coefficient (PCC)** over a given category:

```
Sales Quantity and Return Quantity correlation for Color =
VAR __CORRELATION_TABLE =
    VALUES ( 'Product'[Color] )
VAR __COUNT =
```

```
        COUNTX (
            KEEPFILTERS ( __CORRELATION_TABLE ),
            CALCULATE ( SUM ( 'Sales'[Sales Quantity] ) * SUM (
'Sales'[Return Quantity] ) )
        )
    VAR __SUM_X =
        SUMX (
            KEEPFILTERS ( __CORRELATION_TABLE ),
            CALCULATE ( SUM ( 'Sales'[Sales Quantity] ) )
        )
    VAR __SUM_Y =
        SUMX (
            KEEPFILTERS ( __CORRELATION_TABLE ),
            CALCULATE ( SUM ( 'Sales'[Return Quantity] ) )
        )
    VAR __SUM_XY =
        SUMX (
            KEEPFILTERS ( __CORRELATION_TABLE ),
            CALCULATE (
                SUM ( 'Sales'[Sales Quantity] ) * SUM ( 'Sales'[Return
Quantity] ) * 1.
            )
        )
    VAR __SUM_X2 =
        SUMX (
            KEEPFILTERS ( __CORRELATION_TABLE ),
            CALCULATE ( SUM ( 'Sales'[Sales Quantity] ) ^ 2 )
        )
    VAR __SUM_Y2 =
        SUMX (
            KEEPFILTERS ( __CORRELATION_TABLE ),
            CALCULATE ( SUM ( 'Sales'[Return Quantity] ) ^ 2 )
        )
    RETURN
        DIVIDE (
            __COUNT * __SUM_XY - __SUM_X * __SUM_Y * 1.,
            SQRT ( ( __COUNT * __SUM_X2 - __SUM_X ^ 2 ) * ( __COUNT *
__SUM_Y2 - __SUM_Y ^ 2 ) )
        )
```

In this example, the measure calculates the correlation coefficient between **Sales Quantity** and **Return Quantity** over the given color of a product.

If you want to find out more about the PCC, check out the following article:
`https://blog.gbrueckl.at/2015/06/calculating-pearson-correlation-coefficient-dax/.`

Although that concludes our brief look at DAX patterns, you'll find plenty more examples on the internet that will help you to broaden your knowledge on this subject. By following established patterns, you will create more reliable and accurate measures and calculated columns using DAX code.

Summary

In this chapter, we learned about creating measures and columns, following the software engineering principle of coding patterns, and how they can turn your DAX code into templates for more reliable and reusable solutions.

We started with an introduction to the Quick Measures feature in Power BI Desktop. We looked at how this feature can be used as a quick and easy way to create DAX measures, without needing to know any DAX code. We saw how it uses predefined DAX patterns that are modified using the responses provided through the Quick Measures dialog.

Having explored the Quick Measures feature, we looked at examples of DAX patterns being used in a number of different areas, including some of those created by using Quick Measures.

In the next chapter, we'll start our look at performance and optimization, starting with a look at how we can optimize our data models.

Section 3: Taking DAX to the Next Level

3

This section comprises some more advanced DAX topics, including a more in-depth look at data model optimization. You'll also take the hood off DAX by looking at the storage engine and how you can use this knowledge to optimize your DAX queries:

- Chapter 12, *Optimizing Your Data Model*
- Chapter 13, *Optimizing Your DAX Queries*

Optimizing Your Data Model

12

In Chapter 3, *Building Data Models*, we looked at the importance of building a well-structured data model. In this chapter, we'll take the practice of data modeling one step further by learning about some of the techniques behind data model optimization. As a tabular data model resides in **random-access memory (RAM)**, reducing its memory requirement is a major consideration in the overall design process.

We will start this chapter with an introduction to the VertiPaq compression engine. We'll look at what it is and how it works, and how this knowledge can help when it comes to optimizing the data in our data models. We'll investigate data profiling and how this can help identify what sort of data we should include in our data models, and we'll look at some of the tools available that can help with this process.

Then, we'll learn about some of the ways we can simplify the structure of our data models with a focus on column cardinality, column storage, and some ideas on identifying the correct columns to store. Finally, we'll round off this chapter with a look at the benefits of using summary tables.

The chapter is broken into the following sections:

- Introducing the VertiPaq engine
- Understanding your data model
- Simplifying your data model
- Creating summary tables

Introducing the VertiPaq engine

The VertiPaq engine is an in-memory columnar database that sits behind Excel Power Pivot, **SQL Server Analysis Services (SSAS)** Tabular, and Power BI. When you load data into a data model, it is loaded, compressed, and stored in RAM using the VertiPaq engine. You may also see it referred to by its newer official name, the xVelocity engine, but it is still widely known by the code name used during its development, and this is how we will refer to it in this book.

Understanding how this database engine processes data when it is loaded into a data model, even at a basic level, is essential if you want to build efficient data models.

 The VertiPaq engine is only relevant when you are importing data into a data model. If you are using DirectQuery to connect to your data, then the VertiPaq engine is not used.

With a traditional database, data is stored in tables, each consisting of a set of rows. Each row is then split into a number of columns that represent individual data items. *Figure 12-1* shows a cut-down version of the **Product** table from our data model, structured as we might imagine it with a traditional database:

ProductKey	Product Name	Color	Class	Unit Cost
1	Contoso 512MB MP3 Player E51 Silver	Silver	Economy	£6.62
2	Contoso 512MB MP3 Player E51 Blue	Blue	Economy	£6.62
3	Contoso 1G MP3 Player E100 White	White	Economy	£7.40
4	Contoso 2G MP3 Player E200 Silver	Silver	Economy	£11.00
5	Contoso 2G MP3 Player E200 Red	Red	Economy	£11.00
6	Contoso 2G MP3 Player E200 Black	Black	Economy	£11.00
7	Contoso 2G MP3 Player E200 Blue	Blue	Economy	£11.00
8	Contoso 4G MP3 Player E400 Silver	Silver	Economy	£30.58
9	Contoso 4G MP3 Player E400 Black	Black	Economy	£30.58
10	Contoso 4G MP3 Player E400 Green	Green	Economy	£30.58

Figure 12-1: A traditional database table

If you wanted to run a query against this table to find all the silver-colored products, then a traditional database would need to scan all the columns of all the rows to find the answer. This isn't a problem when the table has a small number of rows and a small number of columns, as with our preceding example. However, it can become an issue when dealing with a table that has millions of rows and a large number of columns. In this case, our query would result in the database reading and discarding many millions of data items that are not required.

With the VertiPaq engine, data is stored differently. It is a columnar database, and, as such, when data is loaded, each column is stored within its own table structure. Taking the **Product** table from the previous example, a columnar database would store the data as shown in *Figure 12-2*:

ProductKey	Product Name	Color	Class	Unit Cost
1	Contoso 512MB MP3 Player E51 Silver	Silver	Economy	£6.62
2	Contoso 512MB MP3 Player E51 Blue	Blue	Economy	£6.62
3	Contoso 1G MP3 Player E100 White	White	Economy	£7.40
4	Contoso 2G MP3 Player E200 Silver	Silver	Economy	£11.00
5	Contoso 2G MP3 Player E200 Red	Red	Economy	£11.00
6	Contoso 2G MP3 Player E200 Black	Black	Economy	£11.00
7	Contoso 2G MP3 Player E200 Blue	Blue	Economy	£11.00
8	Contoso 4G MP3 Player E400 Silver	Silver	Economy	£30.58
9	Contoso 4G MP3 Player E400 Black	Black	Economy	£30.58
10	Contoso 4G MP3 Player E400 Green	Green	Economy	£30.58

Figure 12-2: An example of a columnar database structure

As we can see, each column of the original table is stored as a physically separate table. Now, if we wanted to find all the silver-colored products, the database would only need to scan down the table for the **Color** column.

If we wanted to take our query one step further to find the unit costs of all silver-colored products, then the database only needs to scan for those products using the **Color** column, retrieve the row ID, and then look up the unit costs for the corresponding row IDs in the **Unit Cost** column. Where we have a large table, the potential time saved using this much more efficient process can be considerable.

In addition to storing the data in our data model in a different way, the VertiPaq engine also tries to reduce the memory requirement by compressing data as it is loaded into a data model. It attempts to compress data using the following algorithms:

- Value encoding
- Dictionary encoding
- **Run-length encoding (RLE)**

Data compression is important, not only because it reduces the amount of RAM required to store a data model, but also because it has the potential to improve overall performance.

Value encoding

When a column contains a number, it will apply the value encoding algorithm to attempt to reduce the number of bits required to store each number. To do this, it will look for a mathematical relationship between the values in the column, which it then uses to transform the values, using fewer bits. When accessing the values in the column, the engine has to apply the opposite transformation, which requires additional processing. However, this is an acceptable trade-off when considering the reduction in memory usage and the reduced number of reads this method of encoding offers.

To illustrate how this form of compression works, let's look at a simple example, which uses subtraction to transform the original values of a column. Suppose, for example, that our **Product** table also includes a value for the minimum stock level. If the maximum value in this column is **50**, then it requires 6 bits to store each value. However, if the minimum value in this column is **40**, then the VertiPaq engine could reduce this requirement to just 4 bits by subtracting **40** from each value in the column.

Figure 12-3 gives an illustration of the value encoding process:

ProductKey	Minimum Stock Level	Value encoding	Minimum Stock Level
1	50	-40	10
2	50	-40	10
3	40	-40	0
4	45	-40	5
5	45	-40	5
6	50	-40	10
7	40	-40	0
8	45	-40	5
9	50	-40	10
10	40	-40	0
	Max value of 50 requires 6 bits	Subtract minimum value	Max value of 10 requires 4 bits

Figure 12-3: The value encoding process

When retrieving the values from the column, the original value is obtained by adding **40** back to the value retrieved. As we already mentioned, this process does require some additional CPU usage. It will also only work on columns that contain integers. It does not work with floating-point or text values. To encode columns that contain text and floating-point values, the VertiPaq engine will use dictionary encoding.

Dictionary encoding

As with value encoding, the purpose of dictionary encoding is to reduce the number of bits required to store the values in a column. Dictionary encoding starts by building a dictionary table that contains a set of distinct values in a column. It then replaces the original values of a column with an integer number that references the index of the original value in the dictionary table.

The dictionary-encoding process is illustrated in *Figure 12-4*:

ProductKey	Color		id	Class		ProductKey		Color
1	Silver		0	Silver		1		0
2	Blue		1	Blue		2		1
3	White	Dictionary encoding →	2	White		3		2
4	Silver		3	Red		4		0
5	Red		4	Black		5		3
6	Black		5	Green		6		4
7	Blue			Dictionary table		7		1
8	Silver					8		0
9	Black					9		4
10	Green					10		5
Original values						Encoded values		

Figure 12-4: The dictionary-encoding process

There are two key advantages of using dictionary encoding, as follows:

- All columns contain only integer values.
- The number of bits required to store values in a column equals the minimum number of bits required to store the ID values in the dictionary table.

The number of bits required to store the ID value in the dictionary table—and, hence, the number of bits required to store the values of a column—depends on the number of distinct values in a column. As such, the number of distinct values in a column (also known as its cardinality) is a very important factor when designing a data model. We will look at this subject in more detail in the next section when we look at understanding your data model.

RLE

Instead of being an additional method of encoding, RLE is used as a method of compression complementary to dictionary encoding and value encoding. Once a column has been compressed using one of these two methods, it attempts to compress the size of the column further by reducing the number of duplicated values it contains.

Let's demonstrate this with an example. From our **Product** table, we have a column that contains the class of a product. First, VertiPaq will attempt to compress the memory requirement of this column using dictionary encoding. We are then left with a column that contains values that are repeated over many contiguous rows. At this point, VertiPaq compresses the column further by applying RLE.

Figure 12-5 illustrates how the RLE process works. The VertiPaq engine replaces the existing column with a new structure. The new structure contains each repeated value just once, along with the number of contiguous rows that contain that value:

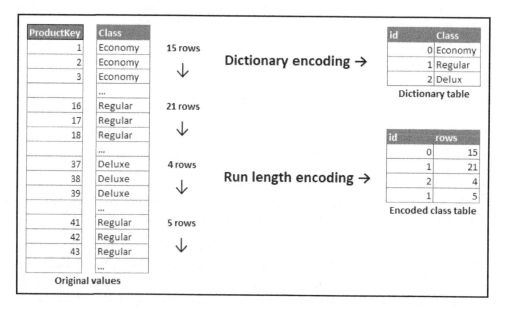

Figure 12-5: The RLE process

In the example shown in *Figure 12-5*, the first 15 products are in the **Economy** class. These are then followed by 21 products in the **Regular** class, four products in the **Deluxe** class, and another five products in the **Regular** class. These rows are encoded in a new column structure, which contains the dictionary ID and the number of contiguous rows that contain values relating to that dictionary ID.

VertiPaq will also apply RLE to value-encoded columns. However, unlike in the preceding example, a dictionary table is not required as the column has already been encoded with value-encoded integers.

The efficiency of this process is dependent on how the values repeat throughout the column. If values repeat for many contiguous rows, then compression will be high. However, if values change frequently, then compression will be lower. If values change too frequently, the compressed column may end up requiring more space than the original. If this happens, VertiPaq will skip the RLE process and will store the original column instead.

Obviously, the sort order and cardinality of a column may have a significant impact on the efficiency of RLE compression, and we will look at these in more detail in the next section.

Understanding your data model

There are a few tools available that will help you to understand your data model in more detail. Some of these are third-party tools, but if you are working with a version of Power BI Desktop released after October 2018, then the Power Query Editor comes with excellent data profiling capabilities built in. In this section, we're going to look at these and how they can be used to help you better understand the data that you are working within your data model.

Data profiling with Power BI Desktop

To access the data profiling capabilities in Power BI Desktop, we need to open the Power Query Editor. The easiest way to do this is by clicking on the **Edit Queries** button in the **External data** section of the **Home** ribbon, as shown in *Figure 12-6*:

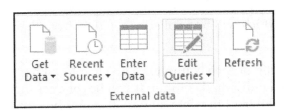

Figure 12-6: Editing queries

This opens the **Power Query Editor**, where we can work on the data loading process for our data model. *Figure 12-7* shows the **Power Query Editor** screen:

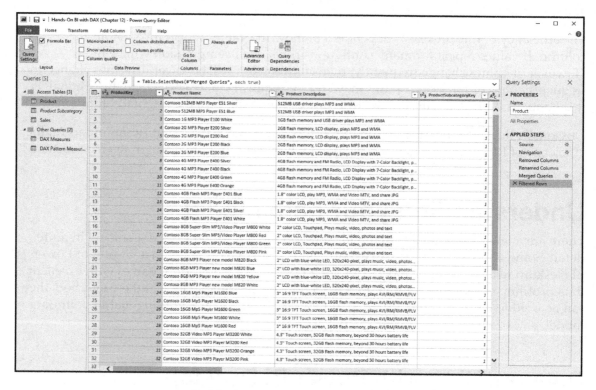

Figure 12-7: The Power Query editor screen in Power BI Desktop

On the left-hand side of the screen, we can see the current list of tables to which we are connected. In the middle is a view of the columns available in the currently selected table. Finally, on the right-hand side, we can see a list of steps that have been applied to the currently selected table, which will be applied when data from the table is loaded into our data model.

Just underneath the heading of each column is a green-colored bar. This indicates the quality of the data in each individual column. If you hover over the bar, you will see a popup that gives a breakdown of the data quality. It shows how many rows have valid data, how many have errors, and how many have missing values, as can be seen in *Figure 12-8*:

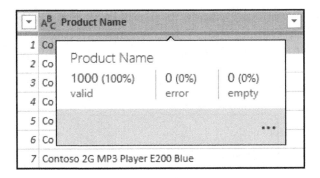

Figure 12-8: The data quality popup dialog

If there are any errors, then the bar will have a proportion colored red, depending on the percentage of overall rows that contain errors. Power Query will not profile columns with errors, beyond flagging the number and percentage of rows that contain erroneous values, as shown in *Figure 12-9*:

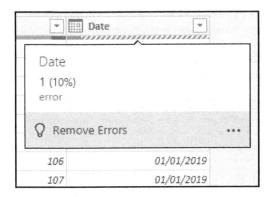

Figure 12-9: The data errors indicator bar

If you click on the **Remove Errors** option, then Power Query will apply an additional **Removed Errors** step to the **APPLIED STEPS** section of the editor. This will remove from the data loading process any rows that are causing errors.

If there are any rows with missing values, these will be shown as a black section of the green bar. Again, the size will depend on the percentage of rows with data missing, and there will be an option to remove these rows from the data load, as shown in *Figure 12-10*:

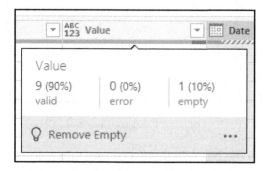

Figure 12-10: The missing data indicator bar

If you click on the **Remove Empty** option, then Power Query will apply an additional **Filtered Rows** step to the **APPLIED STEPS** section of the editor. This will filter out from the data loading process any rows that contain missing values.

In addition to the popup showing data quality details, you can add these as an expanded section to the header of each column, as shown in *Figure 12-11*:

1²₃ ID		A⁸ᶜ Description		1²₃ Value		Date	
• Valid	100%	• Valid	100%	• Valid	90%	• Valid	- %
• Error	0%	• Error	0%	• Error	0%	• Error	10%
• Empty	0%	• Empty	0%	• Empty	10%	• Empty	- %
1	1	Example 1		100		01/01/2019	
2	2	Example 2		101	Error		
3	3	Example 3		102		01/01/2019	
4	4	Example 4		null		01/01/2019	
5	5	Example 5		104		01/01/2019	
6	6	Example 6		105		01/01/2019	
7	7	Example 7		106		01/01/2019	
8	8	Example 8		107		01/01/2019	
9	9	Example 9		108		01/01/2019	
10	10	Example 10		109		01/01/2019	

Figure 12-11: The data quality column header

To enable this view, tick the **Column quality** checkbox in the **Data Preview** section of the **View** ribbon, as shown in *Figure 12-12*:

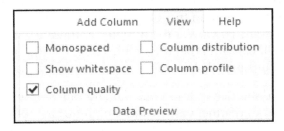

Figure 12-12: Enabling the data quality column header

In addition, in this section of the **View** ribbon, there are checkboxes labeled **Column distribution** and **Column profile** that enable additional views. Let's start by looking at the **Column distribution** view. Tick the **Column distribution** checkbox to enable the view; you will see a new section has been added to the header of each column.

As we can see in *Figure 12-13*, the header of each column now has a small bar chart that shows the distribution of values in the column. It also shows the number of distinct values and the number of unique values contained in the column:

1²₃ ProductKey	A⁸c Product Name	A⁸c Product Description	1²₃ ProductSubcategoryKey	A⁸c Manufacturer
● Valid 100%	● Valid 100%	● Valid 100%	● Valid 100%	● Valid 100%
● Error 0%	● Error 0%	● Error 0%	● Error 0%	● Error 0%
● Empty 0%	● Empty 0%	● Empty 0%	● Empty 0%	● Empty 0%
1690 distinct, 1690 unique	1690 distinct, 1690 unique	589 distinct, 225 unique	22 distinct, 0 unique	10 distinct, 0 unique
1	1 Contoso 512MB MP3 Player E51 Silver	512MB USB driver plays MP3 and WMA		1 Contoso, Ltd
2	2 Contoso 512MB MP3 Player E51 Blue	512MB USB driver plays MP3 and WMA		1 Contoso, Ltd
3	3 Contoso 1G MP3 Player E100 White	1GB flash memory and USB driver plays MP3 and WMA		1 Contoso, Ltd
4	4 Contoso 2G MP3 Player E200 Silver	2GB flash memory, LCD display, plays MP3 and WMA		1 Contoso, Ltd
5	5 Contoso 2G MP3 Player E200 Red	2GB flash memory, LCD display, plays MP3 and WMA		1 Contoso, Ltd
6	6 Contoso 2G MP3 Player E200 Black	2GB flash memory, LCD display, plays MP3 and WMA		1 Contoso, Ltd
7	7 Contoso 2G MP3 Player E200 Blue	2GB flash memory, LCD display, plays MP3 and WMA		1 Contoso, Ltd
8	8 Contoso 4G MP3 Player E400 Silver	4GB flash memory and FM Radio, LCD Display with 7-Color Backlight, p...		1 Contoso, Ltd
9	9 Contoso 4G MP3 Player E400 Black	4GB flash memory and FM Radio, LCD Display with 7-Color Backlight, p...		1 Contoso, Ltd
10	10 Contoso 4G MP3 Player E400 Green	4GB flash memory and FM Radio, LCD Display with 7-Color Backlight, p...		1 Contoso, Ltd
11	11 Contoso 4G MP3 Player E400 Orange	4GB flash memory and FM Radio, LCD Display with 7-Color Backlight, p...		1 Contoso, Ltd
12	12 Contoso 4GB Flash MP3 Player E401 Blue	1.8" color LCD, play MP3, WMA and Video MTV, and share JPG		1 Contoso, Ltd
13	13 Contoso 4GB Flash MP3 Player E401 Black	1.8" color LCD, play MP3, WMA and Video MTV, and share JPG		1 Contoso, Ltd
14	14 Contoso 4GB Flash MP3 Player E401 Silver	1.8" color LCD, play MP3, WMA and Video MTV, and share JPG		1 Contoso, Ltd
15	15 Contoso 4GB Flash MP3 Player E401 White	1.8" color LCD, play MP3, WMA and Video MTV, and share JPG		1 Contoso, Ltd

Figure 12-13: The column distribution bar chart

As we have seen already when looking at the VertiPaq engine, and as we shall see again in the next section, these two values are important when you are looking at what data to include in your data model. Non-integer columns that contain a large number of distinct values will require more memory than those with fewer values as the dictionary that VertiPaq creates will be larger. The lower the number of unique values, then the greater the chance that the column will contain repeating values over contiguous rows, improving the efficiency of compression through RLE.

In theory, when selecting data to load into your data model, you want to avoid columns that contain a high number of distinct values and a high number of unique values. In practice, this may not always be possible, but it is a good indicator when exploring your data.

The final view that we're going to look at is the **Column profile** view. To enable this view, tick the **Column profile** checkbox in the **Data Preview** section of the **View** ribbon. This will add a new view to the bottom of the table display, as shown in *Figure 12-14*:

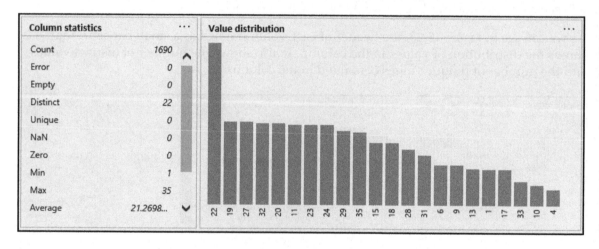

Figure 12-14: The column profile view

As you can see, this view not only gives a more detailed view of how values are distributed throughout the column but also gives an expanded set of statistical data. In addition, you can right-click on any of the columns in the **Value distribution** chart and filter on values or replace values, adding an additional step to the **APPLIED STEPS** section.

Data profiling in SSAS Tabular and Excel Power Pivot

If you are not using Power BI Desktop, then there are other tools you can use to profile data in your data model.

If you are working with SSAS Tabular, then you can use **SQL Server Management Studio** (**SSMS**) to connect to the Analysis Services database and query your data model. You can also use a couple of excellent third-party tools called **DAX Studio** and **VertiPaq Analyzer**.

If you want to try out DAX Studio, then you can find more details at:
`https://daxstudio.org`

If you want to try out VertiPaq Analyzer, then you can find more details at:
`https://www.sqlbi.com/tools/vertipaq-analyzer/`

Using either SSMS or DAX Studio gives you access to **Dynamic Management Views** (**DMV**). The DMVs give you a way to see how data in your data model is compressed. They give you details of how space is being used by tables and columns.

The following DMVs are particularly useful for exploring the data in your data model:

- DISCOVER_OBJECT_MEMORY_USAGE
- DISCOVER_STORAGE_TABLES
- DISCOVER_STORAGE_TABLE_COLUMNS
- DISCOVER_STORAGE_TABLE_COLUMN_SEGMENTS

Figure 12-15 shows an example of DISCOVER_STORAGE_TABLES DMV being queried using DAX Studio:

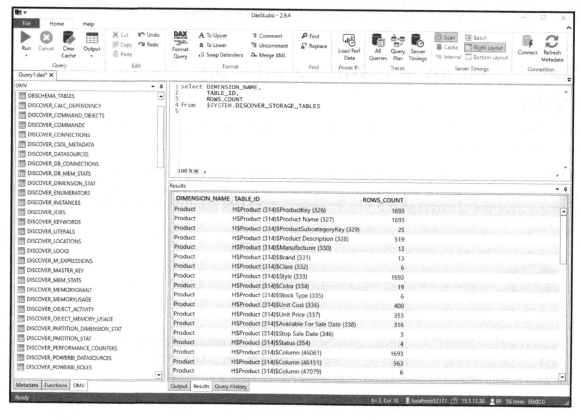

Figure 12-15: DAX Studio being used to query a DMV

DAX Studio is also able to connect to an Excel Power Pivot data model and gives you a good way to access and explore data if your data model is in Excel.

Simplifying your data model

In Chapter 3, *Building Data Models*, we looked at the process of building a data model in some detail. In this section, we will revisit some of the topics we covered, along with what we have just learned about the workings of the VertiPaq engine. Using this combined knowledge, we will focus on some of the ways in which we can optimize the overall memory requirements of our data models and improve performance.

As we saw in the previous section, VertiPaq's ability to compress data is dependent on several factors. As such, there are some elements that you need to consider when building a data model that will have a direct impact on the efficiency of the compression algorithms. These include the following:

- The cardinality of values in a column. This affects VertiPaq's ability to reduce the number of bits used to store a value. If a column has low cardinality, then the dictionary size will be much smaller. Also, consider the granularity of data. If you use a higher granularity than you need—for example, if you are storing date and time when you only need the date—then you will have a much larger column dictionary than you need.
- The number of values repeated in contiguous rows in a column. A column that contains values repeated over many contiguous rows will achieve greater compression than a column that contains frequently changing values.
- The sort order of rows in a table. Although VertiPaq's algorithms will search for the best sort order as part of the compression process, they will consider the physical order of the rows received.
- The number of rows in a table. Do you need all of the data, or can it be filtered before loading?
- The data type of a column. However, this will only influence the dictionary size, so is not relevant for value encoding.

In addition, there are some more general rules that you should follow when building a data model, which will help to reduce the model's overall memory requirement, as follows:

- Understand your source data.
- Keep your data model as simple as possible.
- Use a star schema over a snowflake schema.
- Merge and append tables to simplify the data model.
- Only import rows and columns that are needed in the model.
- Ensure columns are defined with the correct data type.
- Create measures instead of calculated columns, where possible.

Let's look at these rules in a bit more detail.

Understanding your source data

The first step in understanding a data model is to collect some information about the data we have in the data sources from which we will be importing. Specifically, we need to look at the following:

- The number of rows in the tables
- The number of distinct and unique values in each column
- Details of any hierarchies
- The number and complexity of relationships
- The data needed for our analysis

Of these points, the most important is the number of distinct values in each column, also referred to as column cardinality (as opposed to relationship cardinality, which we looked at in `Chapter 3`, *Building Data Models*). As we have seen, column cardinality has an impact on the size of the dictionary created by VertiPaq when it carries out dictionary encoding on a column. The higher the cardinality of a column, the more rows will be stored in a dictionary, and the bigger the size. If you only have a few unique values, then the size of the dictionary will be much smaller, and VertiPaq will be able to achieve a much higher compression ratio.

Keeping your data model simple

Although it is possible to create a very complex data model that contains hundreds of tables with many relationships, there are several reasons why you should avoid this. Firstly, you will end up with a very large field list, making the data model difficult to work with and prone to errors. Even with good compression, a large data model will use excessive amounts of memory and will suffer from poor performance. A large and complicated data model will also make it extremely difficult to write and troubleshoot DAX queries.

Unlike the design of a traditional relational database, where the data structure is highly normalized, we should look to denormalize data when designing a tabular data model. Each table and associated relationship have cost overheads in terms of memory and the passing of filters between tables. Although the best performance might be obtained from a model that uses a single flattened table, this would, in practice, be difficult to use. A more realistic approach would be to design a data model that uses a star schema.

Using a star schema

In Chapter 3, *Building Data Models*, we looked at some of the virtues of using a star schema. With a star schema, the data model consists of a denormalized, or flattened, fact table that sits at the center. This contains the numerical data that we use with measures, on which to base our analysis. Each entity in this table is then connected to lookup or dimension tables that are arranged around the fact table to create the classic star shape. *Figure 12-16* shows an example of this style of data model, and illustrates why it is known as a star schema:

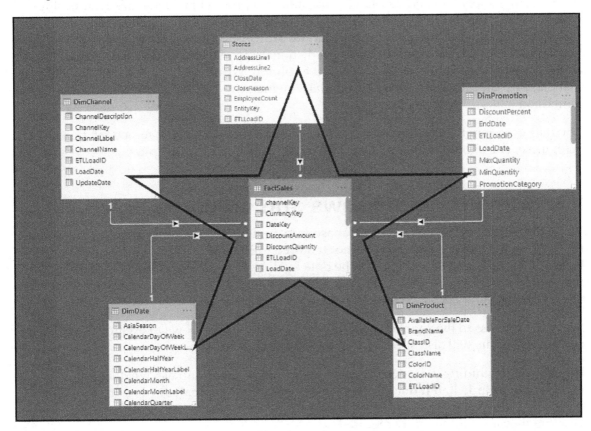

Figure 12-16: A start schema based data model

You may also have a data model where there are dimension tables that are related to other dimension tables, in the form of a hierarchy chain. For example, there might be a product table that is related to a product category table and a brand table. This style of schema is known as a snowflake schema as it resembles a simple snowflake in shape.

Merging and appending tables

You should look to simplify your data model by merging or appending tables where possible. For example, you may have a data source that contains a different table of data for each year. In such a case, you would append the data into a single table as part of the data loading process.

You may find that your data model resembles a snowflake schema. For example, if you pull tables in from a relational database, you might have a product table that has relationships with tables such as product category, color, brand, and class. In a relational database, this structure avoids duplication of data in columns. However, as we have seen already, the VertiPaq engine will automatically create a dictionary for each column, which avoids the memory cost of having duplicated values in a column. We should denormalize the tables that make up the outer edges of the snowflake by merging them together to form a single dimension table.

You may occasionally have tables in your data model that have a one-to-one relationship. With these, you should flatten the data model by merging the tables into one.

Importing required rows and columns only

You will find that many tables in a database contain data gathered over long periods of time, or contain information for areas not required for a particular report. Always filter out historical or unrelated data as part of the data loading process. If you filter out data in your report after it has been loaded, it is still using valuable memory and making your data model larger than it needs to be.

If you have access to the source database, then consider using views to exclude unnecessary rows of data. This will also speed up the data loading process.

When you are building your data model, look at each column and ask whether it is necessary to include it. If it doesn't contribute to the required analysis, do not include it, especially if the values have a high cardinality. Missing columns can easily be added later if you find they are subsequently required.

If you are importing data from a data warehouse, then you will often find multiple date fields that are created by the **Extract, Transform, and Load** (**ETL**) process to record when the row was created, last updated, or when the ETL process last ran. These are rarely needed in a data model and should be excluded from the data model during the load process.

While primary keys may be needed for dimension tables, to create the necessary relationships, they are usually excluded from fact tables. Primary key columns contain unique values, and will not compress very effectively. If you have a fact table with millions of rows, this will consume a large amount of memory unnecessarily.

Similarly, look out for Autonumber columns, columns used as an IDENTITY, or columns that contain **globally unique identifiers (GUIDs)**. These types of columns will all contain highly unique values and will suffer from low compression ratios. Only include these where you know they will be needed for analysis purposes.

Using the correct data type

Always ensure that you define columns in your data model with the correct data type. Certain data types use more memory than others. Where possible, use integers in place of strings, and use dates instead of datetimes. If your data model contains times, only store to the necessary granularity that is really needed. Times stored down to milliseconds require much more memory than times only stored down to minutes. If you don't need to store the time at all, then ensure you use the date data type instead.

You should also look at the possibility of splitting columns. For example, if you do need to include time in your analysis, then you could split a **DateTime** column into the separate date and time columns. This should be done at source or during the data loading process, and not by using calculated columns, as this would only increase the memory overhead.

Finally, consider the granularity of a column. Storing time at the hour level would result in 24 unique values, while storing down to the millisecond would give you 86,400,00 unique values. Remember that the greater the granularity of the values in a column, the higher the cardinality, and the lower the compression ratio that can be achieved for storing the values in that column. The other advantage of a lower granularity is that you are more likely to have repeated values over contiguous rows, further improving the chances of a higher compression ratio.

Do not be tempted to reduce the granularity of dates, such as having a single date for each month. The time intelligence functions in DAX rely on a complete set of calendar dates, and reducing the granularity of dates in this manner would prevent these from working correctly.

Using measures instead of calculated columns

A calculated column will take up more memory than a standard column. Wherever possible, you should avoid having too many calculated columns in your data model. Also, consider ways in which a measure may be used to replace standard and calculated columns. For example, in our **Sales** table, we have **Unit Price**, **Sales Quantity**, and **Sales Amount** columns. However, the **Sales Amount** column could be replaced by a measure. This measure would make use of the **Unit Price** and **Sales Quantity** columns to calculate the sales amount value.

The following DAX expression would create a measure that could be used to replace the **Sales Amount** column in the **Sales** table in our data model:

```
SalesAmountMeasure =
SUMX (
    Sales,
    ( Sales[Sales Quantity] * Sales[Unit Price] ) - Sales[Discount Amount]
)
```

With the **Sales** table containing well over 2 million rows, this has the potential to make a difference to the memory requirement of our data model. Alternatively, if we only want to do an analysis using the **Sales Amount** and are not interested in **Sales Quantity** or **Unit Price**, then it would make more sense to retain the **Sales Amount** column and remove the **Sales Quantity** and **Unit Price** columns instead.

One instance where you might consider using a calculated column to improve performance is where you have a measure that uses a logical expression, based on a column with high cardinality. For example, let's take the following measure:

```
HighSalesAmountCount1 =
COUNTROWS (
    FILTER (
        Sales,
        Sales[Sales Quantity] * RELATED ( Product[Unit Price] ) >= 20000
    )
)
```

This measure counts the number of rows in the **Sales** table where the **Sales Quantity** multiplied by the **Unit Price** from the related product in the **Product** table is greater than or equal to 20,000. As the **Sales** table has over 2 million rows, this filter iteration is a potentially expensive process.

However, we can convert the filter expression into a calculated column using the following expression:

```
HighSalesColumn =
Sales[Sales Quantity] * RELATED ( 'Product'[Unit Price] ) >= 20000
```

Now, we have a calculated column that contains just two unique values of TRUE or FALSE. We can use this new column to revise our previous measure, using the CALCULATE function, to apply a filter with it.

The following is the expression used for the revised measure:

```
HighSalesAmountCount2 =
CALCULATE (
    COUNTROWS ( Sales ),
    Sales[HighSalesColumn] = TRUE
)
```

As this revised measure applies a direct filter to the **Sales** table at execution time, it should be more efficient than the original version of the measure when queried.

Creating summary tables

In the last section of this chapter, we're going to take a look at another way you can optimize your data model, through the use of summary tables. Although the use of summary tables will not necessarily help to reduce the size of your data model in terms of memory usage, they are a great way to improve performance, especially if your data model contains large tables with millions of rows. Any visual that uses a summary table will potentially be much faster than if it were working directly with a larger native table.

There are a couple of ways to create summary tables. If you have access to the source database, then you can create summary tables at the source using SQL views. This has the advantage that, if not needed for analysis, you do not need to import the larger table on which the views are based. If you don't need to import the larger table into your data model, then you may be able to reduce its overall memory requirement.

However, if you don't have access to the source database, or you still need to load the large tables into your data model, you can create summary tables by using calculated tables. You can create aggregation summary tables using the SUMMARY or GROUPBY functions. Alternatively, you can create summary tables that contain subsets of data using the FILTER function.

Let's look at summary tables with some hands-on examples. We'll start by creating an aggregation summary table using the GROUPBY function with the **Sales** table from our data model.

Before we start, the syntax for the GROUPBY function is as follows:

```
GROUPBY ( <Table> [, <GroupBy_ColumnName> [, [<Name>] [, [<Expression>]
[, <GroupBy_ColumnName> [, [<Name>] [, [<Expression>] [, ... ] ] ] ] ] ]
] )
```

In the following example, we will create a summary table that aggregates the **Total Sales Quantity** and the **Total Sales Amount** for each product, by date. For this, we will create a calculated table using the following DAX expression:

```
Sales by Date =
GROUPBY (
    Sales,
    Sales[SalesDateKey],
    Sales[ProductKey],
    "Total Sales Quantity", SUMX ( CURRENTGROUP (), 'Sales'[Sales Quantity]
),
    "Total Sales Amount", SUMX ( CURRENTGROUP (), 'Sales'[Sales Amount] )
)
```

This gives the result shown in *Figure 12-17*:

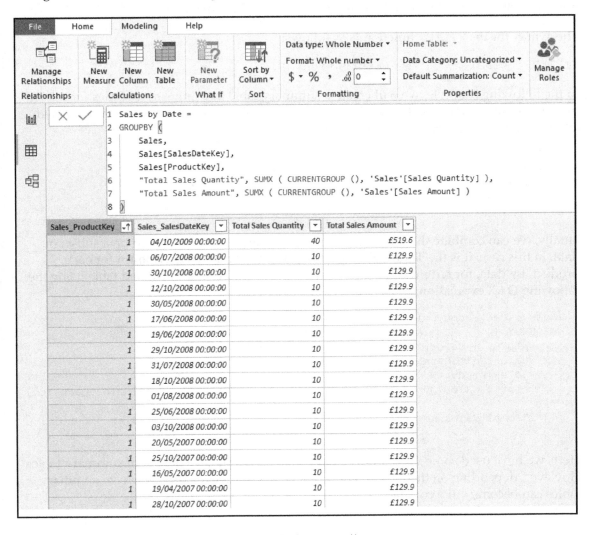

Figure 12-17: Creating a summary table

Next, let's create a subset of the **Sales** table, showing only sales for red products. We can do this using the FILTER function by using the **Sales** and **Product** tables.

The syntax for the FILTER function is as follows:

```
FILTER ( <Table>, <FilterExpression> )
```

In the following example, we will create a summary table that only shows **Sales** for related products in the **Product** table, where the color is **Red**. For this, we will create a calculated table using the following DAX expression:

```
Sales (Red Products) =
FILTER (
    Sales,
    RELATED ( 'Product'[Color] ) = "Red"
)
```

Finally, we can combine these two ideas to create a summary table, based on a subset of data. In this case, it is the **Total Sales Quantity** and the **Total Sales Amount** for each product, by date, for red products only. For this, we will create a calculated table using the following DAX expression:

```
Sales (Red Products) by Date =
GROUPBY (
    FILTER ( Sales, RELATED ( 'Product'[Color] ) = "Red" ),
    Sales[SalesDateKey],
    Sales[ProductKey],
    "Total Sales Quantity", SUMX ( CURRENTGROUP (), 'Sales'[Sales Quantity]
),
    "Total Sales Amount", SUMX ( CURRENTGROUP (), 'Sales'[Sales Amount] )
)
```

Here, we have used some very simple examples to illustrate the concept of summary tables. However, depending on the requirements, the DAX expressions used to create summary tables can become quite complex.

Summary

In this chapter, we learned about some of the techniques we can use to help us optimize our data models. We learned that reducing a data model's memory requirement is a major consideration in the overall design process.

We started off by learning about the VertiPaq compression engine. We looked at what it is and how it works, and why this knowledge is essential if we want to effectively optimize our data models. Next, we learned about data profiling, and how this can help us identify what data to include in a data model. This included a look at the data profiling capabilities of Power BI Desktop, along with some other tools that are available to help with this process.

We then learned about some of the ways we can simplify the structure of our data models looking at column cardinality, column storage, and identifying the correct columns to store. Finally, we looked at the benefits of using summary tables, along with some examples.

In the final chapter of this book, we'll complete our learning by looking at ways in which we can optimize our DAX queries. We'll start by looking at some of the tools that are available and how these can help us with our query optimization.

13
Optimizing Your DAX Queries

For the last chapter in this book, we are going to look at some of the techniques and tools you can use to analyze DAX query performance and identify potential problems.

We will start this chapter by learning about the storage engine and the formula engine. These are the two engines that are used to resolve DAX queries. We'll look at how these engines work together to retrieve data from the data model and return a result. We'll also learn how this knowledge can help to identify and resolve performance issues with DAX queries.

We will then look at some of the tools we can use to investigate the performance of DAX queries. These include DAX Studio, the SQL Server Profiler, and the Performance Analyzer feature in Power BI Desktop. We'll learn how to use these tools and how they can help to find potential bottlenecks and performance issues with our queries.

This chapter is broken down into the following sections:

- Introduction to the DAX calculation engines
- Monitoring performance with DAX Studio
- Using SQL Server Profiler
- Using Power BI Performance Analyzer

Introduction to the DAX calculation engines

Before we start looking at using tools to help us to optimize our DAX queries, we need to understand a little bit about the tabular query engine architecture.

When you execute a DAX query using the in-memory mode, it uses two different engines to run the calculations and come back with a result. These two engines are known as the **Formula Engine (FE)** and the **Storage Engine (SE)**, and they work together in different roles to calculate the result of DAX queries.

 If you execute a DAX query using DirectQuery mode, then the query engine simply coverts the DAX into a SQL statement and sends it to be executed by the external SQL Server. The query engine does no further work other than return the query result that it receives back from SQL Server.

When a DAX query is executed, a combination of the function engine and the storage engine is used to resolve the query and return an answer. In the process, the following steps are taken:

1. The query is transformed into an expression tree.
2. A logical query plan, containing the set of logical operations needed to execute the query, is produced.
3. The logical query plan is transformed into a physical query plan, containing the set of physical operations needed.
4. The physical query plan is executed, and data is retrieved from the storage engine, allowing the result of the query to be calculated.

Steps 2 and 3 are particularly important when it comes to optimizing DAX queries. It is these steps that produce the plans that we can read, allowing us to understand how the query engine resolves our queries. In later sections of this chapter, we will look at some of the tools available to help us to obtain and read these logical and physical query plans.

The formula engine

When your DAX query is executed, it is initially processed by the formula engine. It processes each of the steps presented by the physical query plan and can, therefore, resolve complex DAX expressions. When an operation in the physical query plan requires data from the data model, it passes a request to the storage engine. This is where the two engines begin their interaction in resolving DAX queries.

The formula engine is single-threaded, meaning that it can only use one core to carry out each operation, regardless of how many cores or threads are available to it. As such, it can only perform one request to the storage engine at a time.

In response to the formula engine's request for data, the storage engine will return the data stored in a temporary data cache. Unlike the compressed column stores that are held by the storage engine, data in this cache is uncompressed and held in straightforward in-memory tables.

The formula engine works with either the data structures created by its own operations or with the caches created by the storage engine. The results from the formula engine are not cached in memory so they need to be recalculated each time they are needed. However, the data cache returned by the storage engine is retained and can be reused for queries that follow. This can be especially good for improving performance when you have a measure that needs to calculate many data points for a visual on a report.

The storage engine

The storage engine is officially called the **xVelocity in-memory analytical engine**, but as we saw in the previous chapter, it is better known as the VertiPaq engine. As we have already seen, the purpose of the storage engine is to take requests from the formula engine, scan the columnar database, retrieve the relevant data, and then return the data to the formula engine in the form of a data cache.

Each scan is the result of an internal query that uses a SQL-like language called xmSQL. As we shall see later in this chapter, we can use tools to view the xmSQL queries, which will help us to understand how the formula engine is querying the storage engine.

Unlike the formula engine, the storage engine is multi-threaded. This means that operations carried out by the storage engine can utilize multiple cores if they are available. However, the storage engine only receives requests from the formula engine in a synchronous manner. Being single-threaded, the formula engine must wait for a query request to be completed by the storage engine before it can send the next request. As such, the storage can only make use of its multi-threaded ability when processing a query that involves several column segments, where it can use one thread per segment.

The data cache holds a limited number of results from the storage engine, but if the storage engine receives a request that matches one already in the cache, it will use the cached version rather than scan data in memory. The storage engine is generally faster at scanning than the formula engine, as it is optimized for scan operations. It also has the advantage that it scans compressed data, whereas the formula engine scans data held in a cache, which is uncompressed.

Monitoring performance with DAX Studio

In the previous section, we learned that part of the process of executing a DAX query results in the calculation engine producing a logical query plan and a physical query plan. In addition, when attempting to optimize a slow DAX query it helps to understand which elements are carried out by the formula engine and which are carried out by the storage engine. To help us with both processes, we're going to look at using DAX Studio, a third-party tool that we've looked at briefly in previous chapters.

 To follow along with this section, you will need to download and install DAX Studio, which is available from:
https://daxstudio.org

Once you have installed DAX studio, you will be able to create links to tabular data models in the following products:

- Power BI
- Excel Power Pivot
- **SQL Server Analysis Services (SSAS)** Tabular

If you are working with an Excel Power Pivot data model, then you will need to connect to DAX Studio by launching it from within Excel itself:

1. Once you have your Power Pivot file open in Excel, go to the **Add-ins** ribbon and click on the **DAX Studio** button, as shown in *Figure 13-1*:

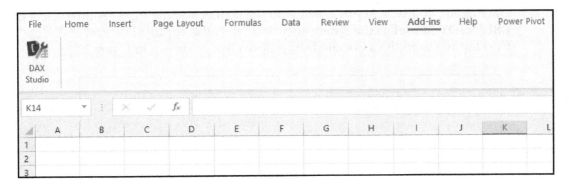

Figure 13-1: The DAX Studio button in Excel Power Pivot

2. DAX Studio should now open showing the connection dialog, as shown in *Figure 13-2*. Select the default option of **PowerPivot Model** for the data source, which should also show the name of the Excel file containing your data model:

Figure 13-2: Connecting DAX Studio to a PowerPivot data model

3. Click on the **Connect** button to open DAX Studio, which will now be connected to your Excel Power Pivot data model.

However, for this section, we are going to work with a Power BI Desktop example. To connect to a Power BI data model, you need to ensure that the required Power BI Desktop file is open, with the data loaded. Unlike with Excel, there is no icon from within the Power BI Desktop application to open DAX Studio, so it should be opened from the Windows desktop:

1. Once again, you will be presented with the connection dialog. This time select the **PBI / SSDT Model** as the data source and select the appropriate Power BI Desktop file from the associated drop-down list, as shown in *Figure 13-3*:

Figure 13-3: Connecting DAX Studio to a Power BI data model

2. Click on the **Connect** button to open DAX Studio, which will now be connected to your Power BI data model.

   Once open and connected to your Power BI data model, you will be presented with a screen like the one shown in *Figure 13-4*:

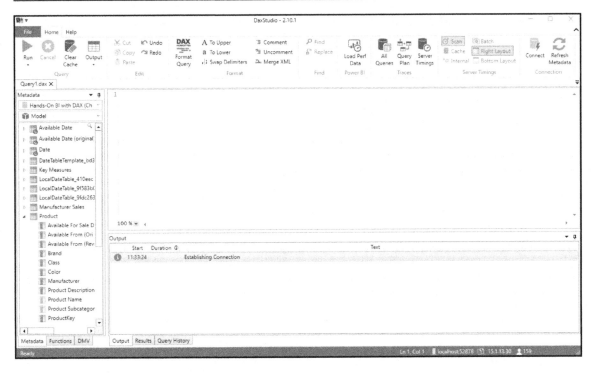

Figure 13-4: The DAX Studio screen

This screen consists of five different sections:

- A Microsoft Office-style ribbon runs across the top, giving gives access to the features available in DAX studio, including those we will be looking at to help us to optimize our data.
- The **Metadata** panel is on the left-hand side and shows the metadata from the loaded data model, including those tables that are hidden away behind the scenes when the data model is viewed from within Power BI Desktop. These tables include the date tables that are automatically created by default to help with the time intelligence functionality. Tables and columns can be dragged on to the editor panel to save typing them. This panel also has tabs to show a list of DAX functions and a list of the **Dynamic Management Views (DMVs)**.
- The query editor panel is where you will write DAX queries and evaluate statements.

- The **Output** panel is where you see information about the queries you run. It also includes tabs to display the results of queries and other tabs are displayed to show query plans and other functions.
- Finally, the status bar runs along the bottom and shows the current connection information. This is useful if you want to connect to the current data model using SQL Server Management Studio.

With our Power BI Desktop file open and DAX Studio connected, we are now ready to start exploring our data and its related use of the formula and storage engines. We do this by entering DAX queries in the query editor panel.

There are two important points to note when entering DAX queries in DAX Studio:

- Each DAX query needs to start with the EVALUATE keyword.
- The output from a query must be a table.

If the output from a query is not a table, then it will need to be wrapped by a function that will convert the output into a table.

Viewing performance with DAX Traces

For this example, we're going to use a very simple DAX query. Enter the following in the query editor and then click on the **Run** button in the **Query** section of the **Home** ribbon:

```
EVALUATE
FILTER (
    'Product',
    'Product'[Color] = "Red"
)
```

This will return all of the columns from the Product table where the value of the Color column equals Red. The result from this query will be displayed on the **Results** tab of the output panel.

We can now start to use the features of DAX Studio to investigate the performance of our DAX query. On the **Traces** section of the **Home** ribbon, as shown in *Figure 13-5*, two buttons enable server timings and show the query plans that we discussed in the previous section of this chapter:

Figure 13-5: Showing the query plan and enabling server timings

Click on both buttons to enable the query plan and server timings features. This will add two new tabs to the output panel. Now re-run this DAX query, but before you do so, click on the **Clear Cache** button on the **Query** section of the **Home** ribbon. It is important to do this before you run any query, to avoid the query engine using data that may already be cached, which would give inaccurate timings.

When the query has run, you will see some information displayed on the new tabs of the output panel. *Figure 13-6* shows the output for the server timings:

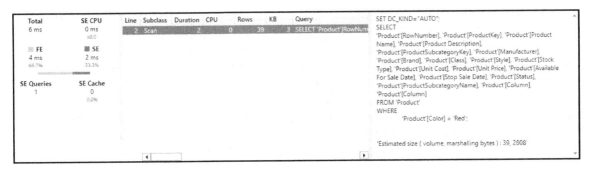

Figure 13-6: The output for server timings

This shows that overall the query took 6 ms to process, with 2 ms being spent by the storage engine retrieving data and 4 ms being spent by the formula engine processing the data returned by the storage engine. We can also see that the query only required a single storage engine query and no cached data was used.

If we switch to the **Query Plan** tab of the output panel, we can see both the logical and physical query plans that were created to execute this query, as can be seen in *Figure 13-7*:

Figure 13-7: The physical and logical query plans displayed in DAX Studio

Unfortunately, the query plan text is displayed in its raw form, so it can be difficult to read without some manual reformatting, especially when looking at query plans for complex DAX queries.

When it comes to identifying bottlenecks and other performance issues with DAX queries, it is important to look out for long-running queries. It is also important to look at how much time is spent processing the query in the storage engine versus the formula engine. Once you have identified potential issues, then you can start to dig into the query plans and the output generated in the output panel, to get an idea of what is going on. For example, you may have a DAX query that uses a filter, which is taking a long time to execute. Looking at the output, you might realize that it is returning far more rows than expected. By altering the place in the query where the filter sits, it may be possible to reduce the number of rows being processed, speeding up the query considerably.

Unfortunately, there is often no right way to write a DAX query. Performance can depend on the structure of the data model or the type of data that you are querying. This is where knowing how to use these tools will help you to understand how a query is being processed. This, in turn, will allow you to experiment with changes to your query and to see how those changes affect query timings and the overall performance of the query.

View VertiPaq metrics

If you are using the latest version of DAX Studio, then it now includes an option to view information and metrics about the currently connected data model, which allows you to make some detailed analysis of the model's design. It gives similar information to the data preview tools that are now in Power BI Desktop.

To access these advanced features, you will need to enable them on the **Advanced** tab of the **Options** screen. To access this screen, click on the **File** tab. Check all of the checkboxes in the **Preview Features** section, as shown in *Figure 13-8*:

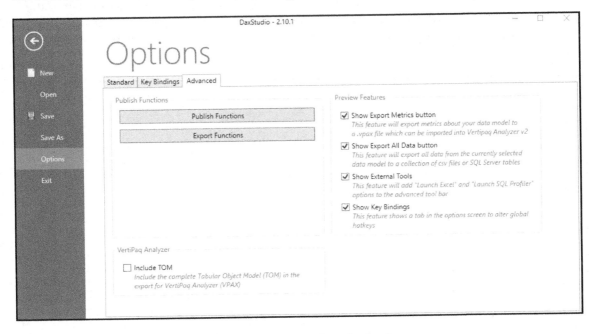

Figure 13-8: Enabling DAX Studio preview features from the options screen

You will now have a new **Advanced** ribbon, as shown in *Figure 13-9*, which includes options to import, export, and view metrics. It also includes a button to launch SQL Server Profiler, which we will cover in the next section:

Figure 13-9: The button to launch SQL Profiler

To view metrics for the currently connected data model, click on the **View Metrics** button on the **Metrics** section of the **Advanced** ribbon.

DAX Studio will do a quick analysis of the data model's structure and add a new tab to the output panel called **VertiPaq Analyzer**. This tab has three tabs of its own: **Tables, Columns,** and **Relationships.** *Figure 13-10* gives an example of what the **Tables** screen looks like:

VertiPaq Analyzer Preview

Tables | Columns | Relationships

Name	Cardinality	Table	Columns	Data	Dictionary	Hier Size	Encoding	Data Type	User Hier Size	Rel Size	% Table	% DB	Segmen
◢ **Sales**	**2,282,482**	**38,516,236**	**38,514,...**	**23,857,...**	**4,485,052**	**10,172,...**	**Many**	-		**0**	**1,760**		**99.64%**	
RowNumber-2662979B-1795-4F74-8F37-6A1BA8059B61	0	-	120	0	120	0	VALUE	Int64	-		0	0.00%	0.00%	
SalesKey	2,282,482	-	15,216,7...	6,086,632	120	9,129,952	VALUE	Int64	-		-	39.51%	39.36%	
SalesDateKey	1,096	-	3,707,032	3,651,840	46,376	8,816	HASH	DateTime	-		-	9.63%	9.59%	
ProductKey	1,689	-	2,987,068	2,933,664	39,852	13,552	HASH	Int64	-		-	7.76%	7.73%	
Unit Cost	397	-	1,163,380	1,150,048	10,116	3,216	HASH	Decimal	-		-	3.02%	3.01%	
Unit Price	350	-	1,116,264	1,103,488	9,928	2,848	HASH	Decimal	-		-	2.90%	2.89%	
Sales Quantity	98	-	35,184	31,584	2,768	832	HASH	Int64	-		-	0.09%	0.09%	
Return Quantity	6	-	1,552	80	1,376	96	HASH	Int64	-		-	0.00%	0.00%	
Return Amount	782	-	367,656	341,472	19,880	6,304	HASH	Decimal	-		-	0.95%	0.95%	
Discount Quantity	23	-	9,468	7,800	1,444	224	HASH	Int64	-		-	0.02%	0.02%	
Discount Amount	8,572	-	2,077,264	1,839,768	168,872	68,624	HASH	Decimal	-		-	5.39%	5.37%	
Total Cost	14,114	-	2,483,944	2,048,520	322,464	112,960	HASH	Decimal	-		-	6.45%	6.43%	
Sales Amount	51,717	-	5,344,424	2,331,128	2,599,520	413,776	HASH	Decimal	-		-	13.88%	13.83%	
Sales Tax	51,378	-	4,004,416	2,331,128	1,262,216	411,072	HASH	Decimal	-		-	10.40%	10.36%	
◢ **Date Table**	**1,096**	**139,394**	**139,394**	**5,496**	**123,450**	**10,448**	**Many**	-		**0**	**0**		**0.36%**	
RowNumber-2662979B-1795-4F74-8F37-6A1BA8059B61	0	-	120	0	120	0	VALUE	Int64	-		-	0.09%	0.00%	
Date	1,096	-	56,952	1,760	46,376	8,816	HASH	DateTime	-		-	40.86%	0.15%	
Year	3	-	1,436	8	1,364	64	HASH	Int64	-		-	1.03%	0.00%	
Quarter Name	4	-	17,184	8	17,096	80	HASH	String	-		-	12.33%	0.04%	
Quarter Number	4	-	1,408	8	1,320	80	HASH	Double	-		-	1.01%	0.00%	
Month Name	12	-	18,004	552	17,308	144	HASH	String	-		-	12.92%	0.05%	
Month Number	12	-	2,096	552	1,400	144	HASH	Int64	-		-	1.50%	0.01%	
Week Name	53	-	19,656	880	18,312	464	HASH	String	-		-	14.10%	0.05%	
Week Number	53	-	2,908	880	1,564	464	HASH	Int64	-		-	2.09%	0.01%	
Day Name	7	-	17,730	424	17,210	96	HASH	String	-		-	12.72%	0.05%	
Day Number	7	-	1,900	424	1,380	96	HASH	Int64	-		-	1.36%	0.00%	

Figure 13-10: Viewing metrics with the VertiPaq Analyzer

The screen gives plenty of information about columns in each table. Each column includes details of the cardinality of the column, the different sizes, and the type of encoding being used to compress data in the column. As we have seen in previous chapters, this type of information can be very helpful when you are working on improving the performance of low-performing queries.

Using SQL Server Profiler

Another tool we can use to help to monitor and improve the performance of our DAX queries is SQL Server Profiler. This tool is installed as part of the SQL Server management tools and can be accessed directly from Windows or from within DAX Studio. SQL Server Profiler allows you to capture trace files that record events generated by an instance of the Analysis Services engine. Using the information it captures, you can do the following:

- Monitor performance.
- Debug queries.
- Find slow running queries.
- Test queries in development.
- Audit activity on an instance.
- Save data to a file or a SQL Server table.

If you want to use Profiler with an instance of Analysis Services, you will need to know some details about that instance, such as the name of the server it is running on.

As Excel Power Pivot and Power BI Desktop also use the Analysis Services engine, it is possible to capture event Traces with them, by saving trace events to a file and then replaying that file using SQL Server Profiler. Also, it is possible to directly connect Profiler to an instance of Analysis Services on an open Power BI Desktop report.

To capture a trace file in Excel, you will need to click the **Settings** button on the **PowerPivot** ribbon. On the **Diagnostic Options section of the PowerPivot Options & Diagnostics** dialog, check the **Enable PowerPivot Tracing for the current Excel session** checkbox, as shown in *Figure 13-11*. You may need to open the Excel Power Pivot data model first, before you can use this option, by clicking on the **Manage** button on the **Data Model** section of the **PowerPivot** ribbon:

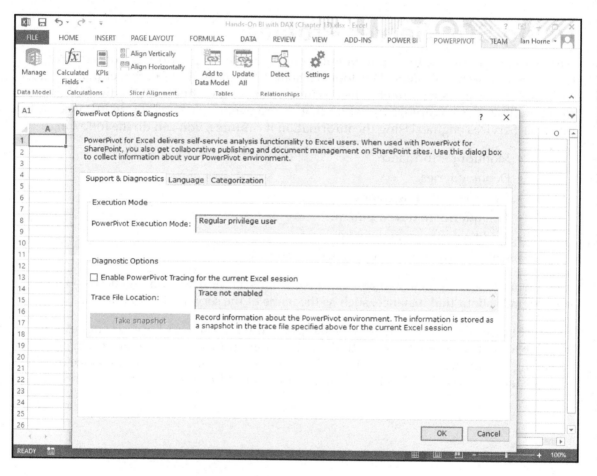

Figure 13-11: Enabling Power Pivot tracing in Excel

To connect Profiler directly to an instance of Analysis Services running on an open Power BI Desktop report, you will need to know the port number that Power BI Desktop is using. If you've already connected to Power BI Desktop with DAX Studio, then the port number will be shown on the status bar as can be seen in *Figure 13-12*:

Figure 13-12: Getting the port number from DAX Studio's status bar

Alternatively, you can find it using this method:

1. Open **Task Manager** and find the **Process ID (PID)** associated with the **msmdsrv** process. This is the process for the Analysis Services engine running within Power BI Desktop.
2. Open Command Prompt and enter the following:

   ```
   netstat -anop tcp
   ```

3. Find the port number in the **Local Address** column for the **PID** that you obtained in *step 1*.

Open SQL Server Profiler and complete the **Connect to Server** dialog as shown in *Figure 13-13*, replacing the port number after localhost on the **Server name** field with the port number you obtained:

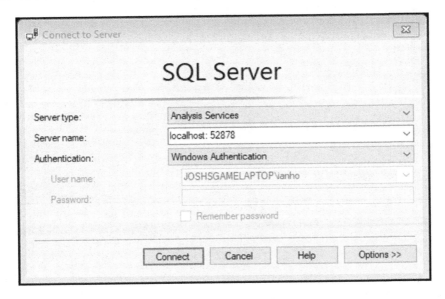

Figure 13-13: Connecting to Analysis Services

In DAX studio, if you have enabled the **Advanced** features on the **Options** screen, there is a **SQL Profiler** button on the **External Tools** section of the **Advanced** ribbon. If you click on this button, then it will open SQL Server Profiler and it will automatically connect to the same instance of Analysis Services that you are connected to with DAX Studio.

Once connected, you can run a trace to catch DAX query plans, queries to the storage engine, and any other events that you might be interested in, relating to your DAX query. As a minimum, consider capturing data relating to the following events:

- Query End
- DAX Query Plan
- VertiPaq SE Query Cache Match
- VeritPaq SE Query End

Figure 13-14 shows an example of the **Events Selection** screen for a trace file, showing these options selected:

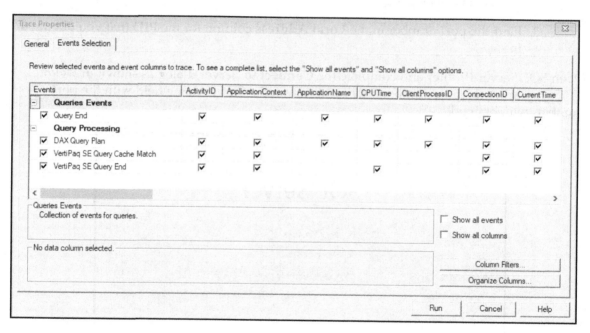

Figure 13-14: Selecting events to capture for a trace file

If you now go back and run a query or create a new visual on the Power BI Desktop report page, then you will see events being created and saved to the trace file. *Figure 13-15* shows an example of the data you can expect to see:

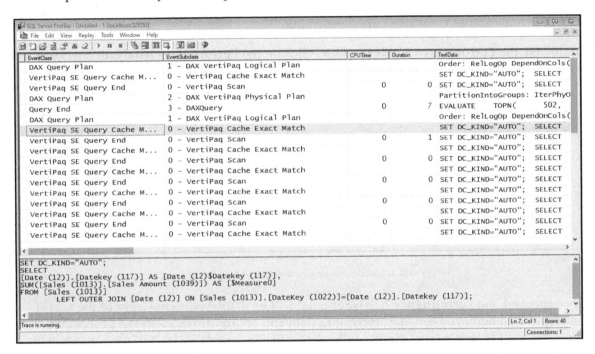

Figure 13-15: An example of events being captured to a trace file

In addition to creating trace files, SQL Server Profiler can also read and display previously saved trace files. For example, we have seen that is possible to save a trace file using Excel Power Pivot.

Trace files give you information about CPU time and duration, which is very useful when identifying bottlenecks. For this, it is important to understand how much time is spent processing a query in the storage versus the formula engine. Using the **Query End** event will give you the total duration of a DAX query, while the VertiPaq events will provide information about the duration spent processing with the storage engine. If you subtract this information from the total duration, it will give you the time spent with the formula engine.

Using Power BI Performance Analyzer

For the last section in this chapter, we are going to look at the Performance Analyzer feature in Power BI Desktop. This feature gives information on how elements of a report, such as visuals and DAX queries, are performing.

To display the **Performance Analyzer** pane, click on the **Performance Analyzer** checkbox on the **Show** section of the **View** ribbon, as shown in *Figure 13-16*:

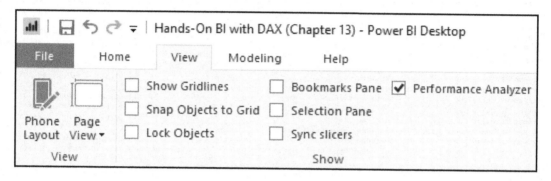

Figure 13-16: Enabling the performance analyzer feature in Power BI Desktop

Once checked, the **Performance Analyzer** pane will be displayed to the right of the report desktop. From here, you can start recording data and see information on the processing times required to update report elements when a user interacts with a report. For example, if you alter a slicer, click on a visual, or adjust a filter, then it will send a query to the data model. Information on the action is then displayed on the **Performance Analyzer** pane.

Data is recorded and displayed in real time, so you will immediately see the **Performance Analyzer** pane updated as you interact with a report.

Each visual contains information on the following categories:

- **DAX query**: The time between a visual sending a query and Analysis Services returning the result
- **Visual display**: The time taken to draw the visual on screen
- **Other**: The time taken to prepare queries, for other visuals to complete, or other background tasks

Figure 15-17 shows an example of the output you get with the Performance Analyzer:

Performance analyzer	X
⊙ Start recording ↻ Refresh visuals ⊚ Stop	
	✎ Clear ⬚ Export
Name	**Duration (ms)** ↓
↻ *Refreshed visual*	-
⊟ Products by Year	228
DAX query	38
Visual display	16
Other	174
⧉ Copy query	
⊟ Sales Amount by Year	312
DAX query	10
Visual display	16
Other	286
⧉ Copy query	
⊞ Total Sales	252
⊞ Total Quantity	189
⊞ Products by Color	276
▦ *Cross-highlighted*	-
⊞ Products by Year	376
⊞ Sales Amount by Year	479
⊞ Total Sales	522
⊞ Total Quantity	429
⊞ Products by Color	183
▦ *Cross-highlighted*	-
⊞ Products by Year	473
⊞ Sales Amount by Year	170
⊞ Total Sales	583
⊞ Total Quantity	622
⊞ Products by Color	537

Figure 13-17: An example of the output from the Power BI performance analyzer

You can see from this where data has been captured for refreshing the visuals and where data was generated when a visual was cross-highlighted.

When identifying bottlenecks in your report, you should be looking for large duration times. If it is the visual display that has a long duration, you should consider whether another type of visual would be better or whether there is some way to reduce the amount of data included in the visual.

If the DAX query has a long duration, then it may need further investigation. It may be due to a slow measure or a poorly designed data model. It is possible to copy the query by clicking on the **Copy query**. You can then paste the query into DAX Studio or SSMS and execute the query from there, using the features we looked at earlier in this chapter.

Finally, it is possible to save the information created by the Performance Analyzer to a `.json` file, by clicking on **Export**.

Summary

In the last chapter of this book, we looked at some of the techniques and tools that are used to help with analyzing the performance of DAX queries and identify potential problems.

We started off this chapter by learning about the storage and formula engines, the two engines used to process a DAX query. We looked at how they work together to retrieve data from the data model, and then process that data to return a result. We learned about how the logical and physical query plans produced by these query engines can help to identify and resolve performance issues with DAX queries.

Finally, we looked at some tools to help us to investigate the performance of DAX queries. We looked at DAX Studio, SQL Server Profiler, and the Performance Analyzer feature in Power BI Desktop. We learned about using these tools to monitor performance by looking at the output of the query engines and how they can be used to create and read Traces files containing events that occur when processing DAX queries.

We have now come to the end of our hands-on journey into learning about the basics of the DAX language. You should now have a good understanding of how DAX can help you, as a business intelligence professional, to gain much deeper insights into your data.

Other Books You May Enjoy

If you enjoyed this book, you may be interested in these other books by Packt:

Learn Power BI
Greg Deckler

ISBN: 9781838644482

- Explore the different features of Power BI to create interactive dashboards
- Use the Query Editor to import and transform data
- Perform simple and complex DAX calculations to enhance analysis
- Discover business insights and tell a story with your data using Power BI
- Explore data and learn to manage datasets, dataflows, and data gateways
- Use workspaces to collaborate with others and publish your reports

Learn T-SQL Querying
Pedro Lopes, Pam Lahoud

ISBN: 9781789348811

- Use Query Store to understand and easily change query performance
- Recognize and eliminate bottlenecks that lead to slow performance
- Deploy quick fixes and long-term solutions to improve query performance
- Implement best practices to minimize performance risk using T-SQL
- Achieve optimal performance by ensuring careful query and index design
- Use the latest performance optimization features in SQL Server 2017 and SQL Server 2019
- Protect query performance during upgrades to newer versions of SQL Server

Leave a review - let other readers know what you think

Please share your thoughts on this book with others by leaving a review on the site that you bought it from. If you purchased the book from Amazon, please leave us an honest review on this book's Amazon page. This is vital so that other potential readers can see and use your unbiased opinion to make purchasing decisions, we can understand what our customers think about our products, and our authors can see your feedback on the title that they have worked with Packt to create. It will only take a few minutes of your time, but is valuable to other potential customers, our authors, and Packt. Thank you!

Index

Made in the USA
Middletown, DE
22 July 2020